Micro Finance and Micro Enterprises in India

Micro Finance
and
Micro Enterprises in India

By

Sanjeeb K. Jena
Lecturer in Commerce,
Aeronautics College, Sunabeda, Odisha

New Century Publications
New Delhi, India

NEW CENTURY PUBLICATIONS
4800/24, Bharat Ram Road,
Ansari Road, Daryaganj,
New Delhi – 110 002 (India)

Tel.: 011-2324 7798, 4358 7398, 6539 6605
Fax: 011-4101 7798
E-mail: indiatax@vsnl.com • info@newcenturypublications.com
www.newcenturypublications.com

Editorial office:
LG–7, Aakarshan Bhawan,
4754-57/23, Ansari Road, Daryaganj,
New Delhi – 110 002

Tel.: 011-4356 0919

First Published: **2013**

ISBN: **978-81-7708-331-6**

Published by New Century Publications and printed at Salasar Imaging Systems, New Delhi.

Designs: Patch Creative Unit, New Delhi.

PRINTED IN INDIA

Dedicated To My Loving Parents

Late Dr. Bhagirathi Jena
and
Late Shrimati Suniti Jena

About the Book

Most people living in rural areas of India draw their livelihood from agriculture and allied sectors. However, the growth and balanced development of other sectors such as industry and services is also necessary to sustain the growth of Indian economy in an inclusive manner.

Micro credit has emerged as a visible credit channel to the poor as their access to conventional credit channels is constrained by the requirement of collateral and high transaction cost. The target groups, therefore, broadly comprise small and marginal farmers, agricultural and non-agricultural labourers, artisans and craftsmen and other poor engaged in small businesses.

Micro enterprises in India provide livelihood, check rural-urban migration, generate export earnings and touch upon the lives of the remotest and most marginalized people. The needs, problems and potential of these enterprises differ not just with the nature of activity (weaving, knitting, wood-carving etc.), but also with the size, geographical location and organizational structure. Not only do micro enterprises generate the highest employment per capita investment, they also go a long way in checking rural urban migration by providing villagers and people living in isolated areas with a sustainable source of employment.

Author's Profile

Dr. Sanjeeb K. Jena is presently Lecturer in Commerce in Aeronautics College (affiliated to Berhampur University), Sunabeda, Odisha. A gold medalist of Utkal University in M.Com. (1990) examination, he obtained his M.Phil. and Ph.D. degrees also from the same university. He has published 16 research papers in referred national and international journals and also authored a book.

Dr. Jena worked in the area of finance with such organizations as Orissa State Housing Board, and UNICEF. He specializes in rural finance, rural development, and micro enterprises.

Contents

Preface

Most people living in rural areas of India draw their livelihood from agriculture and allied sectors. However, the growth and balanced development of other sectors such as industry and services is also necessary to sustain the growth of Indian economy in an inclusive manner. The Government of India is striving to improve the economic and social conditions of rural population and non-farm sector through a host of measures including creation of productive employment opportunities based on optimal use of local raw materials and skills as well as undertaking interventions aimed at: (a) improving supply chain, (b) enhancing skills, (c) upgrading technology and (d) expanding markets and capacity building of the entrepreneurs/artisans and their groups/collectives.

Since Independence, the Government of India and the RBI have made concerted efforts to provide the poor with access to credit. Despite the phenomenal increase in the physical outreach of formal credit institutions in the past several decades, the rural poor continue to depend on informal sources of credit. Institutions have also faced difficulties in dealing effectively with a large number of small borrowers, whose credit needs are small and frequent and their ability to offer collaterals is limited. Besides, cumbersome procedures and risk perceptions of the banks left a gap in serving the credit needs of the rural poor.

This led to a search for alternative policies, systems and procedures, saving and loan products, other complementary services and new delivery mechanisms that would fulfil the requirements of the poor. It is in this context that micro credit has emerged as the most suitable and practical alternative to the conventional banking in reaching the hitherto unreached poor population. Micro credit enables the poor people to be thrifty and helps them in availing the credit and other financial services for improving their income and living standards.

Micro credit has emerged as a visible credit channel to the

poor as their access to conventional credit channels is constrained by the requirement of collateral and high transaction cost. The target groups, therefore, broadly comprise small and marginal farmers, agricultural and non-agricultural labourers, artisans and craftsmen and other poor engaged in small businesses like vending, and hawking.

Micro enterprises in India provide livelihood, check rural-urban migration, generate export earnings and touch upon the lives of the remotest and most marginalized people. The needs, problems and potential of these enterprises differ not just with the nature of activity (weaving, knitting, wood-carving etc.), but also with the size, geographical location and organizational structure.

Micro enterprises have been recognised as engines of economic growth worldwide. In India, these enterprises manufacture products ranging from handloom sarees, carpets, soaps, pickles, papads to machine parts for large industries. Not only do micro enterprises generate the highest employment per capita investment, they also go a long way in checking rural urban migration by providing villagers and people living in isolated areas with a sustainable source of employment.

The dispersed, unorganized and often household-based micro and small enterprises are capital-saving, labour-intensive and environment-friendly. In India, they are the largest source of employment after agriculture and are found in both rural as well as urban areas.

In view of the decline in agriculture's contribution to GDP and the near constant proportion of workers dependent on it, there is need for rapid generation of off-farm employment. There is need for diversification within agriculture (to sericulture, horticulture, pisciculture) to expand the scope for off-farm rural livelihoods. The real potential for employment generation however rests with micro enterprises which comprise weavers, artisans, and people engaged in food processing, hawkers, vendors, carpenters.

I would like to express my sincere thanks to Dr. Jayanta Kumar Parida, Professor and Head, Department of Commerce, Utkal University whose timely assistance, support and guidance enabled me to undertake this work.

I am deeply indebted to my father late Dr. Bhagirathi Jena and my mother late Shrimati Suniti Jena for their inspiration, untiring wishes and enlightened blessings.

I am grateful to my wife Shrimati Meena Bhakat and daughter Aryaditi (Missie) who have been a constant source of inspiration and emotional support.

Sunabeda **Sanjeeb K. Jena**
September 2012

1

Micro Finance and Micro Enterprises in Developing Countries

Because of the limited employment opportunities in both rural and urban areas of the Third World, millions of poor people must make their living through self-employment in the informal economy–the economy of street vendors, petty traders, small-shop owners, scrap collectors, small artisans and microbus drivers. [1] In addition, as Woller and Woodworth (2001) state, the "informal economy differs from the formal economy not just by its 'underground' status, but also in that it is starved by the lifeblood of the formal economy–financial capital".

Despite the global efforts made in the past decades to formalize the provision of financial services to the poor, micro finance and micro enterprise is still considered part of the informal sector economy throughout the world, primarily in developing countries.

According to Ela R. Bhatt (SEWA), "The informal economy in India today employs well over 90 percent of the Indian workforce, provides some 63 percent of the GDP, 55 percent of the savings and 47 percent of the exports" (Jaquette and Summerfield, 2006). [2] In addition, a study by the Inter-American Development Bank indicated that "In the mid-1990s, the micro enterprise sector employed more than 50 percent of the labour force in Latin American countries and…an average of 84 out of 100 new jobs in the region were generated by MEs [3]" (Benería, 2003). Even though these are just two examples of micro finance in different areas of the world, they nonetheless capture its importance and its impact in the developing world.

1.1 Contribution of Micro Enterprises

Most of India's poor live in rural areas, although urban poverty is also a growing problem in virtually all developing regional economies. Most rural poor are engaged in agricultural or related activities as labourers or small-scale farmers in the informal sector. Although the definitions vary according to the country context, it is generally agreed that the informal sector, whether rural or urban, comprises small scale and micro enterprises producing and distributing goods and services in unregulated but competitive markets. These enterprises are generally independent, largely family owned, employ low levels of skills and technology, and are highly labour intensive. These micro enterprises are concentrated largely in low-income low productivity activities, especially in petty trades and services. In many countries, women, who are a significant proportion of the poor and suffer disproportionately from poverty, operate many of these enterprises.

Micro enterprises provide income and employment for significant proportions of workers in rural and urban areas by producing basic goods and services for rapidly growing populations. They account for more than 60 percent of all regional enterprises and up to 50 percent of paid employment. With increasing labour force participation among women in developing countries in the region, a greater number of women depend on micro enterprises in the informal sector for survival. Hence, micro enterprise development is increasingly being seen as an essential ingredient in the promotion of broad based growth, in improving the well being of the poor and women by providing significant income and employment generating opportunities, and by encouraging indigenous investment. Consequently, there is an increasing policy focus on the need to strengthen entrepreneurship and the contribution of micro enterprises to attain economic growth with equity, as well as in addressing gender and poverty reduction issues. Pressure to attain such outcomes has been further increased in the wake of the regional economic and social crises.

Micro finance can provide an effective way to assist and empower poor women, who make up a significant proportion of the poor and suffer disproportionately from poverty. Micro finance can also contribute to the development of the overall financial system through integration of financial markets. Hence, the development of micro enterprises and micro finance are intertwined.

1.2 Micro Credit for Poverty Reduction

It is observed that micro enterprise development has the potential to bring about considerable improvement in incomes of upper poor and non-poor borrowers who are close to the poverty lines [4] (Hulme, D. and Mosley, P., 1996). The extreme poor are either less likely to participate in micro finance programmes or such increases were too small and short-lived to enable sustainable poverty exit. The poor commonly face obstacles in the form of unfavourable market environments, inadequate financial infrastructure, location, market and infrastructure constraints. Poor transport infrastructure is the single most important impediment to rural micro enterprise development, electricity, irrigation and lack of formal education being the other important factors. Low caste and social status may also inhibit entry into entrepreneurial occupations, reducing the range of activities open to extreme poor and some poor households. Some of the social problems being faced by the poor are alcohol abuse, engagement in petty crimes and family instability. Social restrictions on women also limit their economic activities. Interestingly, the female-headed household heads appeared to have more freedom than married women in project selection and mobility [5] (Lepenies, P. H., 2004).

More than half of all women are still in agriculture in the developing world. In South Asia, men are leaving agriculture faster than women, giving rise to increasing concentration of women on land. In India, 86 percent of rural women workers are in agriculture compared with 74 percent of rural mail workers. In addition, 20 percent of rural households are headed by females [6] (World Survey on the Role of Women in Development, 1999). In micro enterprises they own, women work longer hours for less remuneration compared to men. Women's enterprises were also more embedded within the family, relying on family networks for labour and credit. However, as mentioned earlier, in majority of the cases, such micro enterprises were used more as a means of survival than as an instrument of empowering entrepreneurial activity.

Zaman, H. [7] (1999), in a study of BRAC's programme has concluded that while micro-credit interventions can play an important role in reducing vulnerability through a number of channels, a significant impact on poverty reduction is achieved under more restrictive conditions. These conditions revolve around whether the borrower has crossed a cumulative loan threshold. It was shown that the largest effect on poverty arises when a moderate poor BRAC loanee borrows more than Tk. 10,000 in cumulative loan. Vulnerability is reduced by smoothing consumption, building assets, providing emergency assistance and contributing to female empowerment. It was also argued that micro-credit's impact is improved if it is provided jointly with other financial and non-financial interventions like savings, insurance, legal education and flood relief. However, as far as the impact on poverty is concerned, when the credit-financed investment does not generate a significant net profit then an asset is created which can reduce vulnerability but will not reduce poverty as the loan repayment takes place through a reduction in consumption and not from the returns to the investment.

It can be concluded that the impact of micro-credit on poverty is not clear. McGuire P.B. and Conroy, J.D. (2000) [8] suggest that access to credit has potential to significantly reduce poverty, but others argue that it has minimal impact on poverty reduction. There are studies showing that improvements in household incomes are greater for third time borrowers but these gains are small.

1.3 Micro Finance, Micro Enterprises and the Poor

While micro finance is meant to reach the poor there are almost universally acknowledged views that most programs, despite stated objectives, do not reach the poorest of the poor. One of the reasons is related to the fact that loans which are normally given for self-employment presuppose some degree of micro-enterprise and the long-term interest of every implementing agency is to see that members quickly start taking loans for income generation activities. Marguerite Robinson, the author of The Micro Finance Revolution, has expressed her view succinctly when she wrote "I don't want to reach the poorest of the poor, I want to reach the poorest of the economically active. In general, I believe the poorest of the poor are the responsibility of the Ministry of Social Welfare, the Ministry of Labour, private charities and so forth." She has suggested their low confidence becomes even lower if they are unable to repay. In fact, realizing the fact that not all the poor want necessarily to be self-employed and that some of them prefer wage employment, Government of India is implementing parallel programmes for self-employment and wage-employment for the poor.

This then begs the question of how to reach the really poor. There are those that argue that there is greater decease in vulnerability than income-poverty. Even if loans are used by the extremely poor, the tendency appears to be that they are used for consumption's purposes. In some case it is difficult for there to be a dent on poverty because repayments of loans are effected through a squeeze on current consumption rather than a return on an investment. For the poorest women, therefore, the issue is whether they can access loans and also what are the other interventions that are required so that they can be reached.

The focus is on women for two reasons. Firstly, poverty has a female face and the phenomenon of the feminization of poverty is well established. Not only are there numerically more poor women than poor men, but women also experience poverty in more exacerbated forms than men do. In rural areas, particularly among weaker sections of the society, women are illiterate and suppressed, the women empowerment should focus on the following aspects:

1. Drudgery reduction,
2. Gender sensitization,
3. Capacity building, and
4. Promotion of micro enterprises.

While promoting women empowerment in rural areas, the participant women and the communities have recognized the success of the programme through two important indicators. Firstly, the women and their family members considered women's ability to enhance their family income as an important indicator of success apart from the improvement in hygiene, sanitation, education of children and community health. At the community level, the ability of the women to take active part in various social development activities was considered to be the most important indicator of success. In many women empowerment programmes, which did not include promotion of any livelihood activities, women started demanding support for initiating various income generation activities. It can therefore be concluded that income generation or livelihood support activities should be an integral aspect of the women empowerment programme, while dealing with poor rural communities.

1.4 Micro Enterprises for Women Empowerment

"Another component of empowerment for poor women is self-reliance—self-reliance in terms of financial self-sufficiency, and management and in terms of decision-making. For the poor, collective empowerment is more important than individual. With collective strength the woman is able to combat the outside exploitative and corrupt forces like traders and money lenders. Also her respect in the family and community follow soon"; Ela Bhatt, Founder, SEWA-Speech on "Cooperatives and Empowerment of Women" (1992). [9]

Micro finance/micro enterprise programmes have the potential to transform power relations and empower the poor—both men and women. In well-run ME programs, there is a relationship of respect between the provider and the client that is inherently empowering. This is true regardless of the methodology or approach (whether the institution takes a minimalist approach of delivering financial services only or a more holistic or integrated approach). As a consequence, micro finance and micro enterprise have become a central component of many donor agencies' and national governments' gender, poverty alleviation, and community development strategies.

Since SHG based micro finance and micro enterprise programmes cover a large number of women, it is expected that such programmes will have an important bearing on women's empowerment. However, the historical involvement of banks and micro finance institutions in India have ensured that these programmes adopt a minimalist approach and ignore non-financial inputs like literacy, health, awareness, capacity building and skill training. This approach has an impact on the long-term sustainability of such efforts.

Ideally, on a wider canvas, SHGs can become an extraordinary tools for women's empowerment provided the nurturing agencies take care to design their interventions to improve the confidence level of members through better participation in SHG meetings and more interactions take place with outsiders and through this process members develop communication skills and are able to put forward their views confidently, members are involved in decision making processes of group which will later help them to participate in bigger decisions affecting them, their family and their community, groups are initiated into community level actions which will help them in demanding facilities and systems to suit their needs. This process has already started at the family level and will have to be taken to the community level now.

[10]

The shift in approach to micro-credit coincided with a shift from a women in development approach which emphasized equality, efficiency and productive role of women, to a gender and development approach which analyzed the underlying and structural causes for the persistent inequalities between men and women and focused on the power relations between men and women in the household, community, market and the state. This approach does focus on empowerment but there is no shared understanding of what is meant by empowerment and this is understood in many different ways. It can cover everything from welfare measures to interventions that cover participatory planning, decentralized forms of governance and the empowerment of women. While there are detailed discussions regarding the implications and forms of power and its deconstruction into power to do, power over, power with and power within, in simple terms it spans three dimensions:

1. The personal—manifested in an increase in self confidence, self esteem and increased awareness;
2. The relational—distribution of power between men and women as manifested in the access to and control over material, social and political resources and participation in decision making; and
3. The collective—where women who are mobilized can collectively act, demand or determine their future.

Empowerment does imply transformed awareness. It is a complex process, which involves a change in the perception of the women and their relationships. For purposes of this paper, the vision of empowered women that we would like to use is of women who will:

1. Demand their rights from family, community and government;
2. Have increased access to and control over material, social and political resources;
3. Have self confidence, self-esteem and enhanced awareness; and

4. Be able to raise issues of common concern and take action through mobilization and networking. [11]

Although micro-credit programme participation expands mobility into certain public spaces, like NGO office and health centre since such programmes require visits to NGO office and often motivate participants to avail themselves of public health services, such positive effect of participation on the condition for empowerment is small since the women's access to more remunerative wage employment and mobility into the male dominated public sphere is not increased [12] (M. Simeen, 2003).

1.5 Challenges in Promoting Micro Finance and Micro Enterprises

Despite documented successes by several studies, other research efforts show that some micro finance and micro enterprise programs have experienced a wide range of challenges such as limited outreach, excessive overhead cost and high loan losses (Bhatt and Tang, 2001 [13]). To put the challenges in context, the Association for Enterprise Opportunity (AEO) states: "If the micro enterprise development industry was a single business, then it could be characterized as having low market penetration, high costs, increasing competition, inadequate expenditures in R&D and technology, and promising but insufficient returns on investment [14]" (Servon, 2006).

1.5.1 Financial Sustainability: Sustainability is one of the primary issues found among micro finance and micro enterprise service providers. Aside from all the positive outcomes achieved by micro finance institutions and micro enterprise development programs, not all of them are sustainable or able to return a profit. Despite their rapid growth and sound operations, less than half of all programs return a profit and most still require the help of donors and subsidies [15] (Sengupta and Aubuchon, 2008). Issues regarding financial sustainability are predominant on the micro finance field. Many times the costs are not covered by the monetary returns the program obtains via fees or grants in order to maintain its services. Despite these issues, programs assisting micro enterprise development remain a cost-effective method to provide financial services to typically underserved populations.

1.5.2 Market Penetration: Micro enterprise development programs continue to experience difficulty reaching the markets they intend to serve. Edgcomb and Klein estimate the size of the market for the targeted services provided by micro enterprise programs at about 10 million individuals [16] (2005). Assuming this figure is accurate; the field has fallen short of reaching its target market, as it served 626,277 participants in 2005. Part of the reason behind outreach problems might be explained by the client-to-staff ratio, as the majority of micro enterprise development programs are short staffed and the amount of potential clients far exceeds their capacity.

1.5.3 Fragmentation: The difference in mission among programs can be summed up into those that see themselves as either an economic development entity or as a social services entity. Their approach depends largely on the program's founder. The micro enterprise field has historically sold itself as both and many programs sit in the middle of that spectrum. While implementing either of the approaches can be successful, attempting to pursue both can lead to mission confusion. This lack of identity, as well as the lack of standardization, makes definitions of success difficult in addition to making the creation of standards and performance measures difficult to be embraced across the field [17] (Servon, 2006).

The rise of micro finance and micro enterprise services has overturned established ideas of the poor as consumers of financial services, shattered stereotypes of the poor as not bankable, spawned a variety of lending methodologies demonstrating that it is possible to provide financial services to the poor, and mobilized millions of rupees of "social investment" for the poor (Brau and Woller, 2004; Mutua et al., 1996). Despite of these changes, there are challenges that should be addressed. Given the enormous and rapid growth in the field, it is important to analyze to what extent success claims can be confirmed and whether micro entrepreneurs and recipients of micro finance services are in fact experiencing it. [18]

1.6 Role of Self-help Groups (SHGs)

In India, the organization of self-help groups, especially for micro finance and micro enterprise development programmes constitute a widely accepted development strategy for poverty reduction. This strategy is equally shared by government, commercial banks and civil society. The authors argue that, thus far, SHGs have shown a limited effectiveness in terms of their impact on rural poverty and their long-term sustainability. Due to the lack of proper understanding of their potential, the implementers have followed a minimalist approach that has restricted the scope of functioning of SHGs to promoting enterprises that are stereotypically considered feminine.

The universal fascination with SHGs has also resulted in obscuring the potential roles of alternative institutions like co-operatives, private sectors, etc. in poverty removal. The possessiveness of some of the implementers has resulted in the development of SHGs as standalone organizations without having any meaningful interaction with other schemes or community based organizations like watershed user groups, village panchayats, etc. As a result of this, the SHG members have not been able to access substantial development funds, which could otherwise have been available to them. This study advocates that for SHGs to have a marked and sustained impact on poverty it is necessary for them to adopt a more encompassing approach with various community-based organizations and programmes by laying far greater focus on processes, capacity building, convergence with various ongoing programmes, etc.

1.7 Multiple Roles of Rural SHGs

Roles of SHGs can be classified as follows: (1) as micro finance institutions; (2) as part of marketing chains; (3) as networks for neighbourhood welfare; and (4) in natural resource management (NRM). [19] Broadly, the first two roles impact human-made and human capitals while the last two, impact social and natural components. We desist from listing success or failure stories in each of these categories, but the sections below try and evaluate the roles per se.

1.7.1 SHGs as Micro Finance Institutions: Micro finance, the current buzzword in the developmental sector, is often hailed as panacea for the problems of community development. Micro finance commonly works through group systems like the Grameen Bank of Bangladesh, solidarity groups of Latin America, and self-help groups of India. Self-help groups, the most common micro finance institutions in India, are 'small voluntary associations of poor people from the same socio-economic background who come together for the purpose of solving their common problems through self-help and mutual help [20]' (NABARD, 2000). They are mostly autonomous financial institutions, which help members to keep safe their occasional small surpluses in the form of thrift, and grant loans to people in exigencies without any cumbersome procedure. More than 16 million rural households have gained access to bank credit, making the SHG movement the largest social movement in India targeting nearly one-third of India's poor [21] (Das, 2005). The impressive credit recovery rate of 90 percent, low overhead costs and the enormous goodwill earned in the process of BOP transformation enthuse the banking community to nurture more groups to serve the twin purposes of banking and social development.

1.7.2 SHGs as Networks for Rural Well-Being: Expectation about the potential of SHGs in bringing rural well-being seems to originate in (a) the role of social capital in reducing poverty, (b) the debt-resource hypothesis and (c) the poverty environment nexus theory. In reality, these are context specific and have varying strength, depending on diverse factors [22] (Dasgupta et al., 2005). Nevertheless, broad implications of these concepts are discussed below.

1.7.3 SHGs and Social Capital: SHGs are institutions understood as mechanisms to uncover latent shared values, for sanctioning antisocial behaviour and for channelling individual action in collectively desirable direction [23] (World Bank, 2000). But there are arguments to show that the benefits of social capital in reducing poverty has been oversimplified in literature and that it is a weak policy tool to fight poverty (Schuurman [24] 2003, Cleaver [25] 2005). There are studies showing that benefits of group formation may not lead to lowering of poverty itself [26] (Thorp, 2005). Studies evaluating the role of SHGs in poverty alleviation offer contradictory opinions on the problem. While Vatta and Singh [27] (2001), Tankha [28] (2002) and Galab [29] et al. (2003) report that SHG activities have improved the income of women, Panda [30] (2003), Mahajan [31] (2004) and Rajasekhar [32] (2004) opine that the income through SHGs has limitations in meeting the financial requirements of members and does not provide any income security. But the relevance of SHGs as powerful instruments of social, political and economic empowerment of women has been unanimously brought forth in the studies of Antia and Kadekodi [33] (2002), Sinha and Sinha [34] (2002) and Jahan [35] et al. (2004).

When we consider the Indian poor at the BOP, a desirable intervention would be to aim at social transformation (morphing the economic 'pyramid' to a 'diamond') beginning with basic facilities for health care and education provided either by the government or other agencies followed by a three-pronged strategy to make the BOP better savers, producers and then consumers. This involves conservative use of natural resources, poverty reduction and profit making. Combining these strategies in any single effort seems like a difficult balancing act and calls for tackling the basic ecological and social components of a SES. SHG institutions are geared to supplement social capital endowment of a community through fostering mutual trust, co-operation, and cohesiveness among people. The impact of SHGs in nurturing equity across castes, class and gender itself is a lofty and worthy goal to pursue.

1.7.4 SHGs and the Debt-Resource Hypothesis: With the micro finance focus of SHGs, the argument that SHGs can reduce natural resource degradation should be tested based on the debt-resource hypothesis (DRH). [36] It means that if resource degradation increases with indebtedness, and if SHGs can reduce the indebtedness of nature dependent poor, it probably can conserve natural resources. Forming credit and savings group can not only lead to the economic betterment of the community but can also reduce their forest dependence through providing new livelihood options. Nevertheless, DRH itself is not proven as of now.

1.7.5 SHGs and the Poverty-Environment Nexus: Erosion of local resource base can make certain categories of people destitute even while the economy's gross national product (GNP) increases (Dasgupta, 2001). At micro scale, this would mean that poverty reduction is invariably dependant on natural regeneration and biomass. When livelihoods depend directly on natural resources, the sustenance of livelihoods depends on sustained flow of natural resources. Thus, poverty reduction strategies should be making community sustainable suppliers of NC first, and consumers next. Commercial transformation of BOPs also needs assured livelihoods for consistent rates of credit recovery. Retaining a productive and healthy landscape in spite of changed consumption pattern comes through ecological knowledge (HC) and synergistic networks (SC) built through institutions like SHGs. Hence, management of human and social capital through institutions like SHGs is crucial for poverty reduction strategies to stimulate complementary changes in the ecological component of SES.

Are self-help groups (SHGs) institutions capable of enhancing the aggregate of capital components discussed above, enhancing rural well-being? SHGs can be catalysts in building human and social capital, in order to move towards sustainable natural capital management so that livelihood options are available and long standing. Thus, livelihood security can lead to freedom of choice and access to resources, eventually leading to improved rural well-being. This potential role of SHG movement in rural poverty alleviation and dearth of studies assessing the success of SHGs in synergizing a dynamic equilibrium of SES prompted this paper.

1.7.6 Women Support for SHGs: Following support is needed to promote micro enterprises through women SHGs.

1. Motivation of the target communities, particularly women,
2. Formation of self-help groups and their federations,
3. Introduction of drudgery reduction activities,
4. Gender sensitization,
5. Training and capacity building,
6. Micro finance provision of credit facilities and linkage with banks,
7. Development of infrastructure, particularly through the SHG Federations to provide necessary support services and marketing,
8. Trade networking and establishment of market outlets, and
9. Village level information centre/e-*Chaupal* for dissemination of information.

A multi-disciplinary team can interact with the SHGs to explore the potentials for development of various enterprises and extend necessary support for dissemination of technologies, procurement of inputs, training of members and establishment of linkage with the market.

1.8 Use of Indigenous Knowledge for Micro Enterprises

Knowledge is a process for transforming natural landscapes into cultural landscapes (e.g., sacred mountains and lakes), ecological functions and livelihood support systems in the particularly situated socio-economic and biophysical environments. Sustainable livelihood analysis does not pay enough attention to the local placed indigenous knowledge [37] (Scoones, 1998).

Mangetane et al. (2001) noted that people in a community value whatever resource they get from the environment through sustainable production systems. [38] These communities are conscious of the need to self-reliant in capital stocks and management skills. In the view of Dewes (1993), the knowledge of local people was an enabling component of development. In this regard; a large percentage of the earth's genetic diversity has been maintained and managed through indigenous peoples' indigenous knowledge system (IKS). Moreover, IKS often forms the basis for livelihood that has been sustained for generations. [39]

Indigenous knowledge (IK) functions within the given socio-economic and spatial boundaries of the society and plays an active part in the culture of the population concerned, being preserved, communicated, and used by its members to serve some purpose in relation to productive activity within the society (Bell, 1979). [40] It can be transferred by quite elaborate systems, often involving oral transmission using stories and myths.

Indigenous knowledge is a critical factor for sustainable development. Empowerment of local communities is a prerequisite for the integration of IK in the development process. The integration of appropriate IK systems into development programs has already proved to contribute to efficiency, effectiveness and sustainable development impact. [41] IK, like any other knowledge needs to be constantly used, challenged and further adapted to the evolving local contexts. Supporting local and regional networks of traditional practitioners and community exchanges can help to disseminate useful and relevant IK and to enable communities to participate more actively in the development process. While innovative mechanisms for the protection of IK need to be developed, many indigenous knowledge practices can at the same time be integrated into local, national, regional or even global development efforts. [42]

End Notes

1. Woller, Gary M. and Woodworth, Warner (2001), Microcredit as a Grassroot Policy for International Development, *Policy Studies Journal,* 29, 267-282.
2. Jaquette, Jane S. and Summerfield, Gale (2006), *Women and Gender Equity in Development Theory and Practice,* Durham and London: Duke University Press.
3. Benería, Lourdes (2003), *Gender, Development and Globalization: Economics as if People Mattered,* New York: Routledge.
4. Hulme, D. and Mosley, P. (1996), Finance against Poverty, Vol. 1, London: Routledge.
5. Lepenies, P. H. (2004), Exit, Voice and Vouchers: Using Vouchers to Train Micro-entrepreneurs-Observations from the Paraguyan Voucher Scheme, World Development 32 (4), pp. 713-724.
6. World Survey on the Role of Women in Development, (1999), New York, United Nations.
7. Zaman, H. (1999), Assessing the Impact of Micro-credit on Poverty and Vulnerability in Bangladesh, Washington, The World Bank Policy Research Working Paper No. 2145.
8. McGuire P. B. and Conroy, J. D. (2000), The Microfinance Phenomenon, Asia Pacific Review, Vol. 7, No. 1, pp. 90-108.
9. SEWA (n.d.), Shri Mahila Sewa Sahakari Bank Ltd. (Brochure).
10. In this extremely thoughtful paper, Mahmud, S. (2003) has assessed the effect of micro-credit programme on women's empowerment and has concluded that the programme has only a limited direct effect in increasing women's access to choice enhancing resources but has a much stronger effect in increasing women's ability to participate in household level decisions. It improves women's access to resources like self-employment and mobility into certain public spaces like the NGO office and health centre, but the impact is small since their access to more remunerative wage employment and mobility into the male

dominated public spheres is not increased.

11. This is the vision that was developed also for the Indira Mahilia Yojana programme of the Government of India and it encompasses many of the essential factors for such a process.
12. Simeen, M. (2003), Actually How empowering is Microcredit? Mahmud, Development and Change, 34(4), pp. 577-605.
13. Bhatt, Nitin and Tang, Shui-Yan (2001), Designing Group-Based Microfinance Programmes: Some Theoretical and Policy Considerations. *International Journal of Public Administration.* 24, pp. 1103-1125.
14. Servon, Lisa J. (2006), Micro enterprise Development in the United States: Current Challenges and New Directions. *Economic Development Quarterly*, 20, pp. 351-367.
15. Sengupta, Rajdeep and Aubuchon, Craig P. (2008), The Microfinance Revolution: An Overview, *Federal Reserve Bank of St. Louis Review*, 90, pp. 9-30.
16. Edgcomb, Elaine L., and Klein, Joyce A. (2005), Opening Opportunities, Building Ownership: Fulfilling the Promise of Micro enterprise in the United States, *Fund for Innovation, Effectiveness, Learning and Dissemination,* 1-140.
17. Servon, Lisa J. (2006), Micro enterprise Development in the United States: Current Challenges and New Directions, *Economic Development Quarterly*, 20, 351-367.
18. MYRADA (1998), Guidelines for Working with Self-help Groups, Rural Management Systems Series Paper-30 (30A, 30B, 30C).
19. Bhat, M.K. (2000), SHGs: Delivery Mechanism or Empowerment Tool?, Paper presented at the Workshop on Best Practices in Group Dynamics and Micro Credit, 15-17 February, Manesar, Gurgaon.
20. NABARD (2000), Circular, National Bank for Agriculture and Rural Development, New Delhi.
21. Das S. (2005), People's Banking is Here to Stay', Economic Times, February 5, 2005.
22. Dasgupta, S., C.M. Deichmann, and D. Wheeler (2005), Where is the Poverty-Environment Nexus? Evidence from Cambodia, Lao PDR and Vietnam, World Development, 33 (4): 617-638.
23. World Bank (2000), World Development Report 2000/1, New York, Oxford University Press.
24. Schurman, F.J. (2003), The Politico Emancipatory Potential of a

Disputed Concept, Third World Quarterly, 34(6):991-1010.
25. Cleaver, F. (2005), The Inequality of Social Capital and the Reproduction of Chronic Poverty, World Development, 33(6): 893-906.
26. Thorp, R., F. Stewart and A. Heyer. (2005), When and How Far is group Formation a Route out of Chronic Poverty?, World Development, 33(6): 907-920.
27. Vatta, K. and P. Singh. (2001), The Performance of Self-help Groups in Punjab: A Study of Hoshiarpur District, Indian Journal of Agricultural Economics, 56(3): 452.
28. Tankha, A. (2002), Self-help Groups as Financial Intermediaries in India: Cost of Promotion, Sustainability and Impact, Report for ICCO and Cord Aid, Netherlands, pp. 1-89.
29. Galab, S. and N.C. Rao. (2003), Women's Self-help Groups, Poverty Alleviation and Empowerment, Economic and Political Weekly, 38(12 and13): 1274-1282.
30. Panda, S.K. (2003), Micro finance in Economic Empowerment of Weaker Sections, Yojna, 47 (3): 21-25.
31. Mahajan, V. (2004), Deregulating Rural Credit, Paper presented in 'New Priorities: Symposium on a Social Agenda for India'. www.india.seminar.com.
32. Rajasekhar, D. (2004), Micro finance and Poverty Alleviation-Issues Relating to NGO Programmes in South India, ISEC Working Paper No.146, pp. 1-25.
33. Antia, N.H. and G.K Kadekodi (2002), Dynamics of Rural Development: Lessons from Ralegaon Siddhi, A Joint Study by the Foundation for Research in Community Health, Pune and Centre for Multi-disciplinary Development Research, Dharwad, pp. 53-56.
34. Sinha, F. and S. Sinha (2002), Sustainability and Development: Evaluating the Performance of Indian Microfinance, Beyond Microcredit: Putting Development Back into Microfinance. Vistar Publishers, New Delhi, pp. 264-298.
35. Jahan, R., G. Kelkar, and D. Nathan (2004), Redefining Women's Samman: Microcredit and Gender Relations in Rural Bangladesh, Economic and Political Weekly, 39(32): 3627-3640.
36. Biswas, Soumen (n.d.), Expanding NGO-SHG-Bank Linkage Across the Country-Some Issues and Recommendations (mimeo), PRADAN.

37. Scoones, I. (1998), Sustainable Rural Livelihoods: A Framework for Analysis", IDS Working Paper No. 72.
38. Mangetane G.K., Asibey E.A.O. (2001), An Overview of African Indigenous Knowledge for sustainable Development, Scandinavian Seminar College: African Perspectives of Policies Supporting Sustainable Development.
39. Dewes W (1993), Traditional Knowledge and Sustainable Development in Southern Africa. Proceedings of a Conference held at the World Bank, Washington D.C, September 27-28, Environmentally Sustainable Proceedings, Series No. 4.
40. Bell, M. (1979), The Exploitation of Indigenous Knowledge or the Indigenous Exploitation of Knowledge: Whose Use of What for What?, *IDS Bulletin*, 10: 44-50.
41. Atteh, O.D. (1991), Indigenous Local Knowledge as Key to Local-level Development: Possibilities, Constrains and Planning Issues in the Context of Africa, Seminar on Reviving Local Self-reliance: Challenges for Rural/Regional Development in Eastern and Southern Africa, Arusha, Tanzania, 21-24 February.
42. Gorjestani, Nicolas (Chief Knowledge Officer, Africa Region, The World Bank), Indigenous Knowledge for Development: Opportunities and Challenges, This paper is based on a presentation made by the author at the UNCTAD Conference on Traditional Knowledge in Geneva, November 1, 2000.

2

Micro Enterprises in the Indian Context

2.1 Characteristics of Rural India

"Indian society is like a mountain. With the very rich at the top, lush Alpine pastures where skilled workers in the biggest modern industries graze, a gradual slope down through smaller firms where pay and conditions are worse and the legal security of employment means less, a steep slope around the area where the Factories Act ceases to apply, a plateau where custom and the market give poorly paid organized workers some minimum security, then a long steep slope down through casual migrant labour and petty services to destitution. There are well-defined paths up and down those slopes, which are the easiest for some kinds of people", Holmstrom (1984). [1]

India is considered as a country inhabited by poor people. It is true even today, after 63 years of Independence. Mass poverty in India resulted from predominance of rural population, adverse land mass ratio, heavy dependence on agriculture, concentration of industries in urban areas, highly skewed distribution of income and wealth, under utilization of human resources, vicious human psyche and mind set, erosion of ethical values, caste and class based rigid social hierarchy and structures, besides high incidence of poverty and unemployment. The last two viz.; unemployment and poverty pose major challenges to the growth and prosperity of the country. [2]

In the last two decades the rural unrest in different parts of the country is studded with spurts of violence, some of the causes are perennial and chronic rooted in actual social disparity and deprivation. Various attempts by the Government in the past have yielded only marginal success. For a variety of reasons like resource unutilization, social and political conjectures and of course Government Policy, growth happens to be very uneven across the country. This uneven growth has given rise to assetless, unemployed, under-employed and distress-employed population unable to access to the resources of any kind. It seems that economic planning after independence has been more ornamental and less pragmatic and beneficial. The economic growth shows a blind face to the rural people the most in comparison to the urban.

India is a country of villages. Rural population constitutes a major segment in India. According to the 2011 Census, 68.8 percent (83.3 crore) of the total population is from rural areas and is dependent on agriculture and allied activities for their livelihood. [3] Due to inadequate attention on the part of Government to have a farmer-oriented agricultural policy, and the failure of agricultural reforms, employment in agriculture sector is also affecting to a greater extent. It has declined from 2.32 percent in 1972-73 to 1.2 percent in 1983 and subsequently to less than 0.4 percent as on date. Agriculture contributed about 26 percent to GDP in 2005-06 from a level of 56.5 percent in 1951. [4] But this is not the complete picture of the rural economy. The rural economy has a strong base for employment generation. Rural economy still accounts nearly 40 percent of India's GDP including 10 percent of RNFS (rural non-farm sector). Share of agricultural exports also increased considerably. Major contribution to exports comes from the agricultural and allied sectors such as handloom, gem and jewellery, handicrafts, carpets, leather and mineral products, all of which have at least one primary rural production base.

Analyzing the trends in rural non-farm employment, based on the analysis of the data from the quinquennial rounds of the National Sample Survey during the 1990s and 2000s, reveals that though the share of rural employment in total employment has declined from around 90 percent in 1993-94 to 84.1 percent in 1999-2000 [5]; the share of the rural non-agricultural employment has increased from around 14 percent to 17 percent in total employment. Employment in the rural non-agricultural activities has thus been growing much more rapidly than the overall employment, agricultural employment and also urban employment representing fact that there has been a shift from agriculture in which employment has grown at a rate of only 0.74 percent, to the non-agricultural activities. [6]

Micro enterprises established in RNFS contribute about 40 percent of the gross industrial output and 34 percent of total exports. RNFS is the potential sector for employment generation through establishment of micro enterprises. There is a need to match the decline in agriculture sector with the gain in non-farm activities, to absorb the surplus labour arising from agriculture. Eighth Five Year Plan document (Government of India 1992: 122) states that, [7]

"In the long run, however, it must be recognized that agriculture and other land-based activities, ever with a reasonably high rate and possible diversification of growth, will not be able to provide employment to all the rural workers at adequate levels of incomes. One fifth of rural workers are engaged in non-agricultural activities. This proportion has shown a remarkably rapid increase in recent years. Available evidence suggests that this shift is attributable to the growth of productive employment opportunities in the non-farm sector in rural areas, and is not a result merely of the overcrowding in agriculture. Unlike many traditional village industries which constituted only secondary and supplementary occupations, these activities are pushed as main occupations."

Employment in the manufacturing sector has been largely generated by the small scale sector. In the total manufacturing sector, the share of registered small scale enterprises (SSEs) is 48.8 percent. The household and non registered SSEs together contribute 37 percent of the total employment generated which is to the extent of 85.8 percent of the manufacturing sector. The small scale sector produces a wide range of products, from simple consumer goods to highly precision and sophisticated end-products. As ancillaries, it produces a variety of parts and components required by the large enterprises. Rural and traditional sector enterprises largely from amongst the unregistered SSEs and non-farm sector contribute to about 15 percent of the total output of small scale industries but about 40 percent of the work force is employed in this sector. [8]

2.2 Role of Micro Enterprises

Micro enterprise refers to "a very small business that produces goods or services for cash income" [9] (Allerdice et al., 2000). Micro enterprises can be identified on the basis of a number of characteristics. For example, they usually operate in the informal sector of the economy, require little in the way of initial start-up capital and have few employees (usually defined as less than ten, although the definition used by Rogerson (1997) considers micro enterprises to have, at most, one to four employees). Micro enterprises are often home-based (Karekezi [10], 2002a; Rogerson [11], 1997) and as a result, micro enterprise employees are usually family or household members employed on a casual basis (sometimes unwaged). It is also often difficult to distinguish between household expenditure and that of the micro enterprise.

In organizational terms, micro enterprises have been characterized as having low levels of organization and informal accounts, if any (Karekezi, 2002a). According to Karekezi [12] (2002a) the primary legal feature of micro enterprises is that they are not registered with a Registrar of Companies, nor recorded in official or tax records. Such businesses may or may not have the necessary licenses to operate and as a result of their low-profile, informal nature, they are not usually tracked by official government statistics (Allerdice et al., 2000). Micro enterprises operate in a number of economic sectors, including commerce (e.g. retail and trading in new and second-hand goods); manufacture (i.e. production activities) and service (including personal and non-personal services). The distinction has also been made between "survivalist" micro enterprise businesses and "flyers" or "potential flyers" which typically have different needs (Heeks [13] et al., 2001) and, in the case of the latter, greater potential for growth and development.

In order to mitigate the problems of unemployment and poverty, micro enterprises have come up because they fulfil many priorities of development. Micro enterprise refers to "a very small business that produces goods or services for cash income." Small and micro enterprises are generally more labour intensive. They lack technical experience in production, accounting, administration and stock control due to low levels of qualification. Most of the time they are unregistered and family based. Micro enterprises usually operate in the informal sector of the economy, mainly in rural areas. Initially they start with very low amount of capital and have very few employees.

Micro enterprise employees are usually family or household members employed on a casual basis sometimes unwaged. It is also often difficult to distinguish between household expenditure and that of the micro enterprises. In organization terms, micro enterprises have been characterized as having low levels of organization and informal accounts. As a result of their low-profile and informal nature, they are not usually tracked by official govt. statistics. Micro enterprises operate in a number of economic sectors, including commerce (e.g., retail and trading in new and second hand goods), manufacturing and services.

The status of the vast majority of employment in developed countries is within the recognized institutional framework in Government as well as private sector. But in developing countries including India, the vast majority of the population is left to feed for itself and create employment out of its own recourses and skill, thereby creating a dualistic structure of formal and informal components in the employment scenario. The concept of informal or unorganized sector is difficult to define precisely. Most of the time it is defined negatively by pointing out the absence of characteristics that belong to formal activities; of special significance being labour market characteristics, regularity of work, better earnings, existence of non-wage and long term benefits, protective legislation and undue protection.

The United Nations International Year of Micro Credit, 2005 provides an occasion to raise awareness of the importance of Micro enterprise which have emerged as major strategies to combat the twin issues of poverty and unemployment. Due to large size and population around 1000 million, India's GDP ranks among the top 15 economies of the world. [14] But with liberalization and globalization of economy, opportunities for the unskilled and illiterate are not increasing fast enough as compared to the rest of economy leading to a lopsided growth in India. There are more than 300 million people living below the poverty line. The rural people are poor and economically unsound as compared to urban, because rural people depend on agriculture. India is an agriculture dominated country. With the new emphasis given to Micro enterprises, the self employment activities and household enterprises are considered as essential factors for achieving socio-economic development in the developing countries. [15]

Indian economy registered a growth rate of 8.1 percent in 2004, 8.3 percent in 2005 and 7.9 percent in 2006 and 8.7 percent in 2007. Orissa, despite its abundant resources both natural and human, has been one of the poorest States in the country with more than 40 percent of its people living below the poverty line. [16] The rural people of Orissa are working hard throughout the year but not able to develop economically. Because agriculture in Orissa is exposed to various natural calamities like flood, drought, earthquake etc. The trend of development in agriculture is slower than that of industry. Inadequate infrastructure is another hindrance to the production, storage and marketing of agricultural products.

The increase in population and consequent addition to labour force created the problem of unemployment and underemployment. The development efforts of the state have remained largely trapped in the vicious circle of poverty. Women constitute around half of the total population. Hence, they are regarded as the better half of the country. Our society is still male dominated and women are not treated as equal partners both inside and outside four walls of the house. Our age-old socio-cultural traditions and taboos arresting the women within four walls of their houses also make their conditions more miserable. Due to these unfavourable conditions, the development of women entrepreneurship is unexpectedly low in the country. Despite various measures undertaken for protection of women's rights, status of women continues to remain low.

The growth of informal sector gives rise to the growth of micro enterprises which is characterized with small scale operation, family ownership of the enterprise, reliance on indigenous resources, labour intensive and adaptative technology and traditional skills. These micro enterprises (ME), in both rural and urban, form a part of the household sector. These are basically created, managed and financed by the entrepreneur himself/herself and his family members for their self-employment and may be giving employment to a few people outside their family. [17]

2.3 Entrepreneurship in India

Entrepreneurs and entrepreneurship are the lifeblood of any economy, mainly in the context of a developing economy. In India, entrepreneurship is in the state of infancy. One of the most important aspects responsible for economic development and poverty alleviation is entrepreneurship. Local enterprises manifested in the form of small or micro enterprises have become the important source of employment which helps to improve workforce participation as they are basically labour intensive, use local raw materials, traditional skill and indigenous technology.

Entrepreneurship is the active process of recognizing an economic demand in an economy and` supplying the factors of production (land, labour and capital) to satisfy that demand usually to generate a profit. High levels of poverty combined with slow economic growth in the formal sector have forced a large part of the developing world's population to shift for self employment. Micro enterprises contribute significantly to economic growth, equity and social stability. The sector is one of the most important vehicles through which low income people can escape poverty. With limited skills and education the poor people find economic opportunities in micro enterprises.

Micro enterprises mainly deal with initiating, promoting and maintaining economic activities for the production and distribution of income and wealth. It implies recognition of values of individual liberty, innovation, risk taking and independence. In most developing countries, micro enterprises and small-scale enterprises account for the majority of firms and a large share of employment. Small and medium enterprises constitute the most dynamic segment of many transition and developing economies. The role of micro-entrepreneurship in poverty alleviation and economic development in developing countries is promising. It has already been identified that micro-entrepreneurship is a major contributing factor to economic growth.

The person who carries out entrepreneurial activities is an entrepreneur who searches for change, responds to it and exploits it continuously as an opportunity in creating wealth and opportunity not only for self (themselves) but also opportunities to other sections of the society making human lives more comfortable and easier.

Micro entrepreneurs by virtue of their initiatives, earnestness, creativities they accomplish significant advances in national production and obtain incidentally a good slice of the increasing national income as a reward for their untiring conscious effort in the form of profit which they consider the indicator of success.

2.4 Micro Finance for Poverty Eradication

The lesson of successful micro finance model in Bangladesh is the example for any country to tackle the twin problems of mass poverty and unemployment. Micro finance or micro credit movement means the provision of financial services of small quantity to the poor. The Micro Credit Summit at Washington (1997) defined micro credit programme as those extending small loans to poor people for self-employment projects that generate income for themselves and their families. [18] The NABARD task force on micro finance (2000) defined it as the provision of thrift, credit and other financial services and products of very small amounts to the poor in rural, semi urban or urban areas enabling them to raise their income levels. [19]

Micro finance is an effective and financially sustainable tool for eradicating poverty, particularly in developing country. The idea of micro finance rolled around the philosophy of Prof. Mohammad Yunus of Bangladesh who initiated organizing poorest of the poor into self-help groups (SHGs) named Bangladesh Grameen Bank in the year 1976. He explained the theory of survival to the poorest of the poor. In the initial stage SHGs were effective and viable local based organizations for poverty alleviation. The primary focus is a savings and loans. The groups collect regular thrift from the members on pre-agreed terms, form thrift fund; the group provides loans to members. [20]

In a recent meeting, which addressing the industrialists of the country, the Prime Minister of India called upon the corporate leaders to strive for equitable wealth and income distribution across the society. He said "rising income and wealth inequality, if not matched by a corresponding rise of income across the nation, can lead to social unrest." Many of the physical scientists believe that wealth and income can never be uniform in a society and 5-10 percent of the population will remain wealthy and 90-95 percent will be relatively poor. So micro enterprises play a vital role for removing the poverty of the people which will help in economic development of the country. [21]

Rural poverty is the highest in Orissa. Rural people depend mostly on agricultural and forest produce for their subsistence. Agricultural growth is virtually stagnant and employment opportunities are very limited. People in rural areas live precariously from one day to the next. A large number of rural communities particularly in hilly terrains of western and southern Orissa are physically excluded for want of connectivity and other infrastructural support like market, urban areas and the poor in general lack access to growth centres and service centre. The pace of poverty reduction has been sluggish in Orissa and it continues to the most intractable problem for the state in particular and country in general.

There must be a vision to promote micro enterprises. Micro enterprise is an attempt for economic empowerment of the poor, to make them financially independent and to make them an integral part of the market based economy. In India, micro finance was initially promoted by NABARD through the encouragement to form self-help groups. The importance of micro enterprises and poverty alleviation strategies has been a major concern of most successive Governments in any developing countries. Diversified micro credit programmes through institutions are better way to serve poor, to eradicate poverty and to give a better standard of living.

Micro credit has been accepted as the best approach to entrepreneurship development and poverty alleviation both in rural and urban areas. Littlefield, Murduch and Hashemi (2003) clams, "If you are going to provide financial service permanently to people, they have got to be sustainable and that means charging interest rates that cover your costs [22]," Similarly, the IFC (2004) notes, "well managed micro enterprises have convincingly demonstrated that they can become profitable and sustainable institutions while making major contributions to poverty alleviation by increasing economic opportunities and employment". [23]

Micro finance plays a key role for inclusive growth by providing employment and means of livelihood for both the agricultural and non-agricultural population through establishment of micro enterprises. Entrepreneurs engaged in micro enterprises also need technical assistance and support services to enable them set up their own business and grow into larger sizes. The benefits arising out of micro entrepreneurship in most of these countries are compelling, and its potential effects on the developments process are equally promising. It is learnt that micro finance movement is a sustainable and effective tool for poor and disadvantaged sections to access institutional credit through different processes and micro enterprise development as the most effective strategy to address the problems of the overall economy. Keeping this in mind, the ultimate objectives to make poor people self-dependent, pulling them from poverty and to give them standard of livelihood, it is necessary to provide a place for micro credit investment.

Entrepreneurship is the active process of recognizing an economic demand in an economy, and supplying the factors of production (land, labour and capital) to satisfy that demand, usually to generate a profit. High levels of poverty combined with slow economic growth in the formal sector have forced a large part of the developing world's population to shift for self-employment and informal activities. But this is not necessarily negative; micro enterprises contribute significantly to economic growth, social stability and equity. The sector is one of the most important vehicles through which low-income people can escape poverty. With limited skills and education to compete for formal sector jobs, these men and women find economic opportunities in micro enterprises.

They include a variety of firms–village handicrafts makers, small machine shops, restaurants, and computer software firms–that possess a wide range of sophistication and skills, and operate in very different markets and social environments. In most developing countries, micro enterprises and small-scale enterprises account for the majority of firms and a large share of employment. Finally, it has been noted that, "SMEs constitute the most dynamic segment of many transition and developing economies. They are more innovative, faster growing, and possibly more profitable as compared to larger-sized enterprises." [24] Hence, the role of micro-entrepreneurship in reducing poverty in Less Developing Countries is promising. [25]

It has already been identified that micro-entrepreneurship is a major contributing factor to economic growth, however, entrepreneurial ability and leadership tend to be relatively lacking in Less Developing Countries. Collier and Batty [26] (pp. 491/492) have identified five primary reasons for the shortage of entrepreneurs in Less Developing Countries. This includes the limited profit opportunities which exist in less-developing countries because of lower per capita incomes and limited markets, poorly developed capital markets, and infrastructures, adverse social, cultural and religious beliefs and attitudes and above all an unfavourable economic and political climate which usually discourage the development of micro-entrepreneurial talent and initiative.

2.5 Role of the Government

The governments of Less Developing Countries can play an important role in improving the quantity and quality of micro-entrepreneurs in a number of ways. Collier and Batty suggest a number of policies to reduce the shortage of entrepreneurs in Less Developing Countries, such as the establishment of specialist educational institutions offering courses in business management and administration, and the establishment of specialist government agencies and departments to provide advice and assistance to local entrepreneurs about to take up a business venture are likely to aid the process. Additionally, tax relief, subsidies, investment allowances and other incentives may encourage entrepreneurial activities, similarly, the provision of credit facilities to finance appropriate new business ventures might help. Improved business regulations, tax regimes, licensing requirements, financial sector reform and bank supervision will promote better conditions for micro enterprise development.

The present day society consists of two halves: (a) business, and (b) social. The business half has made phenomenal progress because it has benefited from application of entrepreneurial energy in free market, competitive economies. In contrast, the social half, with its bureaucratic and monopolistic structure, has stagnated over the years because it has had very little scope for infusion of entrepreneurial energy in its operations. With rapid growth of citizen sector organizations, the social half will also make fast progress in coming years.

Many of the public sector enterprises (e.g., Housing Development Corporation, Agro-Industries Corporation, Irrigation Development Corporation etc.) and cooperative sector units were established long back in India with primarily social goals in view. However, most of them have turned bureaucratic, ineffective, and loss-making units over the years and failed to achieve the social goals set for them. There is considerable scope for injecting entrepreneurial energy and passion for social development in many of these enterprises through collaborative arrangements or through outsourcing of works to NGOs. In order to be successful in developing such collaborations, the support from policy-makers is often required. In recent years, micro-credit, micro enterprises and self-help groups have emerged as major tools for development of poor people. NGO sector has been playing a major role in these fields. In many areas, mutually aided cooperative societies and linkages with banking institutions have been formed to provide sustainable structure for these initiatives.

2.6 Policy Prescriptions

There is no doubt, poverty is one of the biggest problem in

the world today, and how to solve this problem is one of the greatest task facing everyone of us. When estimating poverty worldwide, the same reference poverty line has to be used, and expressed in a common unit across countries. Therefore, for the purpose of global aggregation and comparison, the World Bank uses reference lines set at US$ 1 per day for the "poorest" or "very poor" people (or those in the extreme economic poverty) and US$ 2 per day for the "poor" people who are living in the upper half of those living below their nation's poverty line (more precisely US$ 1.08 and US$ 2.15 in 1993 Purchasing Power Parity terms). It has been estimated that in 2001, 1.1 billion people had consumption levels below US$ 1 a day and 2.7 billion lived on less than US$ 2 a day. [27]

Rural poverty, aggravated by population growth, has pushed rural folk to migrate to cities. But the failure of the stagnant industrial sector to absorb them has caused many workers to remain unemployed (defined as lacking a job or business and not looking for work because of a belief that no work is available, temporary illness/disability, bad weather, or pending job application/interview) or underemployed.

In many cases many of the world's poor people cannot improve their own lives because they have little access to the financial products and services that help those in the developed world bridge the gap when times are tough. Without life or health insurance, diseases and illness go untreated and the death of an income earner is a dramatic hardship for a family. Without access to loans or credit, shop-owners cannot buy products in bulk and farmers cannot buy machinery or even seeds after a natural disaster or a poor yield the season before. Without access to savings accounts, money is hidden in walls or floorboards where it can be stolen or lost in a flood or fire.

Traditional finance systems have long histories and countless variations. In fact, in most countries they continue to flourish despite the emergence of formal finance systems. Broadly, these can be seen as ranging from traditional institutions such as local money lending and self-finance from relatives and friends, to more formal sources of credit such as trade credit and group-based MFPs promoted by Non-government Organizations (NGOs) (Rutherford [28], 2000; Burman [29], 1995).

Perhaps the most common source of informal finance is loans from family and friends, characterized by uncollateralized credit that carries little or no interest. These are typically small loans, with open-ended repayment arrangements and a strong focus on reciprocity. They are usually intended to meet the consumption and contingency needs of households, rather than to build investment capability.

A commercial variation of such loans is the traditional moneylender. Moneylenders directly draw on traditional patron-client relationships or a set of hierarchical social interactions that are reminiscent of the vertical dimensions of Coleman's [30] (1990) definition of social capital. These relationships are exploitative in nature, as interest rates are set in such a way that full repayment is unlikely (Bastelaer, 1999; Johnson and Roglay, 1997 [31]).

Apart from self-finance, in many countries trade credit is the only other source of operational funds for small and medium enterprises. Personal relationships between the purchaser and the supplier, as well as the links that arise from a shared ethnic background, are critical elements for the extension of trade credit.

These informal sources have played a vital role in meeting the financial, social and safety net needs of the poor in urban and rural areas. Their services are easily accessible, flexible and responsive to clients' specific needs. Furthermore, they have the major advantage of being able to meet the credit needs of the poor more efficiently, as they can handle small sums of money without complex procedures or documentation.

The policymakers and practitioners who have been trying to improve the lives of the poorest and poor people face an uphill battle. Reports of bureaucratic sprawl and unchecked corruption abound. And many now believe that government assistance to the poor often creates dependency and disincentives that make matters worse, not better. Moreover, despite decades of aid, communities and families appear to be increasingly fractured, offering a fragile foundation on which to build.

Amid the dispiriting news, excitement is building about a set of unusual financial institutions prospering in distant corners of the world. The hope is that much poverty can be alleviated–and that economic and social structures can be transformed fundamentally–by providing financial services to low-income households. These institutions, united under the banner of *micro finance for micro enterprise*, share a commitment to serving poor that have been excluded from the formal banking sector.

Micro finance can be described as 'the provision of financial services dealing with very small deposits and loans' (Bastelaer, 1999:6 [32]). As a concept it emerged in the early 1990s with the recognition that poor people needed a wide range of financial services, covering credit, savings, insurance and money transfers (Rutherford, 2000; Robinson [33], 2001). These services have traditionally been provided by informal or indigenous financial institutions, with formal financial institutions having emerged as an alternative in more recent times [34] (Rutherford, 2000).

MEs through MFPs operate on the principle of group-based lending, commonly referred to as 'solidarity groups' [35] (Reinke, 1998). They consist of self-selected, small and homogeneous borrower groups, jointly liable for loans, with varying degrees of participation in program management. Joint responsibility and liability for loans enhance accountability and result in a higher rate of repayment than the standard bilateral loan agreements of formal financial systems. Credit disbursement is organized on the principle of 'social collateral,' where borrowers' reputation or the social networks to which they belong take the place of traditional physical or financial collateral.

In this sense, MEs operate through existing stocks of social capital. The group processes strengthen existing social relations, institutions and shared values and in the process create an environment supportive for the emergence of fresh social capital (Narayan [36], 2000; Mayoux [37], 1999a). They transform 'beneficiaries' into 'clients' through the development and enforcement of contracts between lenders and borrowers and by supporting the ownership and control of resources by the poorest. Some writers have argued that these programmes have resulted in a shift from transferring resources to the poor to emphasizing building sustainable institutions (Edgcomb [38] and Barton [39], 1998). Despite this, almost all group-based MEs incorporate some form of social intermediation, an important factor for promoting sustainable development (Bennett and Goldberg, 1993). Social intermediation is the process in which investments are made in the development of human resources and institutional capital, with the aim of increasing the self-reliance of marginalized groups and preparing them to engage in formal financial intermediation (Bennett [40], 1992; and Barton [41], 1998).

Group-based credit programmes promoted by NGOs allow poor people access to financial services that they have historically been denied. In this sense, they address the market failures of formal financial institutions (Khandker [42], 1998; May and et al. [43]; Wood and Sharif, 1997). MFPs, by extending loans for production, support a virtuous cycle of investment, savings and further investments. In fact, credit is seen as a mechanism for generating self-employment opportunities for the poor and/or improving the productivity of existing enterprises, referred to as the 'promotional' strategy by Hulme [44] (1991:106). This leads to economic empowerment, which is assumed to promote a 'virtuous spiral' of broader social and political change by women (May et al., 1998b, 1999b; Ebdon, 1995). By making consumption credit available during periods of cyclical or unexpected crisis, MEs also play a social protection role (Edgcomb [45] and Barton, 1998:1; Hulme [46] 2000).

Whether they are instruments to tackle market failures or to reduce poverty, MEs practice financial and social intermediation for their targeted clienteles. Further, the group-based approach has been recognized as having the capacity to empower the most vulnerable and marginalized, especially women, by creating a community-based structure that builds mutual support and trust. Such an approach allows for greater economic and social integration for the marginalized section of society, thereby directly addressing issues of vulnerability.

Micro finance and micro enterprise services have the capacity to generate benefits at the community, household and individual levels. Several studies of the micro finance field provide a closer look at the impacts to service recipients and the significance of their micro enterprise. For example, on an issue published by the Community Development Department of the Federal Reserve Bank of San Francisco, Valerie Plummer the Executive Director of Oregon Micro Enterprise Network (OMEN) points: "In rural areas, self-employment has become a central means to cope with structural unemployment, caused by mill and plant closing. And in urban areas where corporate downsizing…affected communities, micro enterprise programs are often able to reach entrepreneurs with increased efficiency and breadth of services". [47]

Despite of the strong base of our rural economy, and all the rhetoric, there is consensus that more than 250 million people remain poor in India, even after 60 years of independence, irrespective of the debate on the methodology and indicators used for poverty estimates. But the harsh reality of employment growth rate is also stated in the different plan documents by narrating that the realm of feasibility is between 2.6 to 2.8 percent. Development efforts were hindered by the growth in rural population and unemployed labour force. According to the UNDP Report 2001, India ranks as low 115 out of total 162 countries. [48]

End Notes

1. NABARD, (1995), Report of the Reserve Bank of India's Working Group on Non-Governmental Organizations and Self-Help Groups, NABARD, Mumbai.
2. Das, Biswaroop (2001), Role and Impact of Micro finance on Poor, Friends of Women's World Banking India, Ahmedabad.
3. Census Data, 2001, Government of India.
4. Tenth Five Year Plan (2002-07), Volume III, Planning Commission, Government of India.
5. NSSO (55th Round), Report on Unorganized Manufacturing Sector in India, 1999-2000, September 2001, New Delhi.
6. NSSO (56th Round), Report on Unorganized Manufacturing Sector in India, 2000-2001 (Report No. 477(56/2.2/1), September 2002, New Delhi.
7. Eighth Five Year Plan Document, Government of India, 1992-93: 122.
8. Economic Review of India, 2006-2007, Government of India, New Delhi.
9. Allerdice, A. and Rogers, J.H. (2000), Renewable Energy for Micro enterprise, National Renewable Energy Laboratory (NREL), Colorado, USA.
10. Karekezi, S. and Majoro, L. (2002a), Improving Modern Energy Services for Africa's Urban Poor", Energy Policy, Vol. 30, pp. 1015-1028.
11. Rogerson, C.M. (1997), Rural Electrification and the SMME Economy in South Africa, EDRC, University of Cape Town.
12. Karekezi, S. and Majoro, L. (2002a), Improving Modern Energy Services for Africa's Urban Poor, Energy Policy, Vol. 30, pp. 1015-1028.
13. Heeks, R. and Duncombe, R. (2001), Information, Technology and Small Enterprise: A Handbook for Enterprise Support Agencies in Developing Countries, IDPM, University of Manchester, UK. Online: http://www.man.ac.uk/idpm/ictsme.htm.
14. World Bank (2005), World Development Report, 2005/6, New York, Oxford University Press.
15. United Nations, Agenda 21, Programme of Action for Sustainable Development, United Nations Conference on Environment and Development, Rio de Janeiro, Brazil, 3-14

June 1992.

16. Basu, Kishanjit and Krishan Jindal (eds.), (2000), Micro finance: Emerging Challenges, Tata McGraw-Hill, New Delhi.
17. Bhat, M.K. (2000), SHGs: Delivery Mechanism or Empowerment Tool?, Paper presented at the Workshop on Best Practices in Group Dynamics and Micro Credit, 15-17 February, Manesar, Gurgaon.
18. World Commission on Environment and Development, 1987, Our Common Future, Oxford University Press, Oxford: 116.
19. NABARD (2000), Circular, National Bank for Agriculture and Rural Development, New Delhi.
20. Harper, Malcolm (2002), Indian Self-help Groups and Bangladesh Grameen Bank Groups: A Comparative Analysis, Discussion Paper, Friends of Women's World, Banking India, Ahmedabad.
21. Times of India, 12th July 2006, p. 6.
22. Littlefield E., Murduch J. and Hashemi S., (2003), Is Micro finance an Effective Strategy to Reach the Millennium Development Goals?, Focus Note 24, CGAP, Washington, DC.
23. ILO (2004), Global Employment Trends, Geneva: ILO.
24. Zaman, H. (1999), Assessing the Impact of Micro-credit on Poverty and Vulnerability in Bangladesh, Washington, The World Bank Policy Research Working Paper No. 2145.
25. Jayaraman, B. (2001), Micro finance-Retrospect and Prospects, Occasional Paper No. 20, NABARD, Mumbai.
26. Collier, M and Batty. P., Micro enterprises and Third World Countries, World Bank Research Paper, Washington, pp. 491-492, 2003.
27. World Development Report, 1996. World Bank, Washington DC.
28. Rutherford, S. (2000), "Raising the Curtain on the Micro financial Services Era", Focus Notes, No. 15, Consultative Group to Assist the Poorest, World Bank, Washington.
29. Bouman, F. (1995), Rotating and Accumulating Savings and Credit Associations: A Development Perspective, World Development, 23(3), pp. 371-384.
30. Coleman, B. (1999), The Impact of Group Lending in Northeast Thailand, Journal of Development Economics, 60, pp. 105-141.
31. Johnson, Susan and Ben Rogaly (1997), Micro finance and Poverty Reduction, Oxfam and Action Aid, U.K.

32. Cameron, Sara (n.d.), India, Convergent Community Action (CCA) in Bihar and Jharkhand (Draft), Reaching the Unreached Case Studies, UNICEF.
33. Robinson, M. (2001), The Micro finance Revolution (The World Bank: Washington, DC).
34. Rutherford, S. (2000), Raising the Curtain on the Micro financial Services Era, Focus Notes, No. 15, Consultative Group to Assist the Poorest, World Bank, Washington.
35. SEARCH (1999), Micro finance Sans Empowerment: Quickfix Approaches to Poverty Alleviation, SEARCH Bulletin (January-March), Bangalore.
36. Narayan, D., Patel, R., Schafft, K., Radcmacher, A. and Koch-schulte, S. (2000), Voices of the Poor-Can Anyone Hear Us? World Bank, Washington, USA.
37. Mayoux, Linda (1998), Women's Empowerment and Micro finance Programmes: Approaches, Evidence and Ways Forward, DPP Working Paper No. 41.
38. Edgcomb, Elaine L., and Klein, Joyce A. (2005), Opening Opportunities, Building Ownership: Fulfilling the Promise of Micro enterprise in the United States, Fund for Innovation, Effectiveness, Learning and Dissemination, 1-140.
39. Barton, C (1998), Micro enterprise Business Development Services: Defining Institutional Options and Indicators of Performance, Micro enterprise Best Practice Project, USAID, Washington DC.
40. MYRADA (1999), A Concept Paper on Federations of Self-help Groups, Rural Management Systems Series, Paper 32, Bangalore.
41. Barton, C (1998), Micro enterprise Business Development Services: Defining Institutional Options and Indicators of Performance, Micro enterprise Best Practice Project, USAID, Washington DC.
42. Khandker, S. (2005), Micro finance and Poverty: Evidence Using Panel Data from Bangladesh, The World Bank Economic Review, 19(2), pp. 263-286.
43. May, P.H., Da Vinha, V.G. and Macqueen, D.J. (2003), Small and Medium Forest Enterprise in Brazil, Grupo Economia do Meio Ambientee Desenvolvimento Sustentável (GEMA) and International Institute for Environment and Development (IIED), London, UK.

44. Hulme, D. (1991), The Malawi Mundi Fund: Daughter of Grameen, Journal of International Development, 3(4), pp. 427-431.
45. Edgcomb, Elaine L., and Klein, Joyce A. (2005), Opening Opportunities, Building Ownership: Fulfilling the Promise of Micro enterprise in the United States, Fund for Innovation, Effectiveness, Learning and Dissemination, 1-140.
46. Hulme, David (2000), Impact Assessment Methodologies for Micro finance: Theory, Experience and Better Practice", World Development, Vol. 28, No. 1, pp. 79-98.
47. Annual Report, 2005, Federal Reserve Bank of San Francisco.
48. Country Report, UNDP, 2001.

3

Poverty Dimensions in India

Of the many afflictions and adversaries humans have to fight, poverty is perhaps the most stubborn and hardest to eliminate. India recognized the challenge of poverty and made its removal as the central aim of its economic planning. Yet, it is also distressingly true that the efforts of the governments have met with a limited degree of success than what was originally anticipated. Regardless of which figure one chooses for drawing the poverty line, a quarter of India's population–more than 250 million people–still live in the abject poverty.

For the first decade and a half after Independence in 1947, it was widely believed that growth would automatically reduce and eliminate poverty. But, by the end of the 1960s, it had become evident that growth alone was not enough, and that active state intervention through re-designed as well as new policies of income and asset redistribution was necessary. However, thanks to some very Indian complexities, social, cultural and governmental, by the end of the 1980s, the focus once again shifted to growth. The new wave of globalization has only added to this impulse.

On the face of it, the results have been most gratifying. The rate of GDP growth in India has spurted in the last four years to 9 percent, making it the second-fastest growing economy in the world, after China. But at the same time, the outcome of this growth has not necessarily been pro-poor. Thus, income and asset distribution have worsened during the last decade. The result is a heightened degree of social unrest, mostly in the countryside. In a nutshell, even the basic subsistence needs of millions of people are not being met. That is the bottom line. [1]

3.1 Facets of Poverty

There is no agreed international definition of poverty. The World Bank states that poverty is hunger. Poverty is also lack of shelter. Poverty is being sick and not being able to see a doctor. Poverty is not having access to school and not knowing how to read. Poverty is not having a job, is fear for the future, living one day at a time. Poverty is losing a child to illness brought about by unclean water. Poverty is powerlessness, lack of representation and freedom. [2]

3.1.1 Poverty is Hunger [3]: The United Nations' Food and Agriculture Organization's (FAO) report "The State of Food Insecurity in the World 2003" showed that the number of people suffering from chronic extreme hunger increased during the last half of the 1990s by 18 million. This means that 84 million people in developing and transition countries are severely undernourished. This increase reversed what had been a steady drop over the previous three decades, a period in which the share of population in the developing world experiencing chronic hunger fell from 37 percent in 1970 to 17 percent in 2000, despite the huge population increase. The problem is not that there is too little food in the world. According to the FAO, 2807 food calories per capita were produced worldwide in 2001, far more than are needed for everyone to be well-nourished. The answer is not to ship more food, except as an emergency response to famines and food crises; but to improve agricultural productivity and, as a priority, to work harder for increased income for the poor and for local food entitlements as a safety net among the rural and urban poor.

3.1.2 Poor Health and Early Death: UNICEF's "State of the World's Children 2005: Childhood Under Threat" reports that every day, about 9,000 children under age five die from primarily preventable diseases, resulting in 10.6 million deaths each year. Many of these children die from dehydration from diarrhoea caused by diseases that can be controlled with inexpensive immunizations. Poverty plays such a central role in most health problems affecting people in developing countries that it has its own designation in the International Classification of Diseases: Code Z59.5—extreme poverty.

3.1.3 Loss of Childhood: According to the International Labour Organization, about 180 million child labours are exposed to "work that is hazardous to children," while "some 110 million children in hazardous work are under age 15"; moreover, "73 million working children worldwide are less than 10 years old." An estimated 8.4 million child labours are trapped in slavery, trafficking, debt bondage, prostitution, pornography and other abhorrent conditions.

3.1.4 Denial of Right to Basic Education: Globally, almost 1 billion adults are illiterate. The World Bank estimates that in 2003 more than 100 million children did not attend school because of their poverty—thus depriving these children of the chance to escape poverty later in life.

3.1.5 Powerlessness: The poor lack access to real markets, which could offer a way out of poverty. Poverty is also the systematic exploitation, theft and abuse by the rich and by the government officials ostensibly there to help the poor must pay larger bribes, as a share of their income, than the rich just to survive. It is the debilitating and deliberately caused psychological feeling of hopelessness and dependence on whatever minimal remuneration may be offered by a particular rich family in one's sphere of life. It is the violence from within the family and without. It is the powerlessness to stop the things that hurt people and their families and keep them poor.

Extreme global inequality is also a problem. According to the most recent World Bank estimates, the average real incomes received by the one billion people in the high income countries are now 14 times those received on average by the 2.3 billion people in the low income countries. They are five times higher than those in the middle income countries. Within countries, inequality may undermine social cohesion and community development, keeping individuals from attaining the capabilities they need to escape from poverty. Social exclusion is a poverty problem in its own right; in addition, the more unequal the distribution of wealth, the larger the fraction of the population that is unable to put up collateral for a loan, so fewer children can attend school and fewer businesses and micro enterprises can expand. The likely result is not only greater poverty, but also slower economic growth, and transmission of poverty across generations. Across countries, there is a danger that rich and poor will become two worlds, separate and unequal, sowing the seeds of future international conflict, terrorist groups, global environmental destruction, spread of disease without regard to borders, and continued human misery among the poor.

3.2 Poverty Traps

The term "poverty trap" is very evocative. The phrase reminds us that where there is a trap, there is likely to be a trapper. Indeed, poverty traps are all too commonly set deliberately by the rich to ensnare the poor. But the poor become trapped when conditions of poverty perpetuate themselves and create further conditions of chronic "structural" poverty. [4] This may be in the form of:

1. Family child labour.
2. Illiteracy.
3. Debt bondage.
4. Under-nutrition and illness.
5. Low-skills.
6. High-fertility.
7. Criminality.

From the inception of the development planning in India the policies of the government have continued to be guided by the firm conviction that rapid economic growth is the prime mover in uplifting the poor by offering them more productive employment and enhancing their income.

However, the outcome of the first 20 years of planning in the country does not seem to have strengthened this conviction as there has been very tardy progress both in terms of economic growth as well as in terms of reduction of income poverty (measured as the number of poor below the income poverty line as estimated by the Planning Commission). It was not until the late seventies that the growth rate of the Indian economy actually picked up. The economy grew at the rate of more than 4 percent per annum in the late seventies, at about 5 percent during the early eighties and accelerated further since the mid-nineties. Currently, the growth rate is hovering around 8 percent.

Although the negative correlation between economic growth and poverty ratio for the entire time horizon (1973-74 to 2004-05) at the macro-level appears quite straightforward, such correlation does not necessarily affirm the pro-poorness of the growth process. In order to judge whether growth process had actually been pro-poor, it is also important to examine the picture at the disaggregate level. The rate of growth of State Domestic Product (SDP) has also been accompanied by a commensurate decline in poverty. Moreover, the all India poverty ratio masks the actual scenario and conceals the variations in poverty and inequality across location, social class, occupation group, gender, religion, etc.

The basis of such variation lies at the unequal economic, social and cultural fabric that has continued to persist even in the post-independence era. It has also to be noted that the reduction in poverty ratio and increase in per capita income do not necessarily imply an improvement in the quality of life and well-being of the poor and the disadvantaged unless factors that determine 'availability' and 'access' to the basic needs and freedoms for them are also taken into account.

3.3 Pro-Poor Growth

The notion of pro-poor growth in the Indian context is not new. The idea of such a growth process found its resonance in Sukhamoy Chakraborty's perception of poverty-reducing growth process. Prof. Chakraborty proposed during the mid-

1970s that, for growth to be poverty reducing, it should happen in a manner which increases income much more for the lowest 30 percent of the population. [5] Such an idea of pro-poor growth in a relative sense has also been applied in the recent work of Kakwani, Khamdker and Son [6], wherein growth has been defined as pro-poor if it benefits the poor more than the non-poor.

Martin Ravallion [7], however, defined pro-poor growth in an absolute sense as an increase in GDP that reduces poverty. These two definitions have generated a lively debate in the academia. Ravallion's definition [8], however, has been much more contested on the ground that it is too broad and just reducing poverty may not be a sufficient condition of pro-poorness as any growth process which reduces poverty but aggravates inequality and disparity may not be conceived as pro-poor. It is identified that the intensity of pro-poor growth as strong or weak depending on whether incomes rise proportionally faster for the poor than the non-poor. Siddiqur Osmani [9] while endorsing Kakwani's criteria of 'pro-poorness' as a policy bias in favour of the poor, proposed to define the bias a little differently–not in relation to how well the non-poor do but in relation to country's past record of poverty reduction after taking into account the initial conditions.

Howard White proposed three criteria of pro-poorness. The first criterion calls for the share of the poor in income growth to exceed their existing share. The second requires that the poor's share in incremental growth surpasses their share in population. The third and the final criterion, in the line of Frances Stewart, requires that share of the poor in incremental growth exceeds some international norm. Quentin Wodon [10] from the World Bank, however, advocated a more robust test of 'pro-poor' distributional changes by giving more weight to the poorer of the poor, as growth may lead to a proportionate reduction of a country's poor but with adverse impact on the very poor. [11]

3.4 State-wise Variations in Poverty

The classification provided by official sources, based on official poverty estimates of the Planning Commission, groups 15 major Indian states with respect to State- Specific Poverty Ratio (Head Count Ratio) above and below the national average and indicates their relative performances in poverty reduction over time. The states could be grouped into four categories on the basis of poverty ratio in the initial year (1973-74), the rate of decline in poverty over three decades, 1973-74 to 2004-05, and other characteristics, like, size of the state, income and population. [12]

Bihar and Orissa have registered a phenomenal decline in effectiveness. Andhra Pradesh has experienced a marginal decline in effectiveness in the post-reforms period. It is noteworthy that with the exception of Assam and Maharashtra, all the states that belong to category I and category II have experienced a decline in terms of anti-poverty effectiveness in the post-reforms period. The economic reforms process does not seem to have yielded benefit for the chronically poor states like Bihar, Madhya Pradesh, Uttar Pradesh and Orissa both in terms of per capita income growth and decline in poverty. Moreover, Gujarat, a prosperous state belonging to category IV, which has performed well both in terms of income growth and poverty reduction throughout the pre-reforms period has registered a decline in anti-poverty effectiveness in the post-reforms period.

The economic reforms also does not appear to have triggered any phenomenal changes in the percentage concentration of very poor [13] across the major states. However, what is really noteworthy is that seven states, namely, Assam, Punjab, Haryana, Kerala, A.P., Gujarat and Karnataka, which had experienced increase in concentration of the very poor in the pre-reforms period, have experienced a decline in such concentration in the post-reforms period with Haryana experiencing a significant decrease. However, for the relatively poorer states belonging to categories I and II the reforms appear to have either negative or imperceptible influence in terms of reduction in concentration of the very poor.

The concentration of very poor has increased post-reforms in U.P., W.B. and Orissa. For Bihar, the decline is marginal and for MP, the decline is modest. Thus, the category I and most of the category II states with relatively higher poverty ratio initially and with a more regressive record of poverty reduction over the successive plans, have persistently failed to root out the concentration of the very poor and hence failed to remove chronic poverty. The picture of regional disparity in terms of poverty reduction would become clearer in the next section where a rural-urban disparity in poverty and inequality has been examined at the all-India level and across the states. [14]

3.5 Regional Poverty and Inequality

Although, income poverty has declined significantly at the all–India level, the decline has not been uniform across rural and urban areas. The poverty reduction in urban areas has usually been sharper than that in rural areas (which is nearly 67 percent of Indian population). It also shows that although the rural income poverty has been declining continuously, income inequality had been growing till 1983-84, declined from 1983-84 to 1993-94 and increased afterwards from 1993-94 to 2004-05. On the other hand, although the urban poverty has been declining continuously, the urban inequality has been rising in an uninterrupted manner. The urban-rural differential in per capita consumption expenditure which indicates a widening disparity from 1.334 in 1973-74 to 1.882 in 2004-05 on account of a higher rate of increase in per capita expenditure in urban areas as compared to rural. [15]

There are several special features of poverty in Orissa [16]:

1. Poverty is also spatially concentrated in Orissa. Some regions such as southern Orissa are very poor.

2. Orissa is vulnerable to repeated natural calamities like droughts, floods and cyclones. The recurrent visitation of natural calamities further exacerbates distress of the people, particularly small and marginal farmers and landless labourers.
3. A large proportion of ST and SC population in western and southern Orissa are highly vulnerable. They live rather precariously from one day to the next. Women and children generally suffer more.
4. A large number of rural communities, particularly in hilly terrains of western and southern Orissa are physically excluded for want of connectivity and other infra-structural support (i.e., markets, urban areas). As a result, the poor in general and SC and ST people in particular lack access to growth centres and service centres (i.e. schools, hospitals).
5. Rural poverty is the highest in Orissa. Rural people depend mostly on agriculture and forest resources to eke out their subsistence. However, agricultural growth in Orissa is virtually stagnant. Agricultural productivity is roughly half that of the national average. Use of improved inputs (e.g., better seeds and fertilizers) is also far below the national average. Employment opportunities are very limited.
6. Though extensive forest resources are an important source of sustenance to a majority of rural poor, they are highly degraded and lack desired financial and managerial inputs. Large forest areas are devoid of regeneration and therefore, cannot provide livelihood support on a sustained basis unless substantial investments are made in them.
7. Want of adequate irrigation facilities (except in certain pockets) is another limiting factor that keeps agriculture undeveloped.
8. Orissa is also deficient in infrastructure (e.g., railways, paved roads ports and telecommunication). Optimal exploitation of its vast natural resources demands heavy investments in infra-structural development.

Besides structural poverty, the State also faces the conjectural poverty due to flood, cyclone and drought and destitute poverty of persons lacking either money or material to survive. In terms of development indicators like literacy rate, infant mortality rate, per capita income, and the living condition of the people of Orissa is far below the national average. Moreover greater inter district variation in the socio economic conditions of the people are found within the State. The State Government's capacity to develop infrastructure is very weak and limited. On the other hand, poor infrastructure inhibits adequate private investment in key sectors of the State economy which continues to languish.

Within Orissa itself, huge disparities exist between the undivided Koraput, Bolangir and Kalahandi (popularly known as KBK districts) and the rest of Orissa. The three districts were sub divided in to eight after 1992-93 and account for around 20 percent of the state's population even though geographically they cover around 30.61 percent of the area. As per the 2001 Census, about 38.41 percent people of these districts belong to the ST communities and this is one of the poorest regions in the whole of India.

The extent of destitution can be estimated from the percentage of population Below the Poverty Line (BPL) which stood at 71.40 percent of the total for the above 8 districts. Thus, it worsens the average for the state as a whole when it is already quite backward when compared to the rest of India. Though special developmental schemes have been implemented in the region it continues to be steeped in poverty. Total flow of funds under various schemes and from other sources to the KBK districts was of the order of ₹ 1,117.32 crore and ₹ 940.97 crore during 2003-04 and 2004-05 respectively. [17]

In the words of S. S. Chattopadhyay, a senior IAS officer, "Even though every new government comes up with a new scheme for the development of KBK, the implementation of it so far has not been done in a manner that would truly benefit the people. There is a joke that in order to reach some of the remote regions in KBK, four modes of travel are required–a car, jeep and boat ride and then footslogging. As a result of this inaccessibility, medical facilities and other basic development infrastructure are absent in the region." [18] (2004). Quite clearly the state has failed to make any dent on poverty of these indigenous people and the huge sums disbursed have just been dissipated or misused.

3.6 Effective Poverty Reduction Strategies

3.6.1 Development and Well-being [19]: People's visions of "development" are reflected in their livelihood strategies and in the livelihood outcomes they strive for. Thus "development" does not happen unless people participate in conceiving and realizing "development". Each form of development cooperation therefore requires an adequate level of insight into and understanding of both the livelihoods addressed and the context with which they interact.

3.6.2 Beyond Material Well-being [20]: SDC's engagements in poverty reduction should enhance "the prospects of living a life in dignity". SDC's engagement is thus value-based. Living up to such a commitment requires a livelihood approach that can capture livelihood diversity in partner countries and provide operational guidance for conceiving and implementing poverty-oriented development support that takes livelihood diversity into account.

3.6.3 Coherence between Definitions of Poverty [21]: Empowerment, understood as sustainable improvement of capabilities of the poor, thus becomes a key element of poverty reduction. Basically, capabilities are not given but acquired by human beings. Capabilities are embedded in livelihood systems. They become functional in pursuing livelihood strategies.

3.6.4 Building on Strengths and Potentials [22]: A livelihood focus in poverty reduction means to build systematically on strengths and potentials of the poor. A livelihood focus also acknowledges the role and impacts of contextual factors and forces resulting from policymaking, institutional change, external shocks and trends, etc. It therefore invites assessment of the extent to which the socioeconomic, political and cultural context is conducive to alleviating poverty.

3.6.5 People's Decision-making: Diversity of livelihood strategies is also a reflection of a diversity of rationalities guiding decision-making. Approaching poverty with a livelihood focus thus means examining explicit and implicit rationalities that shape livelihood strategies pursued by the stakeholders [23] (Syöstrand 1992, Simon [24] 1984).

3.6.6 Sustainable Livelihood: Poverty reduction aims at more sustainable livelihood. The generally accepted definition of sustainable livelihood reads: "A livelihood is sustainable when it can cope with and recover from stresses and shocks and maintain or enhance its capabilities and assets both now and in the future, without undermining the natural resource base. [25]. To become an operational guideline in development collaboration this definition also requires a context-related interpretation of sustainability that acknowledges the role of time, space, and culture".

3.6.7 Culture and Spirituality [26]: Livelihood approaches help to integrate culture into development thinking and practice as an essential dimension. The holistic approach of a livelihood focus provides insights into "how culture matters" without promoting cultural determinism of development.

Spirituality, reaching beyond religious reference frames, forms part of inner development of livelihood, attitudes and goal setting, or livelihood strategies in general, are also informed by spiritual dimensions. [27] People-oriented development thus calls for approaches that further our understanding of the roles of these aspects of sustainable livelihood.

3.7 Poverty and Informal Employment

The relationships between informal employment and poverty is often assumed but not well understood. Despite the heterogeneity within the informal economy and its contribution to growth, there are links between working informally and being poor. Average incomes are lower in the informal economy than in the formal economy. As a result, a higher percentage of people working in the informal sector, relative to the formal sector, are poor. However, there is no simple relationship between working informally and being poor or working formally and escaping poverty [28] (Charmes 1998, Sethuraman1998, and Thomas 1995). For example, millions of South Africans worked all their lives for the gold mining or commercial agricultural industries–yet never escaped poverty, because there was no living wage for unskilled but formal workers, and because upward job mobility was restricted through apartheid legislation. The relationship between informal employment and poverty appears only when informal workers are classified by employment status and by industry or trade. Informal incomes worldwide tend to decline as one move across the following types of employment: from employer to self-employed to informal and casual wage workers to industrial outworker.

The link between working in the informal sector and being poor is stronger for women than for men. A higher percentage of women than men worldwide work in the informal sector. Moreover, there is a gender gap in incomes and wages in the informal sector. This is because women worldwide are under-represented in higher income employment statuses in the informal sector (employer and self-employed) and over-represented in the lower income statuses (casual wage worker and industrial outworker). For instance, relatively few women are employers who hire others; and relatively few men are industrial outworkers. Even within the same trade or industry, men and women tend to be involved in different employment statuses. In many countries, for example, men traders tend to have larger scale operations and to deal in non-perishable items while women traders tend to have smaller scale operations and to deal in food items.

The relationship between informality and growth has been somewhat less explored than the relationship between informality and poverty. When it has been explored it has mostly been in terms of one dimension of the relationship: namely, whether and how individual informal enterprises are likely to grow. The potential for growth of informal enterprises has received particular attention in the related field of micro enterprise development. For the purposes of classification and policy development, informal enterprises can be seen as falling at some point on the following continuum either currently or potentially:

1. Survival activities.
2. Stable enterprises.
3. Dynamic growing businesses.

The risks faced by those who work in the informal economy differ by their employment status, by the industry or trade in which they are engaged, and by the wider social, economic, and political context in which they live and work. However, four broad generalizations can be made in this regard. Firstly, those who work in the formal and informal economics face the same general risks, notably: illness, property loss, disability, old age, and death. However, informal workers often face greater exposure to these general risks given the nature of their work and living conditions.

Secondly, those who work in the informal sector face greater work-related risks than those who work in the formal sector do. Dependent informal workers face little assurance or guarantee of work, low wages or earnings, few worker benefits, and unsafe or unhealthy working conditions. Independent informal workers often have insufficient market information, skills, or power and, therefore, less access to existing or emerging market opportunities. Thirdly, those who work in the informal sector typically have fewer mechanisms –

including access to formal financial instruments–for dealing with risk than those who work in the formal sector do. The opportunities enjoyed by those who work in the informal economy also differ by their employment status, by the industry or trade in which they are engaged, and by the wider social, economic, and political context in which they work. However, as a general rule, informal wage workers enjoy fewer career opportunities than formal wage workers; and informal entrepreneurs enjoy fewer market opportunities and are less competitive that formal entrepreneurs or businesses.

End Notes

1. Ahluwalia, M.S., 'Planning' in Kaushik Basu (ed.), Oxford Companion to Economics in India, 2007, New Delhi, Oxford University Press.
2. The World Bank Poverty Analysis; website: http://web.worldbank.org/wbsite /external/topics/extpoverty/extpa/0,,menupk:430373~pagepk:14 9018~pipk:149093~thesitepk:430367,00.html.
3. Smith, Stephen C., Ending Global Poverty: A Guide to What Works, Website-www.palgrave-usa.com/Catalog/product. aspx?isbn=140 965 4X.
4. Ashe, J., Christopher, E., Cosslett, R. (1993), Credit for the Poor-Past Activities and Future Directions for the United Nations Development Program (UNDP), UNDP Policy Discussion Paper, New York, UNDP.
5. The model for raising the consumption for the bottom-most 30 percent of the population in the Fifth Five Year Plan (1974-79), as developed by Professor Sukhamoy Chakravarty, was based on integration of the Leontief's Input-Output system with the models of macro-economic growth belonging to the family of Harrod-Domar. The consumption demand of the bottom-most 30 percent was mathematically quantified and integrated with the overall rate of economic growth.
6. Kakwani, N., Khamdker S. and H. Son, 'Pro-poor Growth: Concepts and Measurements with Country Case Studies, Working Paper, Number I, International Poverty Centre (IPC), August 2004, available at: < http://www.undp-

povertycentre.org>.

7. Ravallion, Martin, Pro-Poor Growth: A Primer, Policy Research Working Paper, Number 3242, World Bank, March 17, 2004.
8. Ravallion, Martin (2000), Should Poverty Measures be Anchored to the National Accounts?, mimeo, ARQADE, University of Toulouse.
9. Osmani, S., Defining Pro-poor Growth, One Pager, No. 9, January, 2005, available at: <http://www.undp-povertycentre.org>.
10. World Bank Report, 2005.
11. Bandyopadhyay, Kaushik Ranjan, Poverty Alleviation and Pro-Poor Growth in India, Asian Institute of Transport Development, New Delhi, 2007.
12. Datta, K.L. and Savita Sharma, Facets of Indian Poverty, 2002, New Delhi, Concept Publishing.
13. Very Poor is defined as people whose per capita expenditure lies below three fourth of the poverty Line. The distribution of very poor across the states have been obtained on the basis of unit level record for 49th and 55th Round, and Report No. 508 on Consumption Expenditure containing grouped data for the 61st Round. Bihar, MP and UP refer to undivided states.
14. Basu, Kishanjit and Krishan Jindal (eds.), (2000), Microfinance: Emerging Challenges, Tata McGraw-Hill, New Delhi.
15. Dash, Anup (2003), Strategies for Poverty Alleviation in India: CYSD's Holistic Approach to Empowerment through the Self-help Group Model, IDS Bulletin 34(4), 133-142.
16. Government of Orissa (2004), Human Development Report 2004, Orissa, Nabakrushna Choudhury Centre for Development Studies, Bhubaneswar, Orissa.
17. Report of Tour of the KBK Districts, July 2005, Planning Commission.
18. Chattopadhyay, Suhrid Sankar, Anguish in Bolangir, Frontline, Volume 21, Issue 05, February 28-March 12, 2004.
19. Pattnaik, B. (1994), Women Work Participation and Family Welfare, Yojana, May: 28-30.
20. Meyer, Richard L. (2001), Microfinance, Poverty Alleviation and Improving Food Security: Implications for India (Draft). IDS Bulletin, Volume 29, Number 4, October.
21. Meher, R.K. (1999), Development Disparities in a Backward

Region-A District Level Analysis, APH Publishing Corporation, New Delhi.

22. McGuire P. B. and Conroy, J. D. (2000), The Micro finance Phenomenon, Asia Pacific Review, Vol. 7, No. 1, pp. 90-108.
23. Sjöstrand, S. (1992), On the Rationale Behind "Irrational" Institutions, Journal of Economic Issues, 26(4), pp.1007-1040.
24. And Simon, H. A. (1984), Models of Bounded Rationality, Volume 1, Cambridge, MA: MIT Press.
25. Carney, D., Drinkwater, M., Rusinow, T., Neejes, K., Wanmali, S. and Singh, N. (1999), Livelihoods Approaches Compared, London: Department for International Development, DFID.
26. Mahajan, Vijay (2002), Microfinance Policy: Review and Prospective Suggestions, Presentation to the Sa-Dhan Subgroup on Policy, January.
27. Baumgartner, R. and Högger, R. (eds.) (2004), In Search of Sustainable Livelihood Systems-Managing Resources andC. New Delhi, Sage Publications.
28. Charmes J. (1998:12), A Critical Review of Concepts, Definitions and Studies in the Informal Sector, in Employment and Development: A New Review of Evident, edited by D. Turnham et al., Paris, OECD.

4

Sustainable Livelihood Framework

4.1 What is Sustainable Development?

The concept of sustainable development emerged as an important theme in 1987. The Brundtland Commission on Environment and Development in its report "Our Common Future" called for application of sustainability as a criterion for all development initiatives. "In order for development to be sustainable, it must meet the needs of the present without compromising the ability of future generations to meet their own needs [1] ", said the Commission.

This definition is highly generalized and hence has been subjected to a variety of interpretations. Broadly speaking, developed countries lay emphasis on economic and technological aspects. "How to integrate environmental costs into economic decision-making while protecting and enhancing their industrial competitiveness and employment opportunities" is a million dollar question for all. The general feeling is that the current development/growth processes can continue provided the technological innovations are rapid and appropriate enough to reduce environmental side effects.

In contrast, the perspectives of developing countries are understandably different. In their view, poverty is the greatest polluter of environment and hence they must accelerate economic growth to meet the basic needs of the people. And if the industrialized rich countries are really serious about environment, they should realize that it is they who have created the present environment crisis, not the poor countries, and hence they should assist the latter with finance and latest environment friendly technological knowhow to promote economic growth. Interestingly, both sides have a firm faith in economic growth and all that goes with it, such as industrialization, urbanization, and environmental deterioration.

Both pin their hopes in science and aim to achieve the characteristics of sustainable development listed technology to solve the emerging problems. It is simply the question of access to resources particularly finances and technology. One wants maintain the status quo, i.e., its economic and technological superiority and competitiveness; the other wants to change the existing world order to make it more egalitarian. The means for achieving the goals are the same.

The Earth Summit held at Rio de Janeiro in 1992 reemphasized the need for sustainable development, a term perhaps first used at the time of Cocoyoc Declaration in 1970 and gained popularity through IUCN report (1980, 1990) and WCED Report (1987) "Our Common Future". The term sustainability and its corollary sustainable development are being widely used in government policy pronouncements, scientific articles, publications of international aid agencies, professional literatures, seminars, and popular media. While unsustainability of the ongoing development processes is well manifested through environmental problems, declining productivity and such other indicators, how sustainability can be achieved is not very clear. Moreover, there is little unanimity in comprehending this term. It conveys different meaning to different people. In global context, view point of the developing countries differs considerably from that of the developed countries as evidenced during Rio summit. [2]

Recent writing about intergenerational equity has tended to be modest in its definition of sustainability, and so of our responsibilities for the future. This is reflected in the following quotations (cited from Pearce et al. 1989:173-185) [3]. Sustainability might be redefined in terms of a requirement that the use of resources today should not reduce real incomes in the future…sustainability ought to mean that a given stock of resources—trees, soil quality, water and so on—should not decline.

The sustainability criterion suggests that, at a minimum, future generations should be left no worse off than current generations.

We summarize the necessary conditions [for sustainable development] as 'constancy of the natural capital stock.' More strictly, the requirement is for non-negative changes in the stock of natural resources such as soil and soil quality, ground surface waters and their quality, land biomass, water biomass, and the waste assimilation capacity of receiving environment.

In principle, such an optimal [sustainable growth] policy would seek to maintain 'an acceptable' rate of growth in per capita real incomes without depleting the national capital asset stock or the natural environmental asset stock.

The concept since 1980s, particularly after the publication of the report "Our Common Future"—a good many literature is devoted to deal with the concept of sustainable development and its possible application (Barbier, 1967: Brown, et al., 1987; Daly, 1989; Lele, 1989; Pezzy, 1989: Radcliff, 1987; Rees, 1988 among others). Brown et al. (1987) and Lele (1989) summarized the essential elements covered, in various deliberations. In broad terms, these essential elements or objectives and premises cover all the following aspects:

1. Survival of human beings.
2. Survival of all other life forms.
3. Satisfaction of basic human needs.
4. Maintenance of bio-physical productivity.
5. Economic efficiency and growth.
6. Preservation of environmental quality and ecosystem.
7. Inter- and intra-generational equity.
8. Social justice.
9. Self-reliance and people's participation.
10. Stabilization of human population.
11. Promotion of values and ethics.

Sustainable development cannot be a static concept and hence cannot be defined once for all. It is a dynamic process and will be applied by different countries in tune with their own cultural, political and economic perspectives. But unless there is a broad agreement on goals, directions and means, the concept will prove sterile and the business of development will continue as usual with more tensions among the nations, states, regions and localities.

4.2 Conditions for Sustainable Livelihoods

Sustainable development has to be a long-term process, and one may say a continuing process. The economic, political, technological and social structure and superstructure built during the last few centuries the world over particularly in industrialized countries of the world cannot be dismantled in a day. No structure is, however, permanent. Elemental and partial changes do take place as a part of renewal process. This renewal process can be accelerated within the tolerable birth pangs and death agonies that mark any such change. The renewal process must aim to achieve the characteristics of sustainable development. It is four dimensional: (i) Equity among nations–rich nations, poor nations, developed nations, and developing nations; (ii) Equity within countries–between regions, social classes, genders, (iii) Equity between generations; and (iv) Equity between economics and ecology and science and spirituality.

Sustainability is the core concept, without which development effort is wasted. Policies to reduce poverty, whether the actual interventions are at local or national level, must be sustainable and continue to achieve their objectives. Sustainability, in the context of livelihoods approaches, includes not only continuing poverty reduction but, among others, environmental, social and institutional sustainability. Crucial to the success and sustainability of all interventions is the concept of good governance. Policies and services should not exclude the poor, they should meet the needs of the people and they must be properly managed and regulated at all levels.

The vulnerability context may include population trends, resource trends, (including conflict), national/international economic trends, trends in governance (including politics), technological trends, human health shocks, natural shocks, economic shocks, conflict, crop/livestock health shocks, and seasonality of prices, production, health and employment opportunities.

Human capital represents the skills, knowledge, ability to labour and good health that together enable people to pursue different livelihood strategies and achieve their livelihood objectives. At a household level, human capital is a factor of the amount and quality of labour available; this varies according to household size, skill levels, leadership potential, health status, etc.

Social capital is taken to mean the social resources upon which people draw in pursuit of their livelihood objectives. These are developed through: networks and connectedness, membership of more formalized groups, and relationships of trust, reciprocity and exchanges that facilitate co-operation, reduce transaction costs and may provide the basis for informal safety nets amongst the poor. Some people choose to distinguish between social capital and 'political capital', derived from access to wider institutions of society, though both are included here.

Natural capital is the term used for the natural resource stocks from which resource flows and services (e.g. nutrient cycling, erosion protection) useful for livelihoods are derived. There is a wide variation in the resources that make up natural capital, from intangible public goods such as the atmosphere and biodiversity to divisible assets used directly for production (trees, land, etc.).

Physical capital comprises the basic infrastructure and producer goods needed to support livelihoods. Producer goods are the tools and equipment that people use to function more productively. Infrastructure consists of changes to the physical environment that help people to meet their basic needs and to be more productive. The following components of infrastructure are usually essential for sustainable livelihoods:

affordable transport; secure shelter and buildings; adequate water supply and sanitation; clean, affordable energy; and access to information (communications).

Financial capital denotes the financial resources that people use to achieve their livelihood objectives. There are two main sources of financial capital: available stocks, which can be held in several forms such as cash, bank deposits, liquid assets such as livestock and jewellery, or resources obtained through credit-providing institutions; and regular inflows of money, including earned income, pensions, other transfers from the state, and remittances.

Transforming structures and processes are the institutions, organizations, policies and legislation that shape livelihoods. They operate at all levels, from the household to the international arena, and in all spheres, from the most private to the most public. Structures are the organizations, both private and public; those set and implement policy and legislation, deliver services, purchase, trade and perform all manner of other functions that affect livelihoods. Processes determine the way in which structures and individuals operate and interact. They include macro, sectoral, redistributive and regulatory policies, international agreements, domestic legislations, markets, culture, societal norms and beliefs, and power relations associated with age, gender, caste or class.

Livelihood strategies are the range and combination of activities and choices that people make/undertake in order to achieve their livelihood goals (including productive activities, investment strategies, reproductive choices, etc.). This is a dynamic process in which people combine activities to meet their various needs at different times. Links between urban and rural centers will need to be explored, as will the implications for decision-making and asset usage of split families. It is important to recognize that people compete (for jobs, for markets, to secure better prices, etc.). There is no 'solution' to this problem. However, its existence does underscore the importance of extending choice and opportunities for the poor and building up their ability to take advantage of these opportunities, and thinking about safety nets for those who remain unable to achieve their livelihood objectives in what will always be a competitive environment.

End Notes

1. WCED, 1987, Our Common Future, The Report of the World Commission on Environment and Development, Oxford University Press, Oxford, New York.
2. Panda, S.K. 2003, Micro-finance in Economic Empowerment of Weaker Sections. Yojana, 47 (3): 21-25.
3. Pearce, D., Markendya, A. and Barbier, E.B., 1989, Blueprint for a Green Economy, Earthscan, London.

5

Micro Finance and Self-help Groups (SHGs)

5.1 Supporting Vulnerable Groups through Micro Finance

Recognizing that capital was a major bottleneck for enhancing the income levels of the vulnerable people, efforts have been made to enhance access to capital for them. Various finance corporations for scheduled castes, scheduled tribes, backward castes, minorities, women and so on were created to make finances available to these segments. But these institutions have done badly due to over subsidizing of loans and lop sided planning. In India, the strategy of using micro-credit to generate livelihoods for the poor was adopted by the government in a big way, starting with the Small Farmers' Development Agency in early 1970s and the setting up of the network of Regional Rural Banks, (RRBs), since 1976 to serve marginal and small farmers and artisans. The nationwide Integrated Rural Development Program (IRDP) was also based on the idea of offering subsidized loans to the poor for acquisition of assets. The experiment failed, even though 56 million worth of loans were disbursed. Reasons for this were leakage of benefits to the non-poor and those who sanctioned loans and lack of backward and forward linkages. Loan repayment rates were an abysmal 20 percent.

Disillusionment with the IRDP led a number of NGOs working in livelihood promotion, such as MYRADA and PRADAN to come up with alternative ways to enable the poor to access credit from banks. The Reserve Bank of India and NABARD approved the experiments with Self-help Groups in 1992, which led to a pilot project of the bank lending to SHGs. NGOs took lead in linking SHGs with banks in Tamil Nadu. This was evaluated in 1995 and found to be worth replicating nationwide. However, banks were reluctant and it took MFIs such as BASIX to show the way on linking SHGs. Till 1998, MFIs were the leading lenders to SHGs. In 1999, on the recommendations of a task force coupled with the impetus given by NABARD and state governments like AP, led to a steady increase in bank linkage with SHGs. By 2003, over 750,000 SHGs with over 12 million members had received a cumulative of ₹ 2,600 crore of credit from banks. The SHG-bank linkage program became the predominant method of extending micro-credit in India.

Subsequently, a second track developed in micro finance where the micro finance institutions (MFI) lent to the poor, either through SHGs, Grameen style groups or joint liability groups or even individually. SEWA Bank, SHARE, CASHPOR, Spandana and BASIX are examples of such MFIs. A number of NGOs built up substantial direct portfolios, supported by apex lenders such as, the Rashtriya Mahila Kosh and the SIDBI Foundation for Micro credit and others. Later, a third track gathered momentum, mainly in AP, with Mutually Aided Cooperative Societies (MACS) for thrift and credit, some arising out of SHGs and others directly of members. By 2003, there were over 2000 MACS in AP. However, micro credit proved to be less effective as a tool for livelihood promotion in case of poorer households and in remote areas and sluggish economies.

5.2 Cluster Development Initiatives [1]

In both industrialized and developing countries, there is increasing evidence that clustering and networking can help micro (including artisanal), small and medium enterprises (MSMEs) boost their competitiveness. MSMEs in clusters have the qualities to effectively implement support initiatives aimed at enlarging the production base, capturing niche markets, accessing export markets, offering employment opportunities, alleviating poverty and redressing regional economic imbalances.

A cluster can be defined as a sectoral and geographical

concentration of enterprises whether micro or small and medium enterprises (SMEs), but faced with common opportunities and threats that can:

1. Give rise to external economies like presence of specialized suppliers of raw materials, components and machinery; sector specific skills etc.;
2. Lead to the emergence of specialized technical, administrative and financial services;
3. Create a conducive ground for the development of selective inter-firm business co-operation and specialization as well as of co-operation among public and private institutions to promote production, innovation and collective learning.

Ever since the early 1990s of the 20th century, several cluster development initiatives have been undertaken both in industrially developed and developing countries by a range of national and international institutions with a diversity of objectives. United Nations Industrial Development Organization (UNIDO) is one of the early starters that has developed since 1993 an approach to help the public and the private sector co-operate in the design and implementation of cluster development programs to re-vitalize "underachieving" micro enterprise and SME clusters. This program draws lessons from the experience of successful clusters, in developed and developing economies as well from UNIDO's own cluster development initiative in various developing countries.

Indian Milieu: Although SSI clusters are present in the country for decades, targeting growth of SSIs through cluster-based development is a fairly recent phenomenon. It started with the State Bank of India initiative in 1989 and was soon followed by the Small Industries Development Bank of India (SIDBI) in 1991. A study of SME clusters of India undertaken in November 1996 by UNIDO resulted in the first ever database of 138 SME clusters. In 1997 the Abid Hussain Committee recommended "...clusters as the centrepiece. Such cluster can lower transaction costs, help realize informational economies and lower the costs of credit surveillance...". The Committee also felt that "…this is a very practical approach to SSE promotion in India since there already exists a large range of small scale industry clusters across the country…".

However, the real impetus for cluster-based growth of SSIs came in the 21st century. The phenomenon and significance of clusters was clearly recognized and received strong policy support and interest from the Government of India. The list of SME/industrial clusters has subsequently been updated in the year 2003 and it is now estimated that there are 388 SME/industrial clusters. Similarly, Micro Enterprise Clusters, particularly handicrafts and handloom based clusters, have been estimated to be more than 3,000 in number and are also being documented with support drawn from the Ministry of Textiles at the National level as well as from the State Governments.

Some Indian SME clusters are so big that they account for 90 percent of India's total production in selected products, e.g. the knitwear cluster of Ludhiana. Almost the entire Gems and Jewellery exports are from the clusters of Surat and Mumbai. Similarly, the clusters of Chennai, Agra and Kolkata are well known for leather and leather products. However, the majority of clusters in the micro (artisanal) sector are very specialized and small with no more than hundred artisans. However, some artisanal clusters, especially those with the handloom sector are large having over 1000 artisans. However, only a tiny minority of such artisan clusters can be stated as globally competitive.

5.3 Micro Enterprises and Poverty Alleviation

Micro-entrepreneurs can be defined as small businesses with no more than five employees, assets of less than ₹ 10,000 and a turnover of less than ₹ 50,000. They are often treated with hostility when they venture into formal sector financial institutions. These institutions are unwilling or unable to service the financial needs of micro-entrepreneurs, who do not normally have sufficient collateral to satisfy banking requirements or maintain financial records that could allow reasoned financial analysis (Christodoulou, Kirsten and Badenhorst, 1993:9). [2]

Around the world, the SMME sector is gaining increased recognition as an important means by which economic development, social empowerment and job-creation can be facilitated. This holds particular scope for women in that they tend to be the poorest of the poor and have limited formal employment opportunities. The limited employment opportunities contribute to the rising rates of unemployment (Nunes, 1998:1). [3] The economic role of the informal sector is to provide livelihoods for people. It supplies a range of goods and services which the formal sector fails to make accessible to the majority. Consumers are provided with additional goods, which the formal sector does not provide. A manufacturing sector can be created for people to enable them to be employed and develop themselves [4] (Elkan, 1988:172). As in many parts of the world, smaller scale enterprise is believed to have played a significant role in poverty reduction and economic growth.

Micro Enterprise Development Programme intervention for sustainable livelihood is focused on these three broad areas. [5]

1. **Demand-driven Approach:** Activities of programme locations are based on the needs and demands of the market coupled with the ability and potential of micro-entrepreneurs to meet those demands. Programme intervention and entry are based on a thorough understanding on resource potential, people, and market demand for products and services. The successes of these enterprises are dependent on the strengths of a community and their ability to exploit local comparative advantages.
2. **Building Local Capacity:** Activities in the programme are focused on strengthening the capacity of local businesses,

institutions and organizations to promote and develop micro enterprise and employment opportunities.

3. **Sustainable Enterprise Partnership:** The programme promotes strategic alliances and networks between programme partners to support micro enterprise development. These alliances and networks aim to make a consorted effort to mobilize local resources and initiatives to reduce poverty by stimulating micro enterprise growth.

As with the complementary rights-based approach [6], the livelihoods approach may entail broadening the types of stakeholders generally involved in enterprise development, to acknowledge of the needs of:

1. Poor entrepreneurs, including women, the poorest and most disadvantaged and particularly those involved in micro enterprise.
2. Workers in enterprises of all sizes.
3. Other affected poor and disadvantaged people in the households, communities and markets where enterprises are being promoted.

In rural areas, in addition to the legion of subsistence and small farmers, there is a growing percentage of individuals whose primary source of income is trading, cottage industries and a wide range of services. Those who engage in these activities are the landless and arguably, the poorest group in the society [7] (Holcombe, 1995:45). The 1988 World Conference on Micro enterprise referred to the informal sector as "the major development agent for employment creation, income generation and social stabilization in the next decade" [8] (Ashe, Christopher and Cosslett, 1993:18). This sector of the economy is growing in importance in India, but it faces obstacles that affect the growth, profitability and even the sustainability of these smallest economic activities. The role played by the MEs in rural and tribal areas to eradicate poverty by sustainable development can be summed up by the following.

1. **Increasing Access to Basic Needs:** The aim of the SMEs

is extended beyond economic success to explicit social and environmental ends [9] (Macqueen et al., 2005).

2. **Enhancing Security and Resolving Conflicts:** Micro enterprises have proved effective in securing access to natural and financial resources. Conflicts often arise when authorities do not consult local people or recognize their rights.
3. **Overcoming Social Isolation and Powerlessness:** Individual SMEs are often unaware of support opportunities. Micro enterprises pool the knowledge and contacts of their members or provide resources for dedicated people to undertake networking. Larger micro enterprises can create extensive networking opportunities for their members.
4. **Providing Decent Work:** Joint investment through micro enterprises can open up new employment opportunities. They can also attract donor support for better working facilities—where individual enterprises would be politically less fundable and have opened the door to group certification or fair trade that would have proved too costly for individual members. Associations and unions have been at the forefront of the fight to keep SMFEs open and to improve worker conditions. For example, the Gujarat Timber Merchants' association in India has fought the closure of small sawmills due to strong conservation legislation [10] (Bose et al., 2006). Yet, basic salaries, worker health and safety are often worse in SMFEs than in larger enterprises [11] (May et al., 2003; ILO, 2001). Overcoming competitive pressure, scale inefficiencies, inadequate access to capital and disabling policy environments in order to reverse that trend is a major challenge for associations.
5. **Preventing Environmental Degradation:** Local micro enterprises are generally more accountable to local people than large external companies–and there are many examples of good environmental management as a result.

For example, indigenous peoples in the southern states of Mexico, angered by watching their forests degraded by outsiders, fought a successful campaign against imposed concessions and won rights to operate their own micro enterprises adhering to their own environmental values.

6. **Strengthening Cultural Identity:** Cultural identity is extremely important to the many indigenous peoples of the world. It can be defined as: "a set of distinctive spiritual, material, intellectual and emotional features of society or a social group, and that it encompasses, in addition to art and literature, lifestyles, ways of living together, value systems, traditions and beliefs" [12] (UNESCO, 2002). Various methods have been developed to measure cultural and sacred values in landscapes [13] (Putney, 2000) and in forest decision making [14] (Rowcroft et al., 2006). A common way of understanding culture sees it as consisting of three elements: values; norms, rule and principles (what we ought to do) and products (or artifacts). The cultures of forest peoples are not only rich source of diversity, but are also in many cases vital to the sustainable use of forests. [15] (Colchester, 2006). When self-assessing the most important assets within their communities, the Makushi identified culture as a key resource, based in no small part on their sustainable interaction with surrounding forest resources [16] (Ousman et al., 2006).

Jayshree Vyas, Managing Director, SEWA (Self-employed Women's Association), Ahmedabad in 1974 made a detailed study on self employed women and concluded that women workers in the informal sector are economically very active and are mainly involved in production, trading and the service sector. They largely depend on finances from the informal sector like money-lenders, relatives and friends. The poor are ready to contribute and are good repayers of loans if they are served suitably. Suitable mechanism, continued personal relationship, and integrated approach can help poor people's financial institutions to be financially viable and suitable. So banking with the poor needs to be considered as sustainable and potential banking business. [17]

D.S.K. Rao, Faculty Member of BIRD, (Bankers Institute of Rural Development), Lucknow make a case study of Cauvery Grameena Bank, sponsored by State Bank of Mysore (SBM) in 1976. He found that Cauvery Grameena Banks financed SHGs, promoted by NGOs since the launch of the Pilot project by NABARD. The phenomenal repayment rate of almost 100 percent under SHG financing, attracted the attention of NABARD. As the average deposit and loan size of SHGs is larger than that of individual depositors and borrowers, forming and financing SHGs must be profitable to rural banks.

S.M. Sheokand, General Manager, NABARD, Micro Credit Innovations Department, Mumbai, 1992 studied the reorienting banking with the poor in detailed manner. He found that the introduction of the pilot phase of the SHG-Bank linkage programme could be considered as a landmark development in the banking with the poor. The RBI was quick to accept most of the major recommendations and advised the banks to consider mainstreaming lending to the SHGs as part of their rural credit operations. Small affinity groups of poor, with initial outside support can effectively manage and supervise micro credit among its members. The SHG linkage programme offers a win-win situation for the credit delivery system comprising banks of all types, NGOs and SHGs. [18]

Md. Shafiqual Haque Choudhury, Chief Executive of ASA (Association of Social Advancement) Bangladesh in 1997 made detailed study on sustainable micro finance operations through institutional arrangement and observed that micro finance and micro enterprise is a recent innovation for poverty reduction among the poor. [19]

R. Malhotra and D. S. Chauhan, Faculty Associates, BIRD Lucknow in 1997 reviewed the micro finance initiatives taken by OBC (Oriental Bank of Commerce) and proved that micro finance and micro enterprise programs are not only laden with immense potential for socio-economic empowerment but also offer commercially viable and sustainable opportunities for financial institutions. Micro finance is used extensively by the poor to bridge their deficit credit gap for both consumption and production purposes. The effective access of even small amount of credit by the poor can, therefore, become a powerful instrument in poverty alleviation. [20]

Girija Srinivasan, Consultant of Self-help Promoting Institutions (SHPIs) in 1997 made detailed study of SHGs and their linkage to banks. The role of the Self-help Promoting Institutions (SHPIs) in group formation and nurturing and NGOs are building social capital. Social capital is defined as those features of social organization such as networks, norms and trust that facilitate co-ordination and co-operation for mutual benefit.

He examined that NGOs can generate a sound base for their members to develop their credibility as borrowers and encourage financial institutions to develop confidence in establishing a lending relationship with the groups. Thus a sustainable process of liking the poor borrowers to sources of capital and other financial services with formal financial institutions is achieved. [21]

Krishan Jindal, Faculty Member, BIRD, Lucknow made a case study of South Malabar Gramin Bank (SMGB) of successful efforts in micro finance in 1998. SMGB, sponsored by Canara Bank operates five districts of Kerala with a network of 180 branches. The SMGB provide loans to NGOs for on-lending to the self-help groups (SHGs). The role of bank after sanctioning of loan is confined mainly to attending meetings of SHGs on a selective basis and maintaining constant liaison with the NGOs. The recovery of the bank is about 97.7 percent. Presently the risk cost is almost negligible. But the bank feels that the risk cost could be higher in future. [22]

S.R. Hashim, Member Secretary, Planning Commission, Government of India reviewed the importance of micro finance and micro enterprises for economic development of poor people in 2005. He emphasizes that institutions like SHGs and their linkage with the banks are very important for extending credit facilities to the poor people. SHGs occupy pivotal role for mobilization of resources and extending loans to needy poor people for the purpose of poverty alleviation programmes in our country. There is a large scope for employment generation in the self-employment oriented activities. [23]

Micro enterprises are generally grouped into low return survival activities and higher return entrepreneurial activities. Entrepreneurial micro enterprises are larger, more highly capitalized, employ more labour and use more sophisticated technologies. They tend to operate continuously rather than intermittently, reinvest surpluses and have lower closure rates. They are usually primary household income sources and are mostly operated by men. These occupations operate without excessive pressure from competitors. They are also insulated from the seasonal fluctuations in input supplies.

Survival activities, on the other hand, are usually secondary sources of income and are mostly operated by women. They are characterized by low barriers to entry, undifferentiated products, saturated markets and inefficiencies which limit their competitiveness. They often rely on inputs which their owners gather themselves from locally available sources and these supplies vary seasonally. Production processes in survival occupations are also prone to climatic fluctuations and as a result, very few of these enterprises earn income which is close to the poverty line.

Despite the euphoria of micro finance revolution, recent evidence suggests that micro finance alone does not automatically lead to the desired results of promoting enterprises. A clear obstacle to enterprise growth is not only the lack of capital but also rather lack of occupational skills. This is reflected by the fact that a large number of participants are engaged in survival level multiple income generating activities. Undertaking various occupations at the same time allowed them to develop a portfolio of income generating activities and to reduce the risk of income loss when the demand for services or goods of one profession suddenly declines [24] (Lepenies, P. H., 2004). The occupational activities can change easily once market demand varied as long as the profession could be practiced with little investment and required only basic skills.

It is observed that micro enterprise development has the potential to bring about considerable improvement in incomes of upper poor and non-poor borrowers who are close to the poverty lines [25] (Hulme, D. and Mosley, P., 1996). The extreme poor are either less likely to participate in micro finance programmes or such increases were too small and short-lived to enable sustainable poverty exit. The poor commonly face obstacles in the form of unfavourable market environments, inadequate financial infrastructure, location, market and infrastructure constraints. Poor transport infrastructure is the single most important impediment to rural micro enterprise development. Electricity, irrigation and lack of formal education are being the other important factors. Low caste and social status may also inhibit entry into entrepreneurial occupations, reducing the range of activities open to extreme poor and some poor households. Some of the social problems being faced by the poor are alcohol abuse, engagement in petty crimes and family instability. Social restrictions on women also limit their economic activities. Interestingly, the female-headed household heads appeared to have more freedom than married women in project selection and mobility (Lepenies, P. H., 2004).

More than half of all women are still in agriculture in the developing world. In south Asia men are leaving agriculture faster than women, giving rise to increasing concentration of women on land. In India, 86 percent of rural women worker are in agriculture compared with 74 percent of rural mail workers. In addition, 20 percent of rural households are headed by females (World Survey on the Role of Women in Development, 1999). In micro enterprises they own, women work longer hours for less remuneration compared to men. Women's enterprises were also more embedded within the family, relying on family networks for labour and credit. However, as mentioned earlier, in majority of the cases, such micro enterprises were used more as a means of survival than as an instrument of empowering entrepreneurial activity.

In a study involving the women loanees of Grameen Bank of Bangladesh (Hussain M., 1984), it was observed that more than 80 percent of the women had no productive occupations before joining the Grameen Bank. Thus, the Bank had generated new employment for women which increased the labour force participation rate in the area of its operation. The women loanees were found to devote about 28 hours per week for income earning activities compared to about 44 hours for the male workers. The labour was employed mostly in activities financed through micro-credit. [26] Another early study by Chen M. (1984) on BRAC's programme observed that those schemes which build on women's traditional skills and occupations have a greater chance of proving viable than those which require training in new skills. [27] In another study of ASA programmes, Bruntrup, M., et al. (1997) have concluded that economic conditions of the household and women improve, income and assets increase over the period of programme membership but it takes a long time to get out of poverty. [28]

Zaman, H. (1999), in a study of BRAC's programme [29] has concluded that while micro enterprise interventions can play an important role in reducing vulnerability through a number of channels, a significant impact on poverty reduction is achieved under more restrictive conditions. These conditions revolve around whether the borrower has crossed a cumulative loan threshold. Vulnerability is reduced by smoothing consumption, building assets, providing emergency assistance and contributing to women empowerment. It was also argued that micro-credit's impact is improved if it is provided jointly with other financial and non-financial interventions like savings, insurance, legal education and flood relief.

However, as far as the impact on poverty is concerned, when the credit-financed investment does not generate a significant net profit then an asset is created which can reduce vulnerability but will not reduce poverty as the loan repayment takes place through a reduction in consumption and not from the returns to the investment. This study can have a good influence on the designs of other micro-credit programmes. The practitioners can offer more flexible savings products since the savings can have greater impact on reducing vulnerability. Similarly, micro-credit instruments can be offered along with other interventions like food relief for extremely poor women, or health insurance. Such multiple instruments can prove to be very useful to the households facing greater risks of income fluctuations.

It can be concluded that the impact of micro enterprises on poverty is not clear. McGuire P. B. and Conroy, J. D. (2000) suggest that access to credit has potential to significantly reduce poverty, but others argue that it has minimal impact on poverty reduction. There are studies showing that improvements in household incomes are greater for third time borrowers but these gains are small. [30]

This then begs the question of how to reach the really poor. There are those that argue that there is greater decease in vulnerability than income-poverty (Montgomery, et al.). Even if loans are used by the extremely poor, the tendency appears to be that they are used for consumption's purposes. In some case it is difficult for there to be a dent on poverty because repayments of loans are effected through a squeeze on current consumption rather than a return on an investment. For the poorest, therefore, the issue is whether they can access loans and also what are the other interventions that are required so that they can be reached.

5.4 Micro Enterprises and Self-help Groups (SHGs)

Since micro enterprises/SHGs based micro finance programmes cover a large number of poor people, it is expected that such programmes will have an important bearing on their sustainable development. However, the historical involvement of banks and micro finance institutions in India have ensured that these programmes adopt a minimalist approach and ignore non-financial inputs like literacy, health, awareness, capacity building and skill training. This approach has an impact on the long-term sustainability of such efforts. Ideally, on a wider canvas, micro enterprises and SHGs can become an extraordinary tools for poor's sustainable livelihood, provided the nurturing agencies take care to design their interventions to improve the confidence level of members through better participation in SHG meetings and more interactions take place with outsiders; and through this process members develop communication skills and are able to put forward their views confidently. Members are involved in decision making processes of group which will later help them to participate in bigger decisions affecting them, their family, their community, and groups which will help them in demanding facilities and systems to suit their needs. This process has already started at the family level and will have to be taken to the community level now.

The shift in approach to ME coincided with the development approach which emphasized equality, efficiency and productive role of women, to a gender and development approach which analyzed the underlying and structural causes for the persistent inequalities between men and women and focused on the power relations between men and women in the household, community, market and the state. This approach does focus on empowerment but there is no shared understanding of what is meant by empowerment and this is understood in many different ways. It can cover everything from welfare measures to interventions that cover participatory planning, decentralized forms of governance and the empowerment of women. While there are detailed discussions regarding the implications and forms of power and its deconstruction into power to do, power over, power with and power within, in simple terms it spans three dimensions:

1. **The Personal:** Manifested in an increase in self confidence, self esteem and increased awareness;
2. **The Relational:** Distribution of power between men and women as manifested in the access to and control over material, social and political resources and participation in decision making; and
3. **The Collective:** Where women who are mobilized can collectively act, demand or determine their future.

End Notes

1. Mukesh Gulati, UNIDO Cluster Development Program for Micro and Small and Medium Enterprise.
2. Christodoulou, N.T., Kirsten, M.A. and Badenhorst, J. (1993), Financing South African Micro-entrepreneurs, Development Bank of South Africa: Midrand.
3. Nunes, S. (1998), Women and Small Business Development, Pretoria: Ntsika Enterprise Promotion Agency.
4. Elkan, W. (1988), Entrepreneurs and Entrepreneurship in Africa, World Bank Research Observer, 3(2):171-187.
5. Mahajan, V. (2004), De-regulating Rural Credit, Paper presented in 'New Priorities: Symposium on a Social Agenda for India'. www.India.seminar.com.
6. Misra, S. N. and M. Behera (2000), An Evaluation of Anti-poverty Programmes in Mayurbhanj District of Orissa (Mimeo), Nabakrushna Choudhury Centre for Development Studies, Bhubaneswar.
7. Holcombe, S. (1995), Managing to Empower: The Grameen Bank's Experience of Poverty Alleviation, London: University Press Ltd.
8. Ashe, J., Christopher, E., Cosslett, R. (1993), Credit for the Poor-Past Activities and Future Directions for the United Nations Development Program (UNDP), UNDP Policy Discussion Paper. New York: UNDP.
9. Macqueen, D.J., Dufey, A. and Patel, B. (2006), Fair Trade Timber, Background paper presented at an international meeting

on "Enhancing Local Returns from Trade in Forest Products", 27 September 2006 at Royal Botanic Gardens, Kew., IIED, London, UK.

10. Bose, S., Lal, P., Pareek, P.S., Verma, M. and Saigal S. (2006), Forest-based Associations in India–An Overview, Winrock International India and the International Institute for Environment and Development (IIED), London, UK.
11. May, P.H., Da Vinha, V.G. and Macqueen, D.J. (2003), Small and Medium Forest Enterprise in Brazil, Grupo Economia do Meio Ambientee Desenvolvimento Sustentável (GEMA) and International Institute for Environment and Development (IIED), London, UK.
12. UNESCO (2002), Universal Declaration on Cultural Diversity, United Nations Educational, Scientific and Cultural Organization.
13. Putney A. (2000), An Approach to the Identification and Assessment of Non-material Values, Parks Magazine 10(2).
14. Rowcroft, P., Studley, J. and Ward, K. (2006), Eliciting Forest Values for Community Plantations and Nature Conservation, Submitted to Forests Trees and Livelihoods.
15. Colchester, M. (2006), Forest People, Customary Use and State Forests: The Case for Reform, Paper presented at the 11th Biennial Congress of the International Association for the Study of Common Property, 19-23 June 2006 in Bali, Indonesia.
16. Ousman, S., Macqueen, D.J. and Robert, G. (2006), Development from Diversity: Guyana's Forest-based Associations, Guyana National Initiative for Forest Certification (GNIFC) and the International Institute for Environment and Development (IIED), London, UK.
17. Shylendra, H. S. (1999), Micro finance and Self-help Groups (SHGs): A Study of the Experience of Two Leading NGOs, SEWA and AKRSP in Gujarat (India), IRMA research paper No. 16.
18. Sheokand, S. M., SHG-Bank Linkage-The Pilot Phase, Annual Report, NABARD, 1992.
19. Bruntrup, M., Alauddin, S. M., Huda, A. and Rahman, M., (1997), Impact assessment of the Association of Social Advancement (ASA).
20. Annual Report of Oriental Bank of Commerce, 1997-98.
21. Srinivasan, G., (1996), Branch Manager's Dilemma, First prize

winning case study of NIBM, Pune.

22. Kishanjit Bash and Krishon Jindal, Bankers Institute of Rural Development, Lucknow, 2000, Micro Finance: Emerging Challenges.
23. NABARD, NABARD and Microfinance, 2000-2001 and 2001-2002, Micro Credit Innovations Department, NABARD, Mumbai.
24. Lepenies, P. H. (2004), Exit, Voice and Vouchers: Using Vouchers to Train Micro-entrepreneurs-Observations from the Paraguyan Voucher Scheme, World Development 32 (4), pp. 713-724.
25. Hulme, D. and Mosley, P. (1996), Finance Against Poverty, Vol. 1. London: Routledge.
26. Hussain M. (1984), The Impact of Grameen Bank on Women's Involvement in Productive Activities, Dhaka, Grameen Bank.
27. Chen M. (1984), Developing Non-craft Employment for Women in Bangladesh, New York, Seeds.
28. Bruntrup, M., Alauddin, S. M., Huda, A. and Rahman, M., (1997), Impact Assessment of the Association of Social Advancement (ASA).
29. Zaman, H. (1999), Assessing the Impact of Micro-credit on Poverty and Vulnerability in Bangladesh, Washington, The World Bank Policy Research Working Paper 2145.
30. McGuire P. B. and Conroy, J. D. (2000), The Micro finance Phenomenon, Asia Pacific Review, Vol. 7, No. 1, pp. 90-108.

6

Institutional Support for Micro Entrepreneurs

6.1 Cluster Approach for Micro Enterprises

Opening up of the world economy and removal of trade barriers have made it indispensable for entrepreneurs to adopt and promote a culture of sustained competitiveness. Researches on industrial clusters of small and micro enterprises (SMEs) indicate that they have shown ability to grow, innovate and compete successfully under fast changing demand patterns, even under recessionary conditions. The clusters have assumed further significance in the wake of liberalization process the country is currently undergoing. For, the SSIs now will have to be more efficient to face the competition from within and abroad. Finance, quality improvement and consequent technology up-gradation will be the major source of competition. The industrial clusters provide ample opportunity for such interventions, leading to increased collective efficiency, despite internal competition. Such clusters have also been observed to be leading to flexible specialization resulting into a number of process innovations. All in turn contribute to competitiveness of enterprises in a cluster vis-à-vis non-cluster enterprises.

The cluster approach helps overcome the barriers faced by handicrafts sector. Handicrafts sector also experience the much required upsurge on account of business solidarity that ensues from collective action. The spatial concentration of units (in an industrial cluster) gives way to inter-firm linkages and external economies leading to higher degree of collective efficiency. Therefore, clusters derive benefits, which individual firms can hardly achieve. The handicraft clusters are also observed to follow co-operative behaviour in terms of co-operating on some fronts such as in establishing common facility centres, common brand building for the export market, common purchase or (in effect) mutually guaranteeing each other's financial obligations. Simultaneously, they also compete in some areas such as in production, domestic marketing or non-quota based sale of products, etc.

While the development process could be autonomous in a few dynamic clusters, some other may need induced-development and growth to acquire competitive edge and dynamism. The requirement of assistance may usually not be in terms of subsidies for commercial activities but more in terms of contributing towards awareness generation, developing cluster vision and action plan, creation of common facilities, common branding or marketing, facilitating formation of networks, conducting demonstration projects, strengthening industry associations, capacity building of the cluster actors, etc.

The social development approach of micro finance and micro enterprises is based on the premise that people should earn money by investing in viable micro enterprises. They should earn profit from their enterprises. Major share of the profit should be reinvested in enterprises for their growth. The other share of the profit should be spent on social development i.e., health, education, housing, sanitation etc. By earning profit from the viable micro enterprises, people will increase their paying ability for services delivered to them under different social development projects run by NGO and States/ Central Government. For the NGOs and Government, it can be a process of gradual withdrawal and for people, decrease dependency on the NGOs and Government.

6.2 Need for Government Intervention

Orthodox economists tend to subscribe to one or both of the following positions in answer to the question: should governments intervene in the operation of the informal economy? The first position is that markets operate efficiently, that government interventions lead to inefficiencies and distortions, and that the informal sector will, in any case, decline with economic growth. The second is that the informal sector is beyond the reach of the government, in part because those who operate in it want to avoid regulation and taxation. Many heterodox economists, on the other hand, subscribe to the notion that the informal economy is here to stay and requires appropriate regulations, laws, and policies to correct for biases in existing regulations, laws, and policies that favour the formal economy and disadvantage informal workers.

Those who subscribe to the notion that governments should intervene in the informal sector base their arguments on some mix of equity, efficiency, or political economy principles. Those who make the case on equity principles argue that the poor, especially women, who are concentrated in the informal sector, face uneven market power and discrimination; have insufficient market information or skills; and have inadequate insurance against risk (unemployment, illness, disability, old age). They argue that the current process of normalization–whereby more and more people are working under informal arrangements–threatens to do away with decades of social progress.

They recommend the need for a new contract between the state, business, organized labour, and other social actors (including organizations of informal workers or producers). Those who make the case for state intervention on efficiency principles argue that the informal sector contributes to GDP; produces a large share of consumer goods, particularly those bought by middle and low-income groups; represents a potential source of capital goods; and provides a training ground for entrepreneurs. They also recognize that growth in the informal sector is more labour-intensive and, therefore, more labour-absorbing or job-creating than growth in the formal economy. They argue that governments should intervene to promote productivity and growth in the informal economy.

Those who make the case for state intervention on political

economy principles argue that governments do intervene in markets and in ways that are often biased–either deliberately or inadvertently—towards large industries: notably, trade and industry policies and fiscal policies. Why, they ask, should policies directed or biased towards smaller businesses be singled out as distortionary? They also note that most economic policies, whether targeted or not, impact on the informal sector and that the impact of given policies on the informal sector is often different from that on the formal sector. In sum, governments do intervene in markets. The outcomes or impacts of government policies depend on the industry or sector, type of intervention, and the relative power of different economic actors.

6.3 Other Interventions

If the government does not intervene, or even if it does, who else could or should intervene? There is a range of different stakeholders with interests in how the informal economy operates, and how workers are organized within it. A brief stakeholder analysis should help to set the stage for the policy analysis that is to follow:

1. **International System**: The international system has become involved in helping to "set the rules of the game" for the global economy. For example, the World Trade Organization (WTO) was established to regulate global product markets; the International Labour Organization (ILO) has been charged with regulating labour markets; and a new "financial architecture" to regulate capital markets is being designed. Currently, there is a debate as to whether the WTO (through trade sanctions) and/or the ILO (through labour conventions) should promote international labour standards. None of these international institutions has been charged with understanding or addressing how product, labour, or capital markets affect informal wage workers or informal operators.
2. **Employers or Companies**: In response to mounting

pressures from consumer groups and others, the corporate sector has begun to adopt "voluntary" codes of conduct to self-regulate their treatment of labour. Not willing to entrust the corporate sector to monitor itself, existing consumer groups, non-governmental organizations, and worker organizations as well as new third-party monitoring groups have begun to monitor corporate behaviour. However, the codes of conduct and related monitoring efforts have not been extended, except in a few rare cases, to cover home workers and other isolated informal workers.

3. **Industries or Sectors**: Both informal own account operators and informal wage workers typically earn less than their counterparts in the formal economy and less than informal owner operators (hereafter referred to as micro-entrepreneurs). Yet, as has been argued, they often contribute to growth in different industries. How can they share in the benefits of growth in the specific industries or trades in which they operate? One mechanism is to tax the aggregate output of designated industries to finance benefits for the informal workforce in those industries.
4. **Private Insurance Industry**: One dimension of welfare reforms over the past decade in many countries, particularly in Latin America, has been the privatization of social insurance: that is, social insurance funds to cover pensions, health insurance, and other contingencies have been consolidated and replaced, wholly or partially, by individual savings plans. One dimension of economic reforms over the past decade in several countries including India has been the privatization of the insurance industry that, before the reforms, remained in government control. An associated concern is that workers with low wages/earnings and irregular employment–like many of those in the informal economy–are unlikely to be able to save (and contribute) enough to subscribe to private insurance schemes to protect themselves against even

common core contingencies. Also the privatization of insurance has led to the loss of government-mandated coverage for informal workers. In India, so long as insurance companies were public corporations—that is, until 2001—they had special schemes for workers in the "unorganized/informal sector".

5. **Consumers and the Public**: The collective action of consumer groups, student groups, church groups, and others in fair trade campaigns have contributed significantly to building awareness and building pressure on the corporate sector regarding the rights of workers in the global economy. However, from an informal sector perspective, these campaigns can have contradictory outcomes. To begin with, the campaigns usually focus on the conditions of workers in export processing zones and sweatshops but not on the working conditions of home workers or the self-employed. Secondly, the campaigns often do not consider the counterfactual–the quantity and quality of alternative work opportunities–when calling for a ban or restrictions on production in certain industries, companies, or countries. Consulting informal workers might help predict and prevent some of these contradictory outcomes.
6. **Formal Trade Unions**: Formal trade unions have traditionally organized around the conflict of interest between formal wage workers and employers. As such, they find it very difficult to deal, as comrades or colleagues, with informal workers whose employment status is uncertain. Given the recent expansion of employment in the informal sector and the decline in their membership, some formal trade unions have begun to consider and debate whether or not to intervene A few have begun to organize informal workers, and others to collaborate with organizations of informal workers. However, many issues have yet to be resolved.
7. **Informal Worker Organizations**: There are growing

numbers of informal worker organizations around the world, including unions, cooperatives, and other types of associations. However, many remain small, weak, and isolated and most are not recognized as legitimate worker organizations by formal trade unions in their respective countries or by the international trade union movement. Over the past decade, partly in response to globalization, some of these organizations have begun to organize internationally. For example, two international alliances of grassroots organizations working with home-based workers and street vendors, respectively, were established in the early 1990s.

8. **Non-Governmental Organizations**: Large numbers of NGOs around the world provide services to, advocate on behalf of, and/or organize the working poor in the informal economy. However, rather than recognizing and organizing them as producers, traders, or wage workers, most NGOs treat those they work with as "the poor" and organize them as "clients". For instance, few micro finance institutions, which have grown significantly in number and influence over the past decade, classify their clients by trade or occupation group or address the non-financial needs of their clients as workers, producers, or traders.
9. **Individuals, Families, and Communities**: In the absence of formal systems of social protection, the working poor rely on informal systems of social protection (e.g. support from friends and relatives, social or kinship networks, rotating savings-and-credit societies) as well as their own resources (e.g. use of savings, sale of assets, sending children to work). However, the benefits from such informal sources are seldom adequate and often uncertain, especially during widespread or prolonged crises; and the associated costs and risks are often quite high. Furthermore, women worldwide do a disproportionate amount of this unpaid 'community work'.

Orissa has one of the richest traditions of handicrafts in the country, which goes back to the time of antiquity. The ancient rock-cut caves and beautiful stone carving engraved in the temples of medieval Orissa provide a glimpse of the rich traditions of crafts, art and sculpture in the ancient past. Those handicrafts had flourished side by side with royal patronage and ritualistic needs of the people of Orissa. In a poor and industrially backward state like Orissa, these traditional industries like handloom and popular handicrafts hold a considerable promise for economic empowerment and provide a gainful employment to the technically little qualified, less educated and emaciated poor in the rural non-farm sector. It is found that the second major employment provider sector is handloom and handicraft sector after the agrarian sector in the state.

Apart from that the handloom and handicraft products of Orissa are appreciated all over the world because of its exquisite designs, exclusive forms, natural motifs and superb colour combination. Orissa occupies a unique place in India in respect of handicrafts and arts. The subject matter of Orissa handicrafts is still derived from the cosmographic myths and legends of the Indian culture and civilization as described with fabulous imagination in the epics and the sacred scriptures. The present handicrafts are largely the visual manifests produced with remarkable fidelity to the historical continuance of thousands of years of Oriya culture. These traditional crafts have, however, historically passed through many stages of ups and downs. In post-independent era, when the planners and policy makers gave importance to the industrialization and employment generation to accelerate the pace of economic development in the country, they could realize the importance of traditional industries in uplifting the rural economy. The setting up of Khadi and Village Industries Commission, Handicraft Board, Handloom Board, Coir Board, Central Silk Board etc. is the primitive steps in the 1950s and 1960s to develop and transform the rural economy of the country.

Orissa is known for its exquisite handicrafts (52 in number), and the roots of those are intertwined with the rituals and traditions. It is observed that the production matrix of the handicrafts in Orissa is structured in such a manner that the artisan-workers notwithstanding their superb skill and artisanship always remain at the receiving end. In contrast, the trader/merchant capitalists and the middlemen by virtue of their control over the marketing of the craft goods occupy the top position of the production ladder. While the artisans entrepreneurs, who themselves are the master craftsman occupy the middle positions as they cannot afford to take care of marketing of the craft goods on their own. Nor they viably manage the craft units independently without taking work orders or job works from the trader entrepreneurs. To protect the interest of the artisans and to popularize and enhance the marketability of the craft items, the government has taken steps for the promotion of both primary craft cooperatives and apex marketing society. But due to ignorance and low-level of education of artisans, the primary craft cooperatives at grass-root level virtually function like a trader entrepreneurs units of the chief functionaries.

Barring the case of a few artisan workers in the selected handicrafts like stone carving, wood carving, patta paintings etc. have high potential export value, the working and living conditions of craftsmen in other handicrafts of the state are found to be very distressful and the craft has now lost its popularity and in verge of extinction; and annihilation due to the dominance of middlemen and trader entrepreneurs. It is very difficult on the part of those artisans to get craft based employment round the year; and the income from these crafts are so low that 70 percent of these artisans live below poverty line. Thus, it is necessary to appreciate these emerging challenges and gear up the handicraft sector of Orissa by exploiting the inherent strength of the artisans in the interest of rapid economic growth and eradication of poverty.

6.4 Government Initiatives under Different Plans

Recognizing the special needs and problems of tribal several development measures were initiated under five-year plans. The Five Year Plans of the Government of India laid stress on the various development measures to be undertaken by the Central and the State Governments to improve the living standard of the tribal and make an effort to bring them on par with the other developed societies in the country.

The First Five Year Plan of India (1951-56) did not attempt to establish long range development programmes for the tribals, but concentrated more on the immediate problems that had to be solved. In the First Plan, the Union Government had allocated ₹ 12 crore and the various State Governments had provided another ₹ 11 crore for tribal development programmes and much emphasis was laid on education, Economic upliftment, growth of communication system and provision of medical and housing facilities.

A variety of development programmes in the tribal area were initiated during the Second Five Year Plan (1956-61). The total amount allocated in the Second Plan for the welfare of the tribal people was to the tune of ₹ 45 crore. Under the sphere of economic upliftment of the tribal, schemes such as land settlement, land reclamation, distribution of seed and setting up of demonstration farms, establishment of service cooperatives and forest cooperatives and improvement of communication facilities were broadly undertaken.

The Third Five Year Plan (1961-66) undertook the policy of establishing Tribal Development Blocks on a very large scale. These blocks were set up in all the tribal areas for their development in an integrated manner. These blocks focused as the development of certain core sectors like agriculture, education health, communication, cottage industries and so on. These economic upliftment programmes gave priority to the economic rehabilitation of persons engaged in shifting cultivation, working of forests through cooperatives consisting of members of Scheduled Tribes and formulating Multipurpose Cooperatives for meeting the credit requirements of tribal agriculturists and artisans for marketing their products.

During the Fourth Five Year Plan, six pilot projects for tribal development under the name of Tribal Development Agencies were undertaken in the Central Sector in a few tribal areas located in certain states. The total outlay for these projects under the Fourth Plan (1969-74) was to the tune of ₹ 12 crore.

In the Fifth Five Year Plan (1974-78) for the first time, a strategy of earmarking funds for the development of specific areas of concentration of tribal population was evolved–a landmark phase by adopting a new strategy for tribal development. The instrument of Tribal Sub-plans was developed to ensure flow of benefits from all sectoral programmes and to provide integrated delivery of services in the tribal areas. In the tribal sub-plan areas, an outlay to the tune of ₹ 644 crore from State plans (including ₹ 120 crore of Special Central Assistance) was made.

The major objective of the Sixth Five Year Plan (1980-85) are to eradicate poverty and to mobilize all latent energies for the creation of a more dynamic and more equitable society. The main thrust of the policy for the development of Scheduled Tribes during the Sixth Plan is four-fold, namely (i) integration of services at the delivery point to the beneficiary with a view to develop self-reliance in him; (ii) development of services from the bottom-upward instead of top-downwards; (iii) development of skills to diversify the occupations; and (iv) introduction of latest technology based on local materials and local skills to reduce drudgery of workers and also to remove the social stigma attached to their present profession.

Under the Sixths and Seventh Plans there were substantial increases in the flow of funds for the development of STs resulting in the expansion of infrastructure facilities and enlargement of coverage. In addition two national level organizations were set up such as Tribal Cooperative Marketing Development Federation (TRIFED) and National

Scheduled Caste and Tribe Financial and Development Corporation (NSCTFDC). Flow of funds rose from ₹ 5,535 crore in the Sixth Plan to ₹ 10,500 crore in the Seventh Plan.

In the Eighth Plan efforts were intensified to bridge the gap between the levels of development of STs and other sections of the society and ₹ 15,800 crore were made available during the Plan period.

The Ninth Plan aimed to empower STs by creating and enabling environment conducive for them to exercise their right freely, enjoy their privileges and lead a life of self confidence and dignity with the rest of society. This process essentially encompasses 3 components viz., social and economic empowerment and social justice.

The Tenth Plan emphasized to reduce the gaps in education, health, and economic development. Despite all efforts even after more than sixty years of planning, economic progress of tribal could not bring anywhere nearer to the main stream of the society as the gap in their socioeconomic status has widened. The percentage of rural tribal population below poverty line was as high as 52 percent as against an all India figure of 37 percent during 1993-94 leaving a gap of 15 percent. The corresponding figures for 1999-2000 were 46 and 27 leaving a gap of 19 percent. Tenth Plan calls for determined action to ameliorate their conditions. Their unproductive uneconomic holdings, use of traditional technologies for cultivation, watering, input use, non diversification of crops and poor harvesting techniques has been continuing.

6.5 Institutions Promoting Handicrafts at National Level

In order to provide and protect the artisans' skills inherited, government both at the centre and states, have set up Handicrafts emporium at important cities and at district level. These artisans are also encouraged by various government institutions to participate in national and International exhibition to show their skills. Various institutions involved for promotion of handicraft are given below.

6.5.1 Development Commissioner (Handicrafts): The Office of the DC (Handicrafts) is an attached office of Ministry of Textiles, Government of India. It is a central nodal office to work for socio-economic upliftment of the artisans and supplement the efforts of the State Government for promotion and development of handicrafts within the country and abroad and It has 6 Regional Offices at New Delhi, Kolkata, Lucknow, Chennai, Mumbai and Guwahti, and 5 Regional Design and Technical Development Centres at New Delhi, Mumbai, Kolkata, Bangalore and Guwahati. There are 52 handicrafts marketing and service extension centres in addition to above. Various Institutions (like Indian Institute of Carpet Technology, Bhadohi (UP), National Centre for Design Product Development Society, New Delhi and Moradabad, Metal Handicrafts Service Centre (Society), Moradabad) are also working for the development of handicrafts in association with this office.

- Provides assistance under various schemes covering areas like training, design development, technology upgradation, market promotion, exhibition, publicity, exports etc. for promotion and development of Handicrafts as well as welfare of the craft persons. Their schemes are mainly implemented by State Handicrafts Corporation/Primary Handicrafts Societies/NGOs.
- Looks after implementation of schemes of Development Commissioner (Handicrafts) of the States of Eastern Region including Orissa.
- Provides support for design and technology development for promotion of handicrafts in North Eastern and Eastern Region states including Orissa.

6.5.2 Tribal Cooperative Marketing Development Federation (TRIFED): For the socio and economic welfare of tribal population Government of India established an independent corporation called TRIFED whose activities were confined to purchase of forest products and sell them at their retail counters. Since 1999, TRIFED expanded their activities by encouraging tribal artisans in production of arts and crafts which they have inherited from their forefathers. Tribes shop are set up to show case tribal arts and crafts by procuring the crafts from tribal artisans at remunerative prices and sell the same at these shop and organizing periodic exhibitions at different places all over India and abroad. The ultimate objective of TRIFED is socio-economic development of tribal people in the country by way of marketing development of the tribal products on which the lives of tribals depends heavily as they spend most of their time and derive major portion of their income from collection/cultivation of Non-timber Forest Produce (NTFP). Some of the services which TRIFED offers are as follows:

1. To facilitate, coordinate and promote the marketing of the tribal products;
2. To undertake/promote on behalf of its members or the government or government organizations, inter and intra-state and international marketing of tribal products;
3. To act as an agency for canalization of export and import and facilitate, wherever necessary inter-state trade of tribal products under any scheme formulated by Government of India or any other State agencies.
4. To develop market intelligence related to supply, demand, price trends, supply/market chain, value addition and processing facilities, product quality specifications, product applications, market trends, buyers for the tribal products and disseminate the information to the members as well as planners, researchers and associate organizations and business circles etc.;
5. To assist in capability and capacity building of the members relating to the marketing development of the tribal products;
6. To provide consultancy and advisory services to the members relating to the activities in furtherance of their objectives;
7. To act as advisors, consultants and project managers to

government projects relating to marketing development of Tribal products in the form of capacity building, infrastructure development, special programs;

8. To expand and extend the markets for tribal products through marketing development and promotion programs;
9. To assist in the development of new products through product development, product innovation, product designs, new product applications and special R&D drives for tribal products;
10. To collaborate, associate with similar and allied international bodies in trade fairs, tribal product marketing development, tribal research and funding;
11. Agencies to further the interests of tribal product marketing;
12. To collaborate, network, associate with similar and allied international bodies/agencies, societies, (NGOs, co-operatives, foundations, organizations—private and government), institutions for development of marketing.

6.5.3 National Bank for Agriculture and Rural Development (NABARD), Mumbai: Considering the importance of rural non-farm sector as a means to enhance employment opportunities for the rural population, NABARD apart from its multifarious refinance functions has launched some promotional schemes for interventions in areas such as entrepreneurial development, skill up-gradation, technology up-gradation, marketing support, with emphasis on development of clusters, formation of self-help group. Their promotional schemes are mainly implemented by voluntary agencies and NGOs. Four districts of Orissa such as Ganjam, Gajapati, Baragarh and Sundargarh have been taken up by NABARD under DRIP programme. The major activities undertaken by NABARD are as follows:

1. Strengthening of Rural Haats: The 'Scheme for Strengthening of Rural Haats', introduced in 1999 in DRIP districts, was extended to all districts, village bazaar boards, SHG, NGO and to PRI/PACS during the year. The

ceiling under the scheme was increased from ₹ 3 lakh to ₹ 5 lakh and coverage extended to include permanent structure/s as per local requirements. During 2008-09, grant support of ₹ 185.90 lakh was sanctioned to 46 haats, 10 each in AP and Manipur, 5 in TN, 4 in UP, 3 each in Bihar, Maharashtra and Orissa, 2 in Nagaland and 1 each in Arunachal Pradesh, Assam, Meghalaya, Mizoram, Rajasthan and WB. Cumulative grant assistance of ₹ 330.81 lakh has been sanctioned for strengthening infrastructure in 101 rural haats across 22 States.

2. NABARD has been supporting both Rural Entrepreneurship Development Programme (REDP) and Skill Development Programme (SDP) as a proven tool for generating self-employment opportunities in rural areas. During the year, 2,083 REDP/SDP involving a total amount of ₹ 1,303.60 lakh were sanctioned, benefiting 50,264 rural youth. Cumulatively 11,905 REDP/SDP involving grant support of ₹ 6,039.54 lakh covering 3 lakh persons were supported as on 31st March 2009. Besides, an amount of ₹ 88.03 lakh was sanctioned to RUDSETI for capital expenditure.
3. The scheme for supporting Women Development Cells (WDCs) in Regional Rural Banks (RRBs) and co-operative banks, in operation since 1995-96, was modified and made performance-linked with effect from 1 April 2007. During 2008-09, 33 WDCs were set up in 19 RRBs, 12 DCCBs and 2 SCARDBs. As on 31 March 2009, 102 WDCs in 56 RRBs, 43 DCCBs and 3 SCARDBs were sanctioned under the modified scheme. Under schemes for Marketing of Non-Farm Products of Rural Women (MAHIMA) and Assistance to Rural Women in Non-Farm Development (ARWIND), grant support of ₹ 6.02 lakh and ₹ 6.82 lakh, respectively, was released till 31 March 2009.

6.5.4 Small Industries Development Bank of India (SIDBI), New Delhi: In addition to their re-finance scheme they are implementing promotional and developmental schemes through NGOs for improving the inherent strength of small scale and tiny sector.

6.5.5 Coir Board, Ministry of ARI, Government of India, Kochi

1. Looks after promotion and development of coir industry in various parts of the country with interventions in the areas covering research and development, training, extension, quality improvement, development of production infrastructure, domestic and export market promotion etc.
2. They also provide assistance under different schemes of Government of India to strengthen the cooperative net-work and welfare of the coir artisans.

6.5.6 Council for Advancement of People's Action and Rural Technology (CAPART): CAPART is an autonomous body functioning under the aegis of Ministry of Rural Development, Government of India since 1986. It is a nodal agency for catalyzing and coordinating the emerging partnership between voluntary organisation and the Government for sustainable development with interventions like housing, skill training, technology up-gradation, establishment of community centres, marketing support etc. Rural artisans sector is one of identified priority areas of CAPART.

6.5.7 National Centre for Design and Product Development, New Delhi: National Centre for Product Design & Development (NCDPD), non-profit organization, set up by Export Promotion Council for Handicrafts (EPCH) and the office of the Development Commissioner (Handicrafts). NCDPD has been involved in inviting prominent designers from oversees and working in coordination with leading design institutes and helping the Indian artisans especially tribals to hone their skills. NCDPD aims to provide cutting edge assistance to the Indian handicrafts industry through international standard design and technical inputs.

6.5.8 Export Promotion Council for Handicrafts, New Delhi: Export Promotion Council for Handicrafts (EPCH) has been established under the Exim Policy of Government of India in 1986-87 and is a non-profit earning organization. EPCH is an apex organization of trade, industry and government sponsored by Ministry of Textile, Government of India for promotion of handicraft from country and project India's image abroad as a reliable supplier of high quality of handicraft goods and ensured various measures keeping in view of observance of international standards and specifications.

6.5.9 Council of Handicrafts Development Corporation, New Delhi: Council of Handicrafts Development Corporation (COHANDS) represents 28 state government corporations of India and functions under the aegis of the office of Development Commissioner (Handicrafts), Ministry of Textiles. COHANDS acts as facilitator for undertaking the integrated design and technical development workshops, interior design and participating in domestic and international fairs, cultural programmes, organizing seminars and symposiums.

6.5.10 Khadi and Village Industry (KVIC): KVIC works under the administrative control of the Ministry of Industry, Government of India under the department of Small-Scale Industries and Agro and Rural Industries. KVIC has a 10 member commission at the policy making level. The Commission consists of six zonal members (one of whom is Chairman), two expert members and two official members (the Chief Executive Officer and the Financial Advisor). The Chairman, CEO and FA are full time members. The headquarters of KVIC is in Bombay and it has its State and Regional Offices in all the States. It has training, production and Sales centres throughout the country. KVIC is having 30 State khadi and village industries board, over 3500 institutions and over 29000 cooperative societies. There are around 14200 sales outlets in the country in KVI Sector. It is having 46 percent women participation in its activities. 30 percent beneficiaries belong to SC/ST. KVI Boards assist over 5 lakh artisans. It has reached 2.35 lakh villages. Some of the major functions of KVIC are as follows:

1. KVIC is charged with the planning, promotion, organisation and implementation of programs for the development of khadi and other village industries in the rural areas in coordination with other agencies engaged in rural development wherever necessary.
2. Its functions also comprise building up of a reserve of raw materials and implements for supply to producers, creation of common service facilities for processing of raw materials as semi-finished goods and provisions of facilities for marketing of KVI products apart from organization of training of artisans engaged in these industries and encouragement of co-operative efforts amongst them. To promote the sale and marketing of khadi and/or products of village industries or handicrafts, the KVIC may forge linkages with established marketing agencies wherever feasible and necessary.
3. The KVIC is charged with the responsibility of encouraging and promoting research in the production techniques and equipment employed in the khadi and village industries sector and providing facilities for the study of the problems relating to it, including the use of non-conventional energy and electric power with a view to increasing productivity, eliminating drudgery and otherwise enhancing their competitive capacity and arranging for dissemination of salient results obtained from such research.
4. KVIC is providing financial assistance to institutions and individuals for development and operation of khadi and village industries and guiding them through supply of designs, prototypes and other technical information.
5. KVIC take steps as to ensure genuineness of the products and to set standards of quality and ensure that the products

of khadi and village industries do conform to the standards.

6. KVIC also undertake directly or through other agencies studies concerning the problems of khadi and/or village industries besides research or establishing pilot projects for the development of Khadi and village industries.
7. The KVIC is authorized to establish and maintain separate organizations for the purpose of carrying out any or all of the above matters besides carrying out any other matters incidental to its activities.

6.5.11 National Backward Classes Finance and Development Corporation (NBCFDC)

To look after economic development of member of backward class below poverty line through channelling agencies nominated by the State Government.

1. Government of Orissa has nominated Orissa Backward Class Development Finance Co-operative Corporation Ltd. as the channelling agency to obtain loan from NBCFDC for disbursement to eligible target groups of backward classes.
2. The State government in Industries Department has nominated Orissa State Co-operative Handicrafts Corporation Ltd., Orissa Co-op. Coir Corporation Ltd., Orissa Khadi and Village Industries Board and Orissa Rajya Talgur Samabaya Sangha Ltd. as channelling agencies to avail financial assistance from NBCFDC for upliftment of backward classes of the state in the field of the handicrafts and cottage industries.

6.6 Handicrafts Artisans Comprehensive Welfare Scheme

Handicrafts constitute an important segment of the decentralized/unorganized sector of our economy. Originally, started as a part time activity in rural areas, it has now transformed in flourishing economic activity due to significant market demand over the year. Handicrafts have big potential as they hold they key for sustaining not only the existing set of millions of artisans spread over length and breadth of the country, but also to increasingly large number of new entrants in the crafts activity. Presently, handicrafts are contributing substantially in employment generation, and export. The handicrafts sector has suffered from basic problems of being in the unorganized sector with additional constraints like lack of education, capital, poor exposure to new technologies, absence of market intelligence and poor institutional framework. These problems have been further aggravated due to lack of proper care on the welfare of the artisans. In order to address the welfare needs of artisan in terms of health and insurance, these following two scheme has been envisaged.

6.6.1 Bima Yojana for Handicrafts Artisans: The objective of "Bima Yojana for Handicrafts Artisans" is to provide life insurance protection to the Handicrafts Artisans, whether male or female, between the age group of 18-60 years.

There are two components under the Bima Yojana for handicrafts artisans, which are:

Janshree Bima Yojana:

- Life insurance cover towards natural death shall be a sum of ₹ 20,000 per member.
- For accidental death/permanent total disability, the coverage shall be maximum ₹ 50,000 per member and for permanent partial disability, it shall be maximum of ₹ 25,000 per member.

Shiksha Sahyog Yojana

- Added benefits in the form of an associated scheme of LIC, under which not more than 2 dependent children of the beneficiary studying in the classes IX to XII are given ₹ 300 per quarter/child as educational allowance for maximum period of 4 years or till completion of XII class, whichever is earlier.

Pattern of Financial Assistance:

- Annual premium rate per person under the policy will be ₹ 200.
- The annual premium charged would be ₹ 200 per annum, of which i.e. ₹ 100 is to be borne by LIC from its Social

Security Fund, ₹ 60 is to be borne by the Government of India [by the Office of the DC (Handicrafts)] and remaining ₹ 40 is to be borne by the beneficiary.

6.6.2 Rajiv Gandhi Shilpi Swasthya Bima Yojana: Rajiv Gandhi Shilpi Swasthya Bima Yojana aims at financially enabling the artisans' community to access to the best of healthcare facilities in the country. This scheme will cover Artisan's family of four, comprising self, and any other three members of the family from amongst the dependent parents, spouse and children.

The benefits of the scheme are as follows:

Up to ₹ 1 lakh and in case of death: sum assured: ₹ 1 lakh; Total and irrecoverable loss of any one limb by physical separation: sum assured ₹ 1 lakh; Total and irrecoverable loss of any one limb without physical separation: sum assured ₹ 1 lakh.

6.6.3 Work shed for Handicraft Artisans: The scheme is primarily welfare oriented. It focuses on providing improved working conditions with emphasis on not only ample space for work, but also well ventilated and healthy working environment to the handicraft artisans, leading to better productivity and enhanced contribution to national economy.

Work shed should preferably be located adjacent to the dwelling unit of the handicraft artisan. If due to dense population, a site adjacent to the dwelling unit is not available, the plot should be as near the dwelling unit as possible. The minimum area available should be 30 sq. mtrs. Depending upon the local need, common and community work sheds may also be constructed but effort should be made that minimum availability of space per artisan is around 30 sq. mtrs.

The ceiling of construction assistance under the Scheme will be ₹ 20,000 per unit for rural areas and ₹ 22,000 per unit for urban areas. This assistance will be provided by the Office of the D.C.(H) as government share. Any expenditure in addition to the assistance provided will have to be borne by the beneficiary artisans themselves besides the land/site for construction. In case of common/community working sheds the financial assistance would be considered in proportion to the number of artisans of the group. In this case the overall ceiling will be less than 10 percent as the construction of common/community working centres would involve some common expenditures, hence the reduced ceiling.

Out of the sanctioned amount 50 percent would be released as 1st instalment as Grant in aid as advance to the implementing agencies and remaining sanctioned amount would be released as reimbursement as 2nd instalment on receipt of audited expenditure of accounts by CA and a report from the concerned assistant director/regional director, receipt of the audited statement of full accounts and satisfactory completion report from the regional director/assistant director. All the instalments will be transferred in the bank account of the implementing agency who in turn will transfer it to the selected beneficiaries' accounts as per need. In case of community work sheds, the funds will be transferred to the community account through the implementing agency, as per need.

100 percent Grant from the Office of the D.C.(H) with the ceiling of ₹ 20,000 per unit for rural areas and ₹ 22,000 per unit for urban areas. Any expenditure in addition to the assistance provided will have to be borne by the beneficiary artisans themselves either from own resources or by raising loans besides the land/site for construction.

7

Role of Non-governmental Organizations (NGOs)

7.1 Significance of NGOs in the Informal Sector

With a low level of income and pervasive poverty, development priorities in India increasingly focus on efficient growth policies and provision of basic services to the poor. Poverty analysis in the country underscores the multidimensionality of the process which in turn has significant implications for designing effective poverty alleviation policies. Poverty reflects a state of vulnerability coupled with deprivation. Persistence of crises that the poor routinely face significantly affects their ability to sustain current status, let alone increase the level of welfare.

Within the general framework, poverty alleviation strategies in the country lay emphasis on accelerated growth, generation of productive employment, human resources development, and increased self-reliance. Economic growth is recognized as fundamental to development but not enough to reduce poverty. Economic reforms and structural adjustments, directed at efficiency and growth, need also to promote poverty alleviation by concentrating more on correcting policy distortions that disadvantage the poor. Investing in human resources of the poor, sustainable management of natural resources and the environment, and empowerment of the poor are considered essential for their participation in the growth process. Policy reforms and structural adjustments, primarily aiming at reducing Government interventions and enhancing economic efficiency to create a conducive macro-environment for sustained growth, has created new opportunities as well as challenges for poverty alleviation efforts in the country.

In particular, emphasis on the increased role of the private sector and fostering of macroeconomic incentives for productivity gains within a competitive paradigm requires innovative strategies and adjustments in institutions to mitigate the adverse impact of policy reforms on the poor, especially during the transition period. The grassroots institutions, with their experience and closeness to the poor, are the ones that are ideally located to perform the critical task of making such a process smoother and effective. In this regard, the NGOs in India with their network, experience, and flexibility have been playing a key role within the existing policy environment governing the civil society.

The scope of further enhancing the contributions of NGOs in tackling the developmental challenges, particularly in addressing poverty, depends on a number of factors e.g. more clear understanding of the strengths and limitations of both the Government and the NGOs in addressing poverty issues, the contributions that NGOs can make as development partners, identifying potential areas for mutual collaboration and establishing the necessary framework to support and sustain such collaboration. For success in developing a more fruitful partnership, necessary changes in policies and practices are required for both the Government and the NGOs that set the environment within which NGOs operate.

The magnitude and depth of human deprivation in India is overwhelming. With increasing realization that economic growth, by itself, is not sufficient to lead to a significant reduction in poverty, its alleviation has emerged as an explicit developmental goal. Any piecemeal effort is unlikely to gather the required momentum to initiate a process of cumulative causation that could accelerate poverty alleviating in the country.

Successful attempts at alleviating poverty require strategies to enhance incomes of these poor groups through measures that would not reduce, rather accelerate, the overall growth of the economy. Human factor as the instrument as well as the ultimate objective of the development process has certain implications. First, it involves the enhancement of capacity: capacity to develop socio-political institutions for production and distribution as well as the ability to invest in people to enhance their capabilities in shaping their own future. Secondly, development includes equitable access to benefits through removing socio-economic and other constraints of the disadvantaged groups. Thirdly, development is empowerment providing for built-in mechanisms for equitable growth. Finally, development is concerned with sustainability to ensure effective management of the resources. The above concerns in development require investment in people and improvements in the macro- and micro-environment under which decisions are made by the poor.

Non-government organization (NGO) is a common nomenclature used by international development agencies to cover "third sector" organizations such as non-profit agencies, charities, private voluntary organizations, or philanthropic societies. The major characteristics of NGOs are that they have been established by individuals or groups of other NGOs, not by governments; they should have non-government legal status in their country of registration and be independent of governmental or inter-governmental bodies; be non-profit making; and have a voluntary membership.

The growing disillusionment and the resultant discontent among the masses gave birth to a number of NGOs in 1960s in India. These grassroots movements are concerned with the plight of the exploited sections of society. They are part of the democratic struggle at various levels. The role of NGOs is neither antagonistic nor complementary with the existing sectors. It is a role at once more limited and more radical, taking up issues that the political parties are unwilling to take up, coping with a large diversity of situation that governments and parties are unable to cope, encompassing issues that arise from not merely local and national but also international forces at work. The individual efforts are expressed in micro terms but it deals with conditions that are caused by large macro-structures. The NGOs are thus a part of a large movement for global transformations in which non-State actors on the one hand and non-territorial crystallizations on the other are emerging and playing new role. Most important role Indian NGOs play in of a 'watch dog'. [1].

The growing involvement of NGOs in promoting SSE is a consequence of the way the state in many developing countries has retreated from its dominant position in the development process in the face of financial necessity, aid donor pressure and electoral demand. New strategies have had to be adopted in order to fill the gap left by the state and still maintain levels of economic activity. The local business community is expected to play an increasingly dynamic role in this process, and incomes generating small businesses have a key role in mobilizing local resources, creating appropriate employment and generating new opportunities.

Donor agencies have long been conscious of the failure of government sponsored enterprise agencies in providing relevant, cost-efficient support for ME, especially in rural areas and marginal urban communities. In the past government efforts to promote ME have been expensive, bureaucratic and relatively ineffective. The situation was aggravated in that governments have traditionally been suspicious of the small business sector, and legislation has generally favoured larger concerns. Consequently, over the last decade donor agencies have increasingly turned to NGOs to supplement existing programmes and initiate new innovative approaches to enterprise development, including micro-loan schemes and rural enterprise programmes. NGOs are seen as being particularly effective in this role because of their flexibility and cost-efficiency, their contacts in the local community and freedom from government control.

Thus in communities with little entrepreneurial heritage or involvement in the small business sector aid advisers and policy makers see NGOs as appropriate mechanisms with which to promote MEs. NGOs provide a wide range of services including: the provision of credit, management and business skills training, entrepreneurship development programmes, extension and advisory services, technical assistance, market information and linkages, legal support and policy lobbying. In general most NGOs concentrate on handicraft and agro-based activities; although it appears that there are no particular type of business that are excluded from receiving NGO support as long as they are morally acceptable.

Although for many years mission organizations have been directly involved in income generating, employment creating ventures to provide work for their parishioners and sustain their own educational work, NGO involvement in the promotion of small business is a relatively recent phenomena. This shift in focus raises difficult issues for those working in NGOs, partly because of their limited skill base in this field, but more pertinently because advising on how to run viable profit orientated businesses is tangentially at odds with their traditional role as welfare providers and community developers. On one hand evidence suggests that NGOs are an appropriate vehicle with which to promote MEs, while on the other hand a number of researchers have questioned whether NGOs have any particular advantage over banks or government sponsored enterprise agencies when working with such small businesses. The reason for NGO's comparative advantage in this area is because of their:

1. Cost-efficiency and flexibility.
2. Capacity to induce trust among the local community, particularly because of their neutrality and commitment to development.
3. Ability to collaborate successfully with the local community, and work at grassroots level to mobilize human resources.
4. Willingness and capability to specialize in areas of particular competences rather than trying to perform the role of a multipurpose development agency.
5. Being less subject to political controls than traditional

public development institutions and their ability to act as a bridge between the community and the government.

6. Willingness to take risks and start new experimental projects.

But despite these apparent advantages it is also clear that NGOs, with the limited resources and lack of exposure to business practices, lack the necessary skilled staff and technical competences to work effectively with the small business community. Research suggests that they suffer from potentially high per-beneficiary costs, and their non-profit welfarist ethos often means they focus on the poor rather than the viable and the profitable, consequently there programmes are rarely sustainable or replicable. [2] (Tendler, 1989). They tend to see income generating activity as an additional welfare support measure for the community, and as a consequence support is targeted to the neediest, rather than those who could be expected to make best use of it (Hailey and Harper, 1989). [3]

In term of accessibility to common people the NGOs are in superior position to GOs but their advantageous position unfortunately is lately recognized i.e. during the Sixth Plan only since earlier strategy was confined to welfare and charity work alone. Both Sixth (1980-85) and Seventh Plans (1985-90) [4] on realizing the importance of participatory development categorically, emphasized on active role of NGOs to make people more self-reliant and self-content. In recognition of catalytic role performed by NGOs in the matter of empowerment of weaker section of community, the Planning Commission Organized "National convention of Voluntary Organizations" on March 7 and 8 in 1995 which further institutionalized relationship between government and voluntary organizations. [5]

7.2 Achievements of NGOs Relating to Women's Issues

One of the distinguishing activities of NGOs is to work for weaker section, the women and children, old, downtrodden or backward communities. Depending on organizational capacity the NGOs can involve themselves in any type of socio-economic activity, but while carrying out their mission the category of beneficiaries are to be given due weightage. From different relevant sources it can be ascertained that NGOs took interest in women-issues even during pre-colonial period but it gathered momentum only after 1970 when world voices became louder. It is well admitted that NGOs have done women's service to the cause of women and children takcn up very sensitivc issues to stop atrocities simultaneously women organizations too have involved themselves in women issues.

Both NGOs and women organizations working on women-issues are to devote attention before total women empowerment is attained. To alleviate poverty from amongst rural people successful implementation of "Poverty Alleviation Programme" is essential in the same way parallel schemes are to be evolved to reduce urban poverty in order to maintain balance in overall poverty scenario. Here, it may be mentioned that to give thrust to women's welfare programme under the Five Year Plans provision was made for grant-in-aid to women organizations too. During the Sixth Plan an amount of ₹ 237 lakh was earmarked for such programme. [6]

Roles of GOs, NGOs and women organizations are complementary not supplementary. It is through better coordination desired result can be achieved. Their struggle for "gender equality" will be more forceful and accelerate momentum when academicians, social scientist und social thinkers join their hands for this noble cause. All the combined forces will definitely help restore lost glory of women. It is to be noted that women as a whole need sympathetic support of patriarchy for smooth continuation of civilized society, women of informal sector living below poverty line are badly in need of care, attention and love, as they are the victim/sufferers of present social system. By bringing them under social security measures a new society can be evolved, where discrimination in any form will cease to exist and women will get their due recognition in society and in this aspect NGOs are to play very significant role. While working together problems may arise but when they all arc working for common cause, judicious minds should take care of situation so that there is real improvement in status of women, rather than deterioration caused by nepotism, corruption and ill practices.

7.2.1 Bharat Integrated Social Welfare Agency (BISWA): BISWA is a community based organization in the voluntary sector, working directly with the poor and marginalized. The mission of BISWA is "to make a real and lasting social, economic, psychological and spiritual impact on individuals, help build strong cohesive communities and generate substantial productive employment opportunity by increasing availability of a wider range of services". BISWA believes that right to equal opportunity is the basic right of all human beings.

Poor people do neither have life choice nor better opportunity for their sustainability. Ensuring that a poor household has stable livelihood, will substantially increase its income and over a period of time asset ownership, self-esteem and social participation. The 'bottom of the pyramid' comprising nearly 4 billion out of the 6 billion people in the world, do not have the purchasing power to buy even the bare necessities of life–food, clothing and shelter. But as soon as they are enabled to get steadier incomes through livelihood support, they become customers of many goods and services, which then promote growth. In addition to, the Organization also aims at restoring social and political stability through promoting livelihoods.

Since its inception, the Organization is dedicated towards creating an environment through positive economic and social programmes for development of women and youth in rural areas and urban slums to enable them to realize their full potential. In this venture, promotion of awareness on human rights, encouraging women participation in decision making process, facilitating access to health care and quality education, vocational guidance, credit linkage, marketing linkage, social security, strengthening systems aimed at all forms of discrimination against women, mainstreaming a gender perspective in the process of activity, building partnership with government, civil society will be our primary focus and function. The basic objectives on which the BISWA works to develop the artisans in different clusters are as follows:

1. Organizing rural artisans into an appropriate organizational form (a self-help group or federation) and spread awareness about group entrepreneurship, better business practices and markets for their products etc.
2. Providing and implement a road map that makes artisans aware of the technical alterations that can expand market and/or lower costs without compromising the basic nature of their products.
3. Enabling artisans to build a marketing network to sell their products or initiate a fair bargain while entering into an existing one.
4. Enabling artisans to set up a production centre appropriate for local and international conditions.
5. Promoting inter-sectoral linkages.

7.2.2 Promotion of Non-Banking Financial Company (NBFC): Pursuing the road map prepared in the year 2003 for BISWA micro finance programme, a Non-banking Financial Company (NBFC) was established to cater to the financial needs of the clients. Under the present legal status of BISWA, it was very difficult to meet the financial needs of the promoted SHGs. Considering the volume and the enhanced intake capacities of the clients and the growth plans of the Organisation; in April 2006 the chairman BISWA has promoted a Non-banking Financial Company named as Credible Securities and Finance Private Limited, later on, the name has been changed to Credible Microfinance Private Limited.

7.2.3 Product and Services: Micro finance is the provision of financial services to individual who cannot provide collateral required by formal banks to receive loans. Credible Microfinance Pvt. Limited has extended its credit facility through 3-types of lending model:

- NGOs/SHPIs (partners of BISWA);
- MBTs (promoted by BISWA);
- Self-help groups (promoted by BISWA).

7.2.4 Micro Enterprises Development Approaches: The objective of the programme is to bridge the gap and permit a flow of finance to be absorbed by different service providers on a commercially viable basis. This will eventually improve the quality of life of all the people in the chain and decrease the percentage of family living below poverty line thereby achieving the Millennium Development Goals (MDGs) by 2015.

The micro enterprise programmes focus on:

- Techno skill up gradation of self-help group members;
- Encouraging procurement of marketable products;
- Networking among federations in order to cater to the market demand;
- Common brand building of the products; and
- Encouraging after sales service.

7.2.5 Micro Marketing: BISWA, through its field experience, has realized that successful marketing of rural products and services is a very crucial factor to bring a significant change in the economic status of the targeted households. Thus, through the past years BISWA has put its efforts to find a suitable market for optimal return for the products of the clientele groups. Specifically, BISWA is facilitating the group and individual production of handicrafts, handlooms and other consumable items. In future BISWA aims at establishing a brand name and reach out to the clients at national level including the metropolis and big cities.

This will ensure maximum profit and radical change in the economic status of the households remaining at the lowest strata of the society. It has been promoting livelihood and MEs through SHGs. This effort has used the local resources in a systematic manner and produced desired cost effective consumer products. The products are usually marketed among local households and nearby SHGs under cross marketing strategy. BISWA has made a preliminary effort to consolidate the existing cross marketing system and bring several networks of SHGs based on their products and promote those in existing regular markets. To strengthen this strategy, BISWA has been supporting SHGs and Federations of SHGs through micro finance and providing technical know-how and management skill input to the entrepreneurs.

Many handicrafts development programs have been implemented for the upliftment of rural artisans. It covered more than 2000 numbers of artisans from 5 districts. The artisans, engaged in dhokra, wood carving, lacquer, leather, appliqué, cane and bamboo, stone carving, cow dung toys, tribal painting, bell metal, and vegetable dye crafts, belong to SC, ST and OBC categories and live under below poverty line.

In the year 2007-2008, Kalanikatan was associated as a Cluster Developing Agency (CDA) with support of DH&CI. It has implemented six numbers of cluster development programs under Craft Village Scheme on dhokra casting, tribal jewellery, lacquer craft, wood craft, art leather and terracotta crafts at Nabarangpur district. Specially, an integrated cluster development program on terracotta craft, assisted by NABARD, implemented in Nabarangpur District.

Notwithstanding some deficiencies, there exists a strong realization among both Government and NGOs, of the need to develop stronger and improved collaboration. Given the imperatives of poverty alleviation and efficacy of the NGOs in dealing with these issues, increased Government-NGO collaboration is a pragmatic way of addressing some of the poverty problems. In particular, Government-NGO collaboration in providing relief, literacy, and health care and family planning services, has a long history of success in the country. Within the broad framework, a number of initiatives can be taken to further promote and expand Government-NGO collaboration:

1. **Multiple and Innovative Roles of NGOs:** In addition to traditional service delivery, the roles of NGOs are now more diversified particularly in response to increased vulnerability of the poor due to implementation of structural adjustment and economic reform programmes. With more cross-sectoral involvement for an integrated focus, NGOs are now equipped to contribute more and in new areas than before.
2. **Capacity Building of NGOs:** With diversity in functions and inter-sectoral involvement, the capacities of many NGOs, except the large and established ones with proven abilities, are stretched. Selective and appropriate capacity building efforts of NGOs can be effective in preparing them to meet challenges.
3. **Government-NGO Dialogue on Development Issues:** Since NGOs work mostly at the grassroots level, they have the ability to assess the impact of poverty interventions and obtain feedback from the poor. Such assessment and feedback can be effective in planning and designing strategies to address the expectations of the poor based on lessons of experiences.
4. **NGO Involvement in Policy Consultations and Project Cycle:** It can be institutionalized to optimize their contribution. One way is to devise formal partnership mechanisms at various levels and strengthen the existing ones.
5. **Enabling Legal and Regulatory Environment:** NGOs can operate effectively and efficiently if a conducive legal and regulatory environment exists to promote rather than constrain their potential like monitoring NGO activity to facilitate dialogue rather than control NGO activities and ensure that NGO advocacy is fruitful and not misdirected.
6. **Alternative Financing Options for NGOs:** While many NGOs are mostly dependent on grants for their activities, alternative financing options need to be explored and

expanded. With greater emphasis on diversification and revenue generating mechanisms by the NGOs in recent years, provision of credit funds and other sources to support their activities becomes critical. The effective involvement of NGOs in areas where they have comparative strengths and support, and capacity enhancement in areas where they appear to be weak should form the basis for Government-NGO collaboration.

However, it is important to realize certain limitations of the NGOs in promoting such collaboration. The NGO outreach is often regarded as limited and fragmented which largely excludes the extreme poor groups. Some of these limitations are the outcome of weak institutional capacity while others are conditioned by low replicability potential, e.g. good leadership, which is not often found in Government agencies or even in all NGOs. In some cases, these may reflect the small size and limited availability of resources for a particular NGO or even a part of deliberate NGO strategy to achieve effectiveness by developing close relations with the beneficiaries to gain acceptability.

7.3 Government-NGOs Collaboration

With respect to national development, the Government and NGOs share common goals e.g. poverty alleviation, human resources development, women's development, protecting the environment and sustainable resource management and building a democratic civil society and others. The institutional approach to address the issues, however, differs due to variations in perceptions as well as responsibilities, expertise, experience, resource base and administrative/management structure. An effective collaboration should recognize these differences and exploit the full potentiality of respective advantages. Within the institutional and other requirements of poverty alleviation efforts, the NGOs have several major advantages:

1. NGOs are valuable facilitators in bringing about closer grassroots beneficiary involvement in development. NGOs

can often motivate and mobilize the poor in a way that the Government cannot do because of their close working relationships with the poor and better understanding of the social dimensions that impinge on beneficiary participation in poverty alleviation efforts.

2. NGOs have the capacity to target on specific population groups in specific locations.
3. NGOs have the flexibility to become creative with capacity for experimentation and innovation.
4. NGOs are able to deliver services in a cost-effective way to communities which are not easily accessible by the Government.
5. NGOs have a voluntaristic ethic that is difficult to replicate in Government agencies.

Above all, within the emerging paradigm of adjustments and private sector-led development, NGOs constitute the vehicle for the Government to shed roles and functions that can be fulfilled with greater efficiency and effectiveness. The Government policy framework for NGO efforts in the arena of relief and rehabilitation, during the 1970s, has been largely supportive. Since then, relations between the Government and NGOs have undergone various phases of polarization with redirection and deepening of NGO interventions into poverty alleviation efforts. With much of the tensions removed, the present efforts aim at promoting Government-NGO collaboration and partnership in alleviating poverty. Initially, collaboration was limited to consultations and informal discussions on poverty alleviation issues. With persistence of poverty and limitations of the Government strategies to tackle poverty directly, the need for greater cooperation with NGOs to supplement Government efforts is now well-recognized.

The main objective of such collaboration is to address the basic needs of the poor and support sustainable development efforts particularly at the grassroots level. A number of sectors of collaboration have been focused upon, which include agriculture, irrigation, fisheries, livestock, forestry, environment, urban development and housing, infrastructure, water and sanitation, health and population, and education and training. Four forms of Government-NGO cooperation are conceived: NGOs as a source of information, consultants, cooperating agencies for execution and co-financiers.

End Notes

1. Puri, Chandrakant, Evaluation of the Role of NGOs in Tribal Development in India, Paper for presentation at 17th APASWC, Japan, 2003.
2. Tendler, J., Whatever Happened to Poverty Alleviation, in J. Levitsky, (ed.), Microenterprises in Developing Countries, IT Publications, London, 1989.
3. Hailey, J. and Harper, M., Management Development for Enterprise Promotion, Paper to IHRD Conference, Manchester, 1989.
4. Noorjahan: *op. cit.,* pp. 127-129.
5. Kurukshetra, February 1995, Vol. XLII, No. 5, p. 3.
6. Mathew. P.M. and Nair. M.S. (1986), Women's Organization and Women's Interest, p. 123.

Appendix

Appendix

Micro Finance and Micro Enterprises: A Case Study of Kalahandi, Balangir and Koraput (KBK) Districts of Orissa

Tribal Economy of Orissa

Orissa has the largest concentration of tribal population in India. The tribal are the children of nature and their lifestyle is conditioned by the eco-system. Orissa due to its diverse ecosystems has a wide variety of tribal population. More than half the tribal population is concentrated in the KBK districts.

The tribal economy is equally distinctive since it is closed and undifferentiated characterized by adoption of primitive technology in economic pursuits. The tribal people earn in their livelihood by undertaking many occupations such as forestry and food gathering, shifting cultivation, settled agriculture, and industrial labour, animal husbandry, fishing, traditional commerce of which household industry including handicrafts is of prime importance. Tribals have been producing different handicrafts both utilitarian and decorative over centuries.

Tribal economy in the earlier days was a barter system through mutual help. Lending, if any, between different members of the community is also governed by customs and interest has not been applied. Thus self sufficient economy of the tribal does not have substantial surpluses to warrant establishment of regular markets nor knew their potentialities for their handicrafts. Slowly market economies began to appear around religious festivals and demands for new items started increasing. This leads to weekly markets. Traders or middlemen came on the scene and slowly these tribal artisans who display their skill, acquired through tradition, used to sell their products to these traders or middleman, unfortunately these artisans are being exploited and are paid paltry amounts.

Even this system is getting eroded due to poor marketing facilities and is unable to with stand competition from manufacturing industries. In order to provide and protect the artisans' skills inherited, government both at the centre and states have developed and implemented various schemes for the upliftment of the indigenous artisans. These artisans are also encouraged by various government and non-government institutions to participate in the entrepreneurial activities through the micro enterprises in the form of SHGs to show their skills and to earn a sustainable livelihood.

The tribal handicrafts are specialized skills which are passed on from one generation to another and these handicrafts are means of livelihood of the artisans. However, in absence of any organized activity in this sector and the products not being adequately remunerative, there is a possible likelihood of the artisans taking up alternate livelihood options (which may involve migration as well). In such a case this age-old activity will die its own death. At this stage, it is very imperative to understand the problems faced by this sector and suggest the strategies for development of tribal handicraft based on which certain policy level interventions need to be taken by the government to sustain the traditional tribal handicrafts.

Orissa is the poorest among all the major states of the country in terms of overall poverty as well as the rural poverty (rural poverty stood at 48.01 percent against the all-India average of 27.09 percent in 1999-2000, Planning Commission). The poverty estimates made by various agencies including the planning commission shows that while the rest of the country has made significant progress in this regard (the percentage of population below poverty line in India has come down from 54.88 percent in 1973-74 to 26.10 percent in 1999-2000, (Planning Commission), the incidence of poverty in Orissa has not changed correspondingly (the percentage of population below poverty line came down from 66.18 percent to 47.15 during the same period in Orissa). The extent, depth and severity of rural poverty in Orissa are very high and its multidimensional facets have been maintained by dynamic interplay of several factors.

The majority of the population (nearly 87 percent), in the state lives in rural areas and is highly dependent on agriculture (73 percent, Statistical Abstract, Directorate of Economics and Statistics, Orissa). Lack of corresponding growth and employment opportunities in other sectors have forced people to depend on agriculture despite a significant drop in relative income from this primary source of livelihood. This has given rise to disguised unemployment and seasonal employment. This trend of occupational base has turned a majority of rural population dependent on uneven income from agriculture, as it is highly dependent on vagaries of nature.

The extent of poverty is not evenly distributed in all regions and among all social groups of Orissa. Some of the regions like tribal-dominated northern and southern regions are characterized by high concentration of tribal population (it was 39.7 percent in southern region and 34.5 percent in northern region in 1983, State Development Report, NCDS). As the incidence of poverty is very high among the ST Population (contributed 38 percent towards total poverty ratio of the state in 1993-94) and the poverty ratio among them hasn't reduced over two decades, these regions remain highly backward. The other feature of regional diversity akin to poverty and backwardness in the state is best demonstrated by the KBK Districts—mostly, poor tribal and rural population of the state who have borne the wrath of repeated droughts due to uneven rainfall in the region inhibit these districts.

There has been no change in the pattern of dependence over primary sector (agriculture and forestry) for livelihood within last decades in these regions due to lack of alternative source of employment (it was 85 percent in 1971, 84 percent in 1991, and 79 percent in 2001, Census Data, Government of India). But the average food grain production in the region is very low owing to several factors like uneven rainfall, low irrigated area compared to gross cultivated area, yield rate etc. (the percent of irrigated area of Kalahandi District was 25.3 compared to 69.1 percent of Cuttack District in 2000-01, Orissa Agricultural Statistics 2000-01, Directorate of Agriculture and Food production). The other major source of tribal and rural poor namely forest resources is fast degrading leading to increase in proportion of daily wage labourers, unemployment, migration etc.

At present, all the eight KBK districts are ecologically disturbed. More than 50 percent of forests of these districts are degraded. Problems of soil erosion and land degradation are common. Water retention capacity of soils is generally poor. These factors, among others, significantly contribute to low land productivity. Employment opportunities in the region are limited. The majority of the population is dependent on forest and subsistence agriculture. Agriculture, which is the major economic activity, does not generate adequate avenues of employment for the rural poor. The agricultural produce is insufficient for providing sustenance throughout the year. The high degrees of dependence of the agrarian population on primary sector and subsequent decrease of income from these sectors have not been accompanied by growth in Industrial output.

The large and medium Industries could not able to come up, leading to seizure of growth in ancillary industries and employment opportunities. On contrary, whatever growth was achieved in the small enterprises sector after 1990s remained concentrated on some industrially developed areas. The Industrial and mining projects developed at the cost of major source of livelihood of rural poor like forest and land, didn't include the unskilled rural poor in the employment opportunities created in this sector.

As a result, many men and women go out to urban areas both inside and outside the State in search of employment. This leaves the old and infirm in villages. However, the promotion of a secure and sustainable livelihood is perhaps the key to improve the economic conditions of the poorest tribal population of this region in the long run. It is in that context that the advent of informal sector has recently assumed a certain degree of prominence. It is based on the recognition that the latent capacity of the poor for entrepreneurship would be encouraged with the availability of small-scale loans and would introduce them to the small-enterprise sector. This could allow them to be more self-reliant, create employment opportunities, and, not least, engage women in economically productive activities. They provide the rural population with access to savings within the local area and with a certain cushion against economic fluctuations, and they encourage a cooperative and community feeling. The groups formed provide joint collateral and serve as instruments for spreading valuable information that is useful for economic and social progress.

The informal economy in this area consists of two large baskets. The first basket contains small, low-capital enterprises run by self-employed persons, drawing on family support and sometimes employing a few hired workers (excluding daily-wage earners or piece-rated workers). The second basket contains casual, daily wage-workers available at street-corner, labour markets or offered by labour agents in sectors like agriculture, mines, brick-kilns and construction as well as piece-rated workers in sectors like handicrafts and handlooms.

The handicrafts of the region are representative of its culture. The state of Orissa is famous for the ethnic beauty of its handicrafts. The motifs and symbols used are steeped in its ancient cultural heritage. The tradition of stone carving, wood carving, pattachitra painting, appliqué work and silver filigree craft began as a part of temple architecture and ornamentation. The somewhat lesser-known traditions of Indian craft are the "folk" crafts dating back to a period that may be referred to as "timeless". These are the living traditions, intrinsically linked with the regional cultural settings from which they arise. It has an age-old heritage that can be traced back to the beginning of the civilization on this subcontinent.

It began with cave paintings, natural dyes in such a manner that they can still visible on the walls of the caves even after centuries. The folk and tribal paintings come from the remote rural and tribal regions. In many a cases the artists of these rustic works are not even educated, but are gifted with beautiful means of expression. Various painting forms coming from these regions began not just as a painting but also as a part of their religious and social rituals performed daily. It began with painting of the walls and the floors of mud houses. They hold the belief that this purifies the ambience and pleased the deities. Various religious symbols are, therefore, seen in the paintings, such as gods and goddesses and their abodes.

All these paintings were produced in a variety of styles and themes. History, sociology and geography infuse the paintings of each region with local flavour. Their style and quality depend on the materials available in the place in which they were executed. These factors help to identify the region to which they belong. Folk art may be defined as the art created among groups that exist within the framework of existing society, but for geographical and cultural reasons, are largely separated from the mainstream sophisticated cultural developments of their time. As a result, they produce distinctive styles and objects as per local needs and tastes. In folk tradition, art is nourishment to the daily life of the people.

The indigenous people of KBK districts are no less than the rest of the other oriyas. The rich craft of terracotta, lacquer works, dhokra casting, bamboo crafts, brass metal works, cane and grass fiber works, handlooms etc is the hallmarks of the rich tradition and culture of this area. The traditional artworks not lonely bind the people to their rich traditions but also provide sustenance in terms of income and social esteem. The economic benefits of this sustainable micro entrepreneurship in these areas are compelling, and its potential effects on the development process are equally promising. In terms of development and social impact, these micro-industries allow significant improvements in quality of life for the micro entrepreneurs.

They can now stabilize the cash flow of their economic activity, bringing security to the enterprise. This allows them to better manage spending, which often generates savings; and this provides better standards of living to their family, and dependents in terms of housing, nutrition, health and education. Finally, an access to banking and increased security promotes a sense of entrepreneurship, and thus their self-esteem and reputation increase. The initial small industrial effort can eventually reintegrate these entrepreneurs into formal networks of the economy and foster the structural and sustainable development of local communities. Despite several challenges ahead, this emerging industry, and the process of sustainable micro entrepreneurship combine to offer a potential alleviation solution to the poverty crisis of the years to come, and into a sustainable future.

As it can be inferred, KBK districts needs micro entrepreneurs in order to sustain local economies. As the slogan "Think Global, Act Local" permeates throughout KBK's progressive culture, micro enterprises' role as a tool for local economic development will become increasingly significant. Given the importance of micro enterprises to the state's economy and the help it provides to many underserved populations, it is imperative to analyze the effects experienced by micro entrepreneurs and continue to explore the field. As the growth of micro enterprises in these areas continues, the voices of the individuals that make up very small businesses must be heard.

Socio-economic Profile of KBK Districts

A poor and backward state like Orissa having a substantial size of depressed population (nearly 40 percent SC and ST population) and a backward subsistence-oriented agricultural economy has failed to bridge the development disparities that have long existed between the people and space at the inter-district level. Till 1992, the State was divided into 13 districts. Among the 13 old and undivided districts only the four coastal districts namely Cuttack, Puri, Baleswar and Ganjam and two districts from the highland region namely Sundargarh and Sambalpur may be characterized as developed or advanced according to the existing development position of the State's economy. Among the backward districts, further, the old and undivided districts namely, Kalahandi, Balangir, Koraput and Phulbani in the highland region are found to be chronically backward and highly underdeveloped.

In recent years, three of the old and undivided backward districts namely, Kalahandi, Balangir and Koraput in the south-western part of Orissa have become vulnerable to recurring droughts and famine like situations, which lead to distress migration of the poor during non-agricultural season. They are also considered very backward districts in the country and are popularly known as KBK districts. Needless to say, in a poor and backward state like Orissa, the KBK region is the most backward and poverty stricken belt. The KBK region now consists of eight districts namely, Kalahandi and Nuapada forming part of undivided Kalahandi; Balangir and Subarnapur forming part of undivided Balangir; and Koraput, Malkangiri, Nabarangpur and Rayagada forming part of undivided Koraput.

Administrative Divisions of the KBK Districts: The undivided districts of Koraput, Balangir and Kalahandi, popularly known as KBK Districts, have since 1992-93 been divided into eight districts, viz., Koarput, Malkangiri, Nabarangapur, Rayagada, Balangir, Subaxzrnapur, Kalahandi, and Nuapada with a view to strengthening and accelerating the process of economic development in the state. It was assumed that smaller districts would be easier to administer and the resources could be more productively utilized at the grassroots level through decentralized administration. These eight districts comprise of 14 sub-divisions, 37 tehsils, 80 CD blocks, 1,437 gram panchayats, and 12,293 villages. The geographical and administrative divisions of these districts are summarized in the Table A1.

Table A1: Geographical and Administrative Divisions of the KBK Districts

Districts	Area (in sq. kms.)	Total Number of (as per 20011 Census)					
		Blocks	TSP Blocks	Sub-divisions	Tahsils	GPs	Villages
Koraput	8,807	14	14	02	07	226	2028
Malkangiri	5,791	07	07	01	03	108	1045
Nabarangpur	5,291	10	10	01	04	169	901
Rayagada	7,073	11	11	02	04	171	2,667
Balangir	6,575	14	-	03	06	285	1,794
Subarnapur	2,337	06	-	02	04	96	959
Kalahandi	7,920	13	02	02	07	273	2,236
Nuapada	3,852	05	-	01	02	109	663
Total KBK	47,646	80	44	14	37	1,437	12,293
Orissa	155,707	314	-	58	171	6,234	51,349

Source: Census of India, 2001.

Demography of the KBK Districts: The KBK districts account for 20.62 percent population over 30.60 percent geographical area of the state of Orissa. 89.45 percent people of this region still live in 12,293 villages. Lower population density i.e., 190 persons per sq. km. in comparison to 269 people per sq. km. for Orissa and 313 for India indicates difficult living conditions and an undeveloped economy of this area. KBK region is a tribal dominated region as 44 blocks out of 80 are included under the Tribal Sub-Plan (TSP). As per 2001 Census, about 54.66 percent people of KBK districts belong to Schedule Tribes (38.41 percent) and Schedule Castes (16.25 percent) as against the state average of only 38.68 percent belonging to both the categories. Some districts, for example, Malkangiri district, have as high Schedule Tribes and Schedule Castes population as 78.80 percent. About 68 percent villages in KBK region have 50 percent or more ST and SC population.

Maximum population of KBK region is the dweller of rural areas (89.95 percent) which is predominated by social and gender disparities in terms of literacy, health and other social-indicators vis-à-vis Orissa. The sex ratio of the KBK region is 997 per 1000 male which is higher than the ratio in Orissa (972 per 1000 male) and the ratio (933 per 1000 male) in India. The higher sex ratio is due to the women dominated society of tribal who constitute the major share of population (38.41 percent) of this region.

Literacy and Education: Literacy rate is one of the important indicators for determining the living condition of the people of a region. A study done by Kar finds that the impact of rural literacy rate on the percentage of rural families living below the poverty line is significant. So, to reduce poverty, education can be a powerful instrument.

As per the estimate made by DPEP, Bhubaneswar in 2002-2003, the total number of out-of-school children was 36.92 percent in undivided Koraput district, 24.90 percent and 30.31 percent in undivided Balangir and Undivided Kalahandi district respectively. The Education Deprivation Index (education deprivation index is the sum total of percentage of out-of-school children plus adult illiteracy rate) shows that Koraput district is the most deprived district with 114.33, Balangir with 82.12 and Kalahandi with 97.96 whereas the state shows it at 74.05.

Health and Family Welfare: The levels of living of the people also depend on the health facilities. The better the health facilities, the better will be the levels of living and life expectancy ratio and the lesser will be the infant mortality rate and maternal mortality rate. Disadvantages of inhospitable terrain, lack of awareness and education, lack of infrastructure, communication and personnel, several diseases and ailments that afflict Orissa, are found either in a more acute and widespread form in the KBK districts.

The cholera epidemic in 2007 shows the dreadful scenario

of health sector in this region. In particular, five diseases: leprosy, diarrhoea, malaria, acute respiratory infections and scabies (*Panchabyadhi*) combined with TB are considered killer diseases of this region. The population suffers from high morbidity on account of under-nutrition as well as endemic malaria and other localized diseases. The facts reveal the disquieting health services available to this poorest population of India. The result of the dismal health sector performance in the KBK region is reflected in the decadal growth rate of population in this region. The crude death rate is high coupled with high death of infants, mothers due to malnutrition and lack of medical facilities at the time of pregnancy and in pre- and post-pregnancy periods.

Agriculture: Orissa is the tenth largest state in area and eleventh in population in the country, accounting for 5 percent of the geographical area and 4 percent of the population of the country. Cultivators and agricultural labourers constitute 65 percent of the total workforce. Agriculture provides direct or indirect employment to 65 percent of the total work force and contributes 26 percent of the net state domestic product. Kharif is the main cropping season and rice is the principal crop during kharif season. Cropping during rabi season is mainly confined to irrigated areas and areas with residual moisture. Other important crops produced in the state are pulses (arhar, moong, biri, kulthi), oilseeds (groundnut, til, mustard and niger), fibres (jute, mesta, cotton), sugarcane, vegetables and spices, mango, banana, coconut and cashewnut are the main horticultural crops of the state. The state has a cultivated area of 62 lakh hectares out of which 27 lakh hectares is high land, 19 lakh hectares medium and 16 lakh hectares low land. Paddy area during kharif is about 42 lakh and during rabi 2.5 lakh hectares.

The state is broadly divided into four physiographic zones namely, coastal plains, central table land, northern plateau and eastern ghats. These are further sub-divided into ten agroclimatic zones namely, north western plateau, north central plateau, north eastern coastal plain, east and south eastern coastal plain, north eastern ghat, eastern ghat highland, south eastern ghat, western undulating zone, western central table land and mid central table land. The state has different soil types ranging from fertile alluvial deltaic soils in the coastal plains, mixed red and black soils in the central table land, red and yellow soils with low fertility in the northern plateau and red, black and brown forest soil in eastern ghat region. The soil types differ widely from highly acidic to slightly alkaline and from light sandy to stiff clays.

The soils are mainly acidic with the degree of acidity varying widely. About 4 lakh hectares are exposed to saline inundation, 3.54 lakh hectares to flooding and 0.75 hectares to water logging. As so, agriculture is the primary economic activity of the KBK region and is the major occupation of the people. 10.64 lakh agricultural families depend directly or indirectly on agriculture for their livelihood. The region has 18.51 lakh hectares cultivable area which is 30 percent of the state's net cultivable area of 61.65 lakh hectares. Of the total cultivable area, uplands constitute about 10.78 lakh hectares which is nearly 57 percent. Household investment in agriculture has been negligible. Due to absence of irrigation facilities farmers are not able to take advantage of the advanced agricultural technologies appropriate to irrigated conditions. As such, agricultural productivity has remained abjectly low. Although cash crops like cotton, maize, onion etc. are becoming increasingly popular, traditional foodgrain crops like paddy, ragi and minor millets, local pulse varieties have remained the main agricultural produce.

The green cover has been depleted everywhere and resulted in global warming. Afforestation and regeneration of degraded forest has formed the need of the hour. The KBK region still has some of the wonderful natural forests of the state. The old Koraput district is covered by Eastern Ghat while the old Balangir and Kalahandi are the part of the Chhatishgarh plateau. The division and land utilization of the geographical area of the KBK districts is discussed in following paragraphs.

Irrigation: The KBK districts are chronically affected by drought due to low and erratic rainfall. Inadequacy of irrigation in this region has been a major impediment for the development of agrarian sector. Increase in agricultural production requires provision of reliable irrigation facility to farmers on a sustainable basis. In term of resource endowments, KBK region has plentiful water and fertile land. In KBK region, coverage of irrigation is much less than the state average. Though these districts have abundant water sources, flow irrigation, i.e., exposure to major and medium irrigation is below state average in spite of a vast potential for developing it.

The basic objective of the irrigation projects in KBK districts is four-fold, viz., (i) to increase food production by increasing yielding capacity of the land, (ii) to increase employment opportunities in agrarian sector and thus to increase the living standard; (iii) to reduce regional disparities through drought proofing; and (iv) to income distribution by generating more income from agricultural and other allied activities. The presence of major rivers, rivulets, springs etc the creation and development of irrigation facilities can be taken a leap in the recent years. Various state and central schemes provide a helping hand to this to enhance a self-sustainable agrarian sector in the KBK regions.

Forest Resources: Historically, the KBK have been rich in forest resources. Traditionally the people have depended on these forests for their needs of timber, firewood, other non-timber forest products (NTFP) and fodder for their cattle. On the one hand, the people and the state agencies have been heavily removing various forest products from these forests. On the other hand, these forests have not received adequate investment. These two processes are continuously reinforcing forest degradation.

Forest sector in KBK plays an important role in the

economy, culture and livelihood of a large number of forest dependent poor and it represents a huge economic resource for the region. However, there has been progressive decline in the forest cover in KBK during the last few decades. The wasteful exploitation is posing potential danger for the economy and environment besides threat to livelihood sector security of millions of forest dependent poor. Massive deforestation is primarily caused by the increase in biotic pressure, and also due to non-response of forest resources to the increased needs of the people. Due to lack of adequate public and private investment, and absence of adequate externally funded forestry development programmes for the KBK, forestry sector has remained precisely unattended over the years.

Livestock Resources: Livestock sector in Orissa is highly livelihood intensive and 80 percent of the rural households own livestock of one species or another to earn stable or supplementary income. The sector contributes 7.25 percent of the state's net domestic product. As the growth potential is comparative low in KBK region, the KBK districts have been included under category B (potential districts) and C (low potential districts). Balangir, Rayagada, and Kalahandi are grouped under the former and the rest five are grouped under the latter group. Livestock and poultry rearing is one of the main activities of the allied activities of the tribals in the KBK districts. Generally, a tribal family keeps 5-10 units of poultry, 4-5 heads of small ruminants, one or two non-descriptive cows and in certain cases one or two pair of working bullocks. Some of them also rear pigs.

Due to the age old practices of the population of KBK region made this area as a major area of producing livestock produces in terms of meat, egg and milk. Dependability on Andhra Pradesh for meat and eggs has been reduced due to higher productivity in this sector.

Housing: The KBK region is an under-developed and poor region in comparison to the other part of the state. The villages of KBK regions are scattered as the majority of the population consists of SC and ST population. The density of population is less in compared to the state average due to difficult terrain and inaccessible areas. Due to poverty, the majority have temporary or semi permanent houses. Due to disintegration of the tribal family after marriage, the average household size is less in comparison to the state share. The average size of household is 4.4 against the state average of 4.8 and country average of 5.4, which indicates the lesser density of population and high death rate.

Mining: KBK's mineral deposits are large, and there is fairly heavy concentrations in respect of bauxite, graphite, manganese, gemstone and limestone also have a significant share, though they are not of high grade variety. The rate of cumulative exploitation (output-resource stock ratio) has remained low, except in the case of Bauxite, Graphite and Manganese ore. However, this has not provided a sufficient condition for establishment of metallurgical and non-metallic mineral based industries on a large scale. Even value addition within the region has remained relatively low.

Industrialization: Industrial structure of KBK districts has hardly shown any improvement as compared to other districts. In most cases, the presence of highly capital intensive industries with cost disadvantages in fuel, interest payment and depreciation has resulted in heavy losses. Moreover, the prevalence of low wages in many industries causes low productivity of labour. Because of poor agricultural base, the emergence of an active local entrepreneurial class has been stifled. The persistently disadvantageous position of the KBK region raises basic questions of neglect and misdirected policies of the Centre as well as the State. Baring some of the big industries like HAL, NALCO, BEDANT Alumina etc., the development of industrial success is very rare in this region. The development of private industrial sector is a scare commodity though the KBK area is full of natural resources.

Lack of proper infrastructure, especially, transport and power, has severely impaired both growth and diversification of industries in this region. So, a serious rethinking on the issue of greater use of power for the industrialization, rather than mere selling it, is essential. In order to activate the industrial sector, development of railways and civil aviation is very much essential. Secondly, to generate income in the rural sector and promote a viable rural industrial base, larger investment in agricultural development needs to be made. Thirdly, for further industrial development, a dynamic small/ micro enterprise promotion policy for this region is needed. Fourthly, KBK districts are endowed with a range of high-grade minerals. But, these are not exploited properly. Mining activities should be upgraded to the status of manufacturing industry wherein mineral processing up to certain stages could be undertaken in this region. Fifthly, modern agro and forest based industries need to be encouraged. Finally, preference should be given to the new areas of industrial activities with special emphasis on location in underdeveloped districts.

Infrastructural Facilities: Nevertheless, it is a good trend to observe that the rural pockets of KBK region in the recent years have witnessed positive transformations of certain key infrastructures such as development of roads, transport and communication networks and if more stress could be put on proper maintenance and supervision of different service infrastructures, it will be easier for a poor and backward region like KBK to accelerate its pace of economic development.

The road length on the KBK districts per sq. km. of area is only 1.28 km. which is below the state average of 1.49 km. Many roads in KBK districts are nothing but earthen tracks with frequent missing links. Because of missing links, many villages even along the existing roads remain cut off from main growth centres (towns and markets) and service centres (schools, hospitals, block offices etc.). The figures with respect to the railway connectivity also provide a very grim and dismal picture. Maximum of the rail roads in this region are meant for carrying the minerals from the mines to the nearest ports or to the industrial sites. The railways passenger sector is a great disappointment for the whole KBK region as the popular passenger mode of transport is still the roadways.

Improvement in infrastructure, particularly connectivity, is necessary for the accelerated development of KBK region along with improved quality of life and reduction of poverty. The roads in KBK districts are intersected by a large numbers of nallas, streams, rivulets and rivers at frequent intervals. The missing links have posed significant challenges for all weather road communication, critical for providing the common man with the access to market places, educational institutions and health centres. As some of the districts are affected by left wing extremism, the lack of connectivity also hampers increased mobility of police and para-military forces to counter the threat.

Other Services: The essential services like post and telegraph, banking etc. also shows a wide inter district variation with respect to the state average. Due to abject poverty and lack of saving habits, the small savings in the financial year 2005-06 in this region is less than 10 percent of the total deposits made by the population of Orissa. The following table shows a comparative view about the postal and banking services in the KBK districts.

The underdeveloped are underdeveloped at all fronts. The mineral rich region of KBK cannot exploit its resources due to the unavailability of the essential services for a civilized and developed society like post & telegraph, internet, banks and electricity etc. In the 21st century, only 66.53 percent of the villages have seen and used the electric bulb which is less in comparison to the state average of 74.09 percent and so the fate of the banking and postal sectors in this regions. The undergrowth of this sector is also a factor for the backwardness of the KBK region.

Handicrafts: KBK, otherwise known for its natural beauty and rich culture, has unfortunately acquired the ill reputation of being one of the poorest districts in the country with acute poverty, hunger and malnutrition. Handloom and handicrafts have the potential to provide gainful employment to the weavers and the craft workers with very little financial investment mainly by exploiting their inherent strength. It is necessary to appreciate these emerging challenges and gear up the handloom and handicrafts industry of Orissa for availing of opportunities, which will bring in rapid economic development and will be of particular significance in eradication of poverty. Since the Indian economy in general has to take care of the surplus workforce under the scenario of unemployment and underemployment, the State has to tap its strength and advantage of handloom and handicrafts sector to bridge the widening gap at the national level under the present state of industrial development.

In a poor and industrially backward area like KBK, these traditional industries like handloom and other popular handicrafts such as stone carving, wood carving, appliqué, *terracotta*, tribal jewellery, jute and sisal fibre, *dhokra* casting, iron crafts, bamboo works, paddy crafts etc. hold considerable promise for economic empowerment and provide gainful employment to the technically little qualified, less educated and emaciated poor in the rural non-farm sector. It is found that next to agriculture, handloom and handicrafts sector is the major provider of employment to the people of this region. Apart from that, handloom and handicrafts products of KBK are appreciated all over the country and outside because of exquisite designs, natural motifs and superb colour combination.

Based on assessment of the socio-economic status, employment and market position, the handicrafts of KBK, which are 23 in number, may be broadly categorized under the following heads:

1. Popular crafts are such as stone carving, lacquer, golden grass, wood carving, wooden painted toys, clay toys, dhokra casting, cane and bamboo work and the like. These are called popular crafts because of their good market potential and they provide employment to a large number

of artisans in the state.

2. Special crafts are typical to the state and localized in the specific regions. For example, the wood painting work of Kalaandi, jute and sisal fibre works of Bolangir, wooden toy making of Subarnapur etc. may be brought under this category.
3. Rare crafts are on the verge of extinction. There are very few artisans left now to run these crafts and keep them alive. These are paddy crafts found in the districts of Koraput, Kalahandi and Bolangir, art leather, lacquered toys, durry and carpet work, wooden inlay work and the like.
4. Languishing craft of six different varieties such as clay terracotta, lacquered terracotta, tin toys, unbreakable toys, tribal jewellery, and the like. Like the rare crafts, these too are in a decaying state as the craftsmen practicing such crafts are not in a position to earn their subsistence due to poor market of the items produced in a very highly unorganized and isolated environment; and
5. The rest other types of crafts such as golden-grass work, embroidery and art textiles and the like are brought under the miscellaneous category.

Culture of Tribals: Orissa occupies a unique position in the ethnographic map of India for having the largest variety of tribal communities. Although they are found in all the districts of the State, yet more than half of their total strength is found in the districts of Koraput, Rayagada, Naurangpur, Malkangiri, Kalahandi, Nauapara, Kandhamal, Baudh, Keonjhar, Sundargarh and Mayurbhanj. The tribes of Orissa in general and KBK districts in particular, are at various stages of socio-economic development. At one extreme are the groups which lead a relatively secluded and archaic mode of life keeping their core culture intact, while at the other extreme there are communities, which are indistinguishable from the general agricultural communities.

Any society-tribal or otherwise, comprises of organized

groups of people who have learnt to live and work together interacting in the pursuit of common goals. Each society has its own rules of business and tricks of trade which helps its people to define their relationship with one another and live and work together. Therefore, a society is a going concern and functions and perpetuates itself on the basis of the rules for living together.

The tribal people express their cultural identity and distinctiveness in their social organization, language, rituals and festivals and also in their dress, ornament, art and craft. They have retained their own way of managing internal affairs of the village mainly through two institutions namely, the village council and the youth dormitory. The dormitory is the core of tribal culture and it reinforces the age-old traditions. In Orissa this institution occurs among many tribal communities in some form or other. The Juangs call it Majang and Darbar, the Kondhs call it Dindaghar, the Bhuyans call it Dhangarabasa and among the Bondos it goes by the name Ingersin. Of all the tribes, the dormitory system is well organized among the Juang. Conspicuous in the village, the Mandaghar is the largest hut. It has wall on three sides and is open in front. The wooden parts and side walls are carried with decorative symbols depicting animals.

The boys hang their changu, a flat tambourine like drum which is used at the time of dancing. In front of the Mandaghar is the small open space where dance takes place almost every night after the day's work is over. The dormitory is so to say a school of dancing and expression of the communal art of the people. The elders of the village assemble at the dormitory house every day for every important event in their corporate life. Here they discuss matters concerning the welfare of the village, settle the distribution of swidden and fix date and time for celebration of the village festivals, etc. In these respects the dormitory may be considered as the centre of social, economic and religious life of the village.

The amazing conglomeration of traditions, beliefs, sorrows

and philosophies that together constitute and vitalize the rituals and festivals of the tribes, has descended from antiquity and has been preserved unimpaired to the present day. Every facet of their life covering round-the-year activities is intimately connected with religious beliefs and ritual practices. It is these aspects of their culture that give meaning and depth to their lives, and solidarity to their social structure. The tribes believe that their life and work are controlled by supernatural beings whose abode is around them in hills, forests, rivers and houses. It is very difficult to standardize the Gods and spirits as their composition continually changes when old ones are forgotten with the introduction of new ones. Their Gods differ from one another in composition, function, character and nature. Some are benevolent; some are neutral and some are malevolent. The malevolent spirits and Gods are cared more than their benevolent counter parts as they can bring misery.

Tribal Rituals and Customs: The religion of the Orissan tribes is an admixture of animism, animalism, nature-worship, fetishism, shamanism, anthropomorphism and ancestor worship. Religious beliefs and practices aim at ensuring personal security and happiness as well as community well-being and group solidarity. Their religious performances include life-crisis rites, cyclic community rites, ancestor and totemic rites and observance of taboos. Besides these, the tribals also resort to various types of occult practices. In order to tide over either a personal or a group crisis the tribals begin with occult practices, and if it does not yield any result the next recourse is supplication of the supernatural force.

Incidence and Severity of Poverty in the KBK Region: KBK is endowed with rich natural resources in the form of vast mineral deposits, forest, fertile land, plentiful surface and ground water resources, long forest line, and picturesque tourist potential. But, such resources have not been exploited adequately for income generation activities. As a result, KBK districts rank very low among the Indian districts in terms of per capita income, and it has become one of the poorest regions of the country. Large proportion of people in the KBK region have very poor living conditions. Frequent drought and floods, incidence of sever malnutrition, and food insecurity and chronic poverty characterize these districts.

Growth of per capita income has a major role in reducing poverty in an economy. Lal-Myint study (1996) found that there was a clear positive effect of per capita income growth on mass poverty reduction in all the countries studied over the period of study (1950-85). For India, Tendulkar and Jain (1995) examined the effects of growth on poverty alleviation for the period 1970-71 to 1988-89. They came to the conclusion that, in comparison to the 1970s, the doubling of annual growth rate of per capita GDP in the 1980s was associated with improvement in both the poverty and social welfare situation. In the context of KBK, it is observed that the KBK region is a low income and slow growing region of the country. Because of low income, larger proportions of people are living below the poverty line in these districts. The per capita income of KBK, as measured by net district domestic product per head of population, was about 15 percent lower than the all Orissa per capita income in 1999.

It is, further, found that among the present eight districts of KBK region, Malkangiri is most backward followed by Koraput, Nabarangpur, Rayagada, Balangir, Subarnapur, Nuapada and Kalahandi in descending order. When we look at the district-wise as well as indicator-wise computed index values of different indicators responsible for the development of agriculture, industry and BIS sector in the region, it is revealed that none of the KBK districts is well-endowed to promote harmonious relationship between agriculture and industry, so as to accelerate the pace of economic development in the region. It may be observed that Kalahandi, Koraput, Nabarangapur and Subarnapur are agriculturally better developed than the other KBK districts. But the districts like Malkangiri and Subarnapur are industrially highly underdeveloped with poor spread of basic infrastructure like urban centres, literacy level, railways, road infrastructure and banking services. Added to this, Malkangiri is, further, observed to be worse in respect of rural electrification, medical amenities and higher concentration of depressed category population.

Agriculture, which is the mainstay of the population in the region, has not yet been modernized to enable the people to pursue a gainful livelihood. On the contrary, in the absence of development of a rural non-farm sector economy, the dependence of population on subsistence and uncertain agriculture instead of showing a diminishing trend has started rising in the recent years. As a result, the majority of the people in the region are now forced to live a life of below subsistence level earning.

It may be noted that in recent years the KBK districts are surmounted with the problems of recurring droughts and erratic rainfall due to increasing deforestation of the region. Excluding a very few blocks of Malkangiri, Koraput and Subarnapur districts the region does not have any irrigation infrastructure of even protective nature to work as shock absorber for the farmers in the case of failure of the monsoon. The tribals and other downtrodden sections of population such as the scheduled castes and other backward and landless castes, who were earlier depending upon the forest resources of the region to supplement their low earnings derived from primary agriculture based occupations become the worst sufferers when the monsoon fails. It is they who form the stream of distressed migrants and seasonal migrant population of the region, be it a normal agricultural year or the drought year.

So, under the prevailing circumstances in order to check distress migration, there is a greater need for the creation of adequate wage work in the short run and a sustainable livelihood in the long run. As shown earlier, creation of wage employment for the poor under different poverty alleviation programmes like JRY, EAS or the present SGSY in the region is too less as compared to the numbers of wage seekers to satiate their needs. The poor wage seekers of KBK region require at least 100 days of government sponsored wage work to bail out them from the clutches of destituteness. Also, as a medium term solution of the problem there is a need for the strengthening of subsistence agriculture by creating watersheds, water harvesting structures, check dams, etc. on the small streams, rivulets and ponds found in the region. No doubt renovation and proper harnessing of the existing water resources through the government sponsored wage work would not only solve the problem of lack of wage work among the distress wage seekers in the short run, but also this would help in creation of irrigation infrastructure in the region.

Added to this, creation of more wage employment in the region would help in afforestation of the deserted and denuded forest area, development of road and communication networks, utilization of the indigenous knowledge and skill in the form of art and craft, and above all proper maintenance of the existing socio-economic infrastructures as well as the creation of new infrastructures such as school buildings, community centres, health centre buildings and the like to create opportunities for social and economic modernization of the region.

The KBK region is also suffering from destitution. Poverty of this category is more critical. As referred earlier, this region has a large number of destitute who lack either money or material to survive. This type of poverty also occurs in other forms. As for instance, there are poor people in the state who have the strength, stamina and capabilities to undertake work but they do not find any opportunities. There are farmers but they do not have land to cultivate. Had there been land at their disposal they could have certainly improved their economic lot. The other types of farmers have lands but they do not have the energy nor the ability to produce anything from the land. These are the farmers who have no access either to credit or to input of agriculture. Economic conditions of such type of poor persons are precarious. However, it is difficult to quantify the number of persons belonging to the category of destitute poverty due to non- availability of data (Lal, 1999). Lal has cited the example of widows who for want of social and economic opportunities remain neglected for years and accept poverty as their fate.

Anti-poverty Programmes: Presently, the KBK region has a very low level of literacy as compared to the State's achievement level and been discriminated in the delivery of public health services due to its difficult accessibility and poor infrastructure. It is revealed from the 2001 Census that due to high morbidity rate and poor living condition of the people, the KBK districts in general furnish a picture of much lower percentage of population in the 60 plus age group as compared to the State average. These districts have comparatively higher infant mortality rates and also higher death rates of population in different age groups due to endemic diseases like malaria, yellow fever, tuberculosis, etc. To tackle these problems and to bridge the literacy gap, there is a need for greater investment on the social sector such as health, education and other welfare-oriented programmes. Removal of regional disparities by utilizing the natural resources has been one of the important planks of the development strategies adopted by the Government during successive Five Year Plans.

The anti-poverty programmes contain programmes both for self-employment and wage employment. The self-employment programmes include Integrated Rural Development Programme (IRDP), Development of Women and Children in Rural Areas (DWCRA), Training of Rural Youth for Self-employment (TRYSEM), and Supply of Improved Tool Kit to Rural Artisans (SITRA). On the other hand, wage employment programmes cover schemes like Jawahar Rojgar Yojana (JRY), Employment Assurance Scheme (EAS), Indira Awaas Yojana (IAY), and Million Wells Scheme (MWS). At present, in order to mitigate rural poverty, various centrally sponsored schemes like SGSY, SGRY, IAY, etc. are in operation. The basic goal is to provide financial support to poor artisans as well as poor families for self employment.

However, due to several economic, social and institutional obstacles, this region in Orissa has not shared gains of development in an equitable manner and continues to languish in abject poverty. Studies undertaken on the impact of various anti-poverty programmes, namely, IRDP, DWCRA, TRYSEM, SITRA, JRY, EAS, IAY and MWS in tribal and backward districts of Orissa such as Mayurbhanj, Koraput and Nabarangpur by the State Government clearly indicates several weaknesses like improper identification of beneficiaries, inadequate and improper supply of assets to beneficiaries, untimely supply of subsidies by government and inadequate supply of loans by banks, inadequate generation of mandays of employment by contractors and their highhandedness in operating the programme, inadequate supervision, monitoring and follow up action either by block staff or bank staff to assess the end use of credit, poor marketing and training facilities available to the beneficiaries, etc. As the result of the weaknesses witnessed in the implementation of the schemes, the impact on generation of output, income and employment in the post-assistance period was marginal compared to pre-assistance period (Misra and Behera, 2000; Kar and Meher, 2001).

Furthermore, the objective of assisting poor people to cross the poverty line through the benefits of the programmes was largely not materialized. The beneficiaries who were able to cross the poverty line were few in numbers. Qualitatively, the programmes did not have adequate impact on the poor as expected.

Particularly, heavy incidence and persistence of poverty in KBK region has been a cause of concern for the State Government as well as the Government of India. Therefore, in consultation with the Government of India, State Government has adopted a special area development approach for this region with a view to focus attention on it and to accelerate development. In order to address severe problems of underdevelopment and regional disparities, the State Government in consultation with Government of India has formulated the Long Term Action Plan (LTAP) and Revised Long Term Action Plan (RLTAP) for the KBK districts.

A revised Long Term Action Plan (RLTAP) of the KBK districts was submitted to Government of India on their advice in 1998. The project was prepared in "sub-plan mode" to address the peculiar socio-economic problems of this chronically poor region, which is also geographically contiguous. This project envisages an integrated approach for speeding up the socio-economic development of this region by synergizing effectively the various developmental activities and schemes under implementation both in Central as well as State sectors. The critical gaps in the development efforts as well as resources are sought to be bridged through Additional Central Assistance (ACA)/Special Central Assistance (SCA) as a special dispensation. Thus, there has to be pooling of resources from different sources like:

1. Normal flow of funds to KBK districts under Central Plan (CP) and Centrally Sponsored Plan (CSP) schemes;
2. Additional funds received from Government of India exclusively for programmes in KBK districts as agreed by the Planning Commission; and
3. Central assistance under programmes of Government of India to be implemented in KBK districts with some relaxation in norms such as Accelerated Irrigation Benefit Programme (AIBP) for earmarked irrigation projects.

A total outlay of funds to the tune of ₹ 6,251.08 crore over a project period of nine years form 1998-99 to 2006-07 is envisaged under the revised project. However, the State Government has been receiving *adhoc* assistance from the Central Government to bridge gaps in resources available for critical sectors on year to year basis. During the first four year RLTAP, i.e. from 1998-99 to 2001-02, the Government of India have released funds to the extent of ₹ 1393.99 crore. This just constitutes 22.30 percent of the plan outlay earmarked under the RLTAP of KBK region for the period 1998-99 to 2006-07. Also it is found that the State Government has failed to utilize the funds released by the Centre possibly due to several constraints.

Against the Central release of ₹ 1393.39 crore during 1998-99 to 2001-02, the State Government has been able to spend ₹ 1042.44 crore (74.78 percent).

No doubt the State Government has taken several initiatives to improve governance and to monitor the implementation of RLTAP programmes in KBK districts. A very senior IAS officer has been posted as the Chief Administrator, Special Area Development (KBK) Project with headquarters at Koraput.

The Revenue Divisional Commissioner (Southern Division) has also been given additional responsibility to act as Deputy Chief Administrator, KBK and to assist the Chief Administrator, KBK. They are responsible for effective monitoring and supervising the implementation of various programmes. However, all the same there is a need for effective grassroots level planning, awareness generation, community level sensitization for sustainable development of the KBK region.

Objectives of the Study

With the above background, this present study made a humble attempt to find out the potential role of micro enterprises and social businesses in addressing the poverty and unemployment problems in the tribal dominated areas of KBK districts. It also identified some areas where improvements are urgently needed. The present study was undertaken with the following objectives:

1. To analyze the socio-economic profile of the indigenous entrepreneurs in KBK Districts of Orissa.
2. To find out the role and the intervention of GOs and NGOs in promoting micro enterprises.

3. To examine the forward and backward linkages of micro enterprises in socio-economic empowerment of indigenous artisans.
4. To trace out the effectiveness of micro enterprising activities in the districts and its impact on the socio-economic conditions of the indigenous artisans.
5. To suggest some remedial measures to improve upon the efficiency and effectiveness of micro enterprises.

Methodology

As the present study is based on primary as well as secondary data, the primary data has to be collected from the artisans engaged in Dhokra painting, terracotta and bamboo works after a preliminary survey combined with pilot testing. For the purpose of primary data collection, three districts namely, Koraput, Nabarangpur and Malkangiri have been taken into consideration. These three districts were selected keeping in view of their rich craft traditions, high demand of artifacts, poverty dominated and unutilized human resources.

Target Group: The target groups of this study will be:

1. Artisans engaged in Dhokra painting, terracotta and bamboo works;
2. Artisan entrepreneurs; and
3. Trader entrepreneurs involved in the production-cum-sale.

Questionnaire Design: The research design phase of the present study had called for preliminary field research at each study site to develop a better understanding of the local context, refine the set of hypotheses, select the most relevant impact variables, and pilot test a draft questionnaire. Preliminary fieldwork included:

1. Discussion of MEs' financial and non-financial services with key members.
2. Discussion of the research design framework and methodology with the research staff of government organizations and NGOs involved in this intervention.
3. Interviews of local practitioners about current socio-

economic trends.

4. Field visits to interview the micro entrepreneur artisans.
5. Collection and review of relevant socioeconomic literature on micro enterprises and its impact on socio-economic development of the artisans.

Towards the end of the preliminary field research, a draft questionnaire was formulated and pilot tested. The draft questionnaire was based on a format that had been developed and tested previously for the AIMS study. Between 1995 and 2002, USAID sponsored the Assessing the Impacts of Micro enterprise Services (AIMS) Project as part of the Micro enterprise Innovation Project. The AIMS core impact assessments, or CIA, are methodologically rigorous, longitudinal impact studies of three micro enterprise support programs: SEWA Bank in India, Mibanco in Peru, and Zambuko Trust in Zimbabwe. For most of the common questions, context-specific data categories and context-specific questions were added to the questionnaire. These modifications grew out of a series of interviews with GO and NGO research staff. Six clients were interviewed initially to test the questionnaire. Later, after translating the draft questionnaire into local language and on the basis of the pilot test, the questionnaire in the form of a schedule was pressed into service to collect the primary responses from the selected artisans.

Sample Design: For Round 1 of the survey in the year 2001, the intention was to draw a sample of 350 households. An attrition rate of 15-20 percent was anticipated in Round 2 of the survey in the year 2006. Finally, this would leave a panel of 225 artisans, 75 each from three crafts viz., terracotta, dhokra and bamboo crafts from whom information from both rounds had been collected.

Area Selection: As noted, KBK has 8 districts. To ease logistics and reduce the cost of the study, it is decided to limit its geographical coverage to three districts, viz., Koraput (for terracotta craft), Malkangiri (for bamboo craft) and

Nabarangpur (for dhokra craft). As a whole, these three districts included in the study are representative of the areas where majority of the indigenous artisans live and depend on the traditional craft for their sustainable livelihood.

Sample Selection: The present study explicitly considers the ways in which micro enterprises may impact on artisans in different levels, viz., at the levels of households, enterprises, and individuals. A simplistic approach would regard credit as beneficial because it leads to higher revenue from a particular micro enterprise, which in turn raises household income and thus confers a variety of other benefits. The household economic portfolio model suggests, however, that impacts can be far more widespread. One of the most important uses of micro enterprise and its credit is to help members deal with—shocks"—unanticipated expenditure needs or disruptions in the income flow. Savings are another important way of dealing with this kind of difficulty, and also generate funds that can be used to attain the other ends for which households sometimes borrow. Since all artisans are producers as well, we hypothesize that there will be greater impact on those who borrow, produce, market as well as save.

Quantitative Data Analysis and Hypothesis: Analysis of the data for both rounds of the survey followed the core AIMS data analysis plan. This called for a set of descriptive tables for data from Rounds 1 and 2, plus two types of statistical analysis-gain score analysis and ANOVA. In addition, other forms of cross-section and longitudinal analyses were carried out. The quantitative analysis tested the core hypotheses about impact at the household, enterprise, and individual levels. For each of these hypotheses, some impact variables were defined.

The most potent statistical test undertaken, the analysis of variation (ANOVA) took into account the possibility that the relationship might be influenced by other factors, known as moderating variables. The impact hypotheses posit that participation in micro enterprise services leads to impacts at three levels: the household, the enterprise, and the individual client. Within each of these levels, a number of possible impacts are hypothesized. The three core impact hypotheses are listed below.

ME Programme has a positive impact at the household level:

1. **Factor 1:** An increase in the level of household income.
2. **Factor 2:** Greater diversification in the sources of household income.
3. **Factor 3:** An increase in household assets, including.
4. **Factor 3a:** Improvements in housing.
5. **Factor 3b:** Increases in major household appliances and transport vehicles.
6. **Factor 4:** An increase in expenditures on children's education.
7. **Factor 5:** An increase in expenditures on food, especially among the very poor.
8. **Factor 6:** An increase in the household's effectiveness in coping with shocks.

ME Programme has a positive impact at the enterprise level:

1. **Factor 1:** An increase in micro enterprise revenue.
2. **Factor 2:** An increase in enterprise fixed assets, especially among repeat borrowers.
3. **Factor 3:** An increase in paid and unpaid employment generated by the enterprise.
4. **Factor 4:** Improvements in the transactional relationships of the enterprise.

ME Programme has a positive impact at the individual level:

1. **Factor 1:** an increase in the client's control over resources and income within the household economic portfolio.
2. **Factor 2:** increased self-esteem and respect from others.
3. **Factor 3:** an increased incidence of personal savings.
4. **Factor 4:** a better position from which to deal with the future through more proactive behaviour and increased confidence.

The data interrelationships by capturing the differences in

change categories based on various feature variables will be tabulated and analyzed by using various advanced statistical tool and techniques. The following statistical tools were used to map the pattern of changes and draw a cohesive conclusion from the emerging pattern of changes in the socio-economic environment.

1. **Cross-section Differences** are examined and evaluated for statistical significance. It was to determine, first of all, whether artisans have more favourable values of the impact variables in two rounds of the study. Next, an analysis of variance (ANOVA) was performed to see whether this difference is statistically significant. If a relationship passes this test, this is taken to indicate possible impact.
2. **Gain Score Analysis**. This form of data analysis compares amounts of change over time in an impact variable between the two rounds. It asks whether the amount of change (or percentage change) over time is more favourable for the treatment group and, if so, whether the difference between the changes is statistically significant.

Limitations of the Study

The assumption that similar type of situation must be prevailing in all areas of KBK district is a major handicap of the present study. The time constraints, so also the locational disadvantages are also another hindrance for the purpose. Although all attempts have been made to overcome such, the findings cannot be universally applied and further detailed study may be undertaken before implementing the suggestions.

The short period of research and the small sample from three districts out of eight KBK districts are the inevitable shortcomings of this study. However, by taking the total number of households (225 HHs), an attempt has been made to understand the socio-economic conditions of the indigenous artisans.

There are several limitations of the framework used to

study the impact of MEPs on the socio-economic life of the indigenous artisans of KBK districts, representing areas in which additional development is needed. First, it has been observed that some enterprises are growth-oriented, others grow little or not at all, and still others may grow to a certain point and stop.

It appears that enterprise growth is not necessarily an objective for all entrepreneurs. A more detailed conceptual model is needed to explain enterprise growth and evolution in terms of household decision making and the environment in which decisions are made.

Second, the usefulness of the household economic portfolio (HHEP) model in analyzing the external environment could be improved by pairing the HHEP framework with a framework that is effective in the analysis of external factors, such as the sustainable livelihoods framework. This would result in a more powerful analytical tool for planning development interventions and assessing their effectiveness. Finally, a conceptual framework is needed to model the impacts of micro enterprise services at the community level and beyond, in the broader society and economy. A general equilibrium approach would be useful in evaluating any macroeconomic changes in prices and production levels, wages and employment, and interest rates and the volume of financial transactions.

Organizations Involved in Promotion of Handicrafts at the State Level

State Handicrafts and Handlooms Development Corporation Ltd.: Various states' Handicrafts and Handlooms Development Corporation, a Government of India undertaking have endeavoured to carry forward rich heritage of all the respective states by reaching out the products developed by the artisan residing in these states and abroad through its network of emporia and a large number of exhibitions, expositions and crafts fairs.

Joint Director General Foreign Trade, Cuttack:

1. Issue of export and import license.
2. Monitor and control export and import as per the Exim Policy.

Small Industries Service Institute (SISI), Ministry of SSI, Cuttack: The main activities of this institute is to render techno-economic and managerial consultancy to existing and prospective entrepreneurs including training facility under EDP, MDP, skill development programmes etc.

They also undertake industrial potential survey, disseminate the information on export organize seminars/ workshops/export management programme/training on packaging etc.

Regional Research Laboratory (RRL), Bhubaneswar: Develop appropriate technology for handicrafts and cottage industries for their sustainable development.

Directorate of Export Promotion & Marketing, Orissa, Bhubaneswar:

1. Assist the exporters in promotion of export from Orissa by disseminating market intelligence and overseas tender/trade enquiries.
2. Take up with Export Promotion Councils for necessary support.
3. Organize seminar/workshops. Give awards to best exporters.
4. Regulate quality and price of industrial products.

Orissa Rural Development and Marketing Society (ORMAS), Bhubaneswar:

1. ORMAS has been organized under Societies Act, 1860 by the State government in Panchayati Raj Department in the year 1990 to provide marketing support to the Swarojgaris assisted under S.G.S.Y.
2. They also promote self-help groups and provide techno-economic consultancy to such groups.

Mahila Vikash Samabaya Nigam (MVSN), Bhubaneswar:

1. M.V.S.N. is an apex Co-operative Society established in 1990-91 by the State government under the administrative control of Women and Child Development Department with the objective of empowering the women.
2. While implementing schemes for social empowerment of women they also provide various support/inputs for self-employment of women in income generating activities.
3. They also act as Nodal Agency for implementation of schemes like NORAD, STEP and NHFDC in the State.

Orissa Scheduled Caste/Scheduled Tribe Finance Development Corporation (OSFDC), Bhubaneswar:

1. Implements various schemes for socio-economic empowerment of SCs/STs.
2. They provide assistance for skill training, EDP, creation of infrastructure, marketing support etc. along with subsidy against bank loan availed by SC/ST artisans for setting up their own productions units.
3. The co-operative societies/SHGs organized by SC/ST and individual SC/ST artisans can be benefited under their schemes.

District Rural Development Agency (DRDA), all district headquarters

1. Under the scheme Swarna Jayanti Gramya Swarojagar Yojana implemented by DRDA assistance is provided for development of skill/infrastructure and setting up of production units by the artisans.
2. Mobilization of artisans into self sustainable SHGs is given priority.

Integrated Tribal Development Agency (ITDA), 21 ITDAs: The main objectives are as follows:

1. To provide assistance to tribal artisans to set up their own production units.
2. To also provide assistance for skill development, creation of infrastructure, marketing support etc.

Orissa Backward Classes Finance and Development Co-operative Corporation Ltd. (OBCFDCC) under the aegis of Minorities and Backward Class Welfare Department, Government of Orissa, Bhubaneswar: This is an apex organisation set up at State level in 1994 under Orissa Co-operative Societies Act, 1962 with the objective of providing loan assistance to the Backward classes to make them self reliant. The organisation has been nominated as a channelizing agency of the loan assistance of NBCDC.

Orissa State Cooperative Handicrafts Corporation Limited: Orissa State Co-operative Handicrafts Corporation Limited has been organized by government in Industries Department as an apex cooperative society to provide marketing support to primary handicrafts cooperative societies/artisans. Steps are also taken by them to export Handicrafts goods. In course of these marketing activities, they study the demand of the product and pass on the feed back to the societies/artisans. In addition to marketing activities, they implement various developmental schemes of both the State and Central Government for promotion of handicrafts and welfare of artisans of the State.

Director of Handicraft and Cottage Industries (DH&CI): DH&CI is the apex body of the Government of Orissa in developing the handicraft and cottage industries.

Intervention Strategies: The intervention strategies adopted by the DH&CI to develop the handicraft sector are as follows:

1. Development of clusters into SHGs/cooperatives to encourage community participation and capacity building.
2. Induction of new artisans through transfer of skill.
3. Appropriate measures for skill up gradation of artisans and technology.
4. Creation of facility for easy and timely access to raw materials.
5. Use of expert service for innovative designs.
6. Establishment of marketing linkage with emphasis on

export promotion.

7. Institutional credit linkage.
8. Strengthening/creation of infrastructure (raw material base/common facility centre/design centre/godown/ market outlets/workshed).
9. Strengthening and streamlining database and information system.
10. Strengthening the existing monitoring and supervision system.
11. Networking at artisan level/cluster level/district level/state-level.
12. Synergy among development partners to ensure dovetailing of funds/efforts for better result.
13. Development of connectivity of craft clusters.
14. Industrial Policy Resolution benefits.

Schemes of DH&CI for Promotion of Handicrafts- Various schemes are implemented by the State Government to provide assistance to the artisans of handicrafts and various societies in order to strengthen their financial base and infrastructure for augmenting production and sale of Handicrafts goods through DH&CI. Necessary funding is made by the State government for imparting skill training through training institutes/master craftsman (MCM) to have strong production base. Margin money assistance is provided to individual artisans to avail bank loan. Marketing support is also provided to the societies/artisans through exhibition. Cluster development is also given priority. The schemes are as follows:

1. Assistance to Handicrafts Cooperatives.
2. Assistance to Individual Artisans.
3. Development of Cluster.

a. Skill training on handicrafts (district level),
b. Skill training on handicrafts (state level),
c. Training on woollen carpet,
d. State level handicraft awards.

4. State Handicrafts Award.

5. State Handicrafts Design Competition Award.

Marketing Support: Exhibitions are organized to promote sale of handicrafts, launching of new designs and to popularize the products. The artisans get an opportunity to sale their products directly to the customers and have interaction with the customers to know the demand and study the taste of the buyers.

A. District Level Exhibition: The following fairs/festivals are regularly held at district level every year. Exhibitions are held during those events to promote sale of handicrafts.

1. Gramashree Mela, Puri during Car Festival;
2. Beach Festival, Puri;
3. Konark Festival, Puri;
4. Bali Jatra, Cuttack;
5. Bali Jatra, Paradeep;
6. Laxmi Puja, Dhenkanal;
7. Laxmi Puja, Angul;
8. Kali Puja, Charampa;
9. Beach Festival, Chandipur;
10. Mayur Festival, Baripada;
11. Kalahandi Utsov, Kalahandi;
12. Parab, Koraput; and
13. Beach Festival, Gopalpur.

B. State Level Exhibition: The following exhibitions are held at state level regularly where handicrafts goods are exhibited and sold by the societies/NGOs/artisans.

1. Adivasi Exhibition.
2. Enterprise 2002, Exhibition Ground, Unit-III, Bhubaneswar.

State level exhibitions are also organized by ORMAS, Mahila Vikas Samabaya Nigam and other organizations, like Director of Tourism, etc. on special occasion.

C. National Level Fairs/Exhibitions: Following exhibitions and fairs are organized at National level where the artisans from the state get scope to display and sell their products.

1. IITF, Pragati Maidan, New Delhi;
2. Ganga Mahotsav, Varanasi;
3. Silpi Gram Utsav, Udaypur;
4. Gwalior Trade Fair, Gwalior;
5. Surajkund Crafts Mela, Surajkund;
6. Taj Mahotsav, Agra;
7. Jhansi Mahotsav, Jhansi;
8. Silpi Mela, Allahabad;
9. Silpi Mela, Madhapur, Hyderabad; and
10. Gift Fair, New Delhi.

D. Craft Bazaar/National Handicrafts Expo: DC (Handicrafts), Government of India organizes craft bazaar and expos at different places of the country to promote sale of Indian handicrafts. The artisans/societies from Orissa participate as per the quota.

E. Urban Haats: Following urban *haats* have been established with assistance from Development Commissioner (Handicrafts) to promote sale of Indian handicrafts by the artisans throughout the year on rotation basis.

1. Dilli Haat, New Delhi;
2. Ekamra Haat, Bhubaneswar, Orissa;
3. Karnal Haat, Haryana;
4. Tirupati Haat, Andhra Pradesh; and
5. Jammu Haat, Jammu & Kashmir.

Artisans from the state participate in the above haats as per the quota fixed by Development Commissioner (Handicrafts).

F. Handicrafts Complex (Kala Nagar): The Handicrafts Complex was set up in 1986 with aim to provide advance training on handicrafts and interrogation of the existing State Handicrafts Design Centre established in 1953 and Handicrafts Show House established in 1973. Subsequently, the State Institute of Handicrafts Training, established in 1961 has been shifted from its earlier rented premises to Handicrafts Complex during 1998.

Provision of Orissa Industrial Policy Resolution for Handicrafts Sector

The government in IPR, 2001 has declared a number of initiatives for promotion of handicrafts and cottage industries in the state, which are as follows:

1. **Sales Tax Exemption:** The finished products of all existing and new khadi, village, handicrafts and cottage industries sold through approved sales outlets of authorized cooperatives/government agencies and recognized by KVIC/OKVIB/Coirboard/Handicrafts Corporation and DIC exempted from payment of sales tax.
2. **Electricity Duty Exemption:** The handicrafts and cottage industries having contract demand up to 100 kva are exempted from payment of electricity duty for a period of 5 years from the date of availing power supply for production.
3. **Patent Registration:** The state shall provide assistance to artisans for patent and intellectual property right provisions @50 percent of the expenditures up to maximum of ₹ 5 lakh.
4. **Land:** Government land wherever available will be allotted for handicrafts and cottage industries at concessional rate.
5. **Cluster Approach for the Artisan Crafts:** Selected existing craft clusters would be developed with involvement of industry associations, financing institutions, and NGOs. For this purpose, common facilities for quality improvement, technology upgradation, market promotion and skill development would be designed and implemented.
6. **Marketing Support:**

- Local khadi and village industrial units including handlooms and handicrafts will enjoy a price preference of 50 percent over local large and medium industries.
- Local khadi, village and cottage industries registered with DH&CI will be exempted from payment of earnest money

and pay 25 percent of the prescribed security deposit while tendering to State government departments and agencies under its control.

- State government departments and agencies under the control of State government will make prompt payment of dues of local khadi and village industries in respect of goods purchased from them.

Workings of Some NGOs in KBK Districts

The sustainable livelihood is the need of the hour for the poverty ridden population of KBK districts amidst the hue and cry of their rights and desperations. In the light of their development, 173 NGOs are working at present in the KBK districts. In the field of development of micro enterprises for the indigenous handicraft artisans, the NGOs like BISWA, Sarvoday Samiti and Kala Niketan etc. are the names to be reckoned with.

Sarvodaya Samiti, Koraput: Sarvodaya Samiti is a state-level, non-governmental, non-political organization. Starting out as Narayanpara Kshetra Samiti in 1959, it renamed itself as Sarvodaya Samiti later. The organization was formally registered in 1970-71 under the Societies Registration Act of 1860. It is committed for the development for the development of tribal, rural and other underprivileged classes of the society. The primary objective of the Samiti is to contribute to the all-round and sustainable development of tribal and other under-privileged communities of the society through social and economic programme interventions. The Samiti has the philosophy that the empowerment is a process of local communities achieving power, self reliance and confidence and the resulting ability to take independent action and the control of decision making on matters concerning their own development.

Currently, the Samiti is engaged in sustainable agriculture and development of khadi and village industries accompanied by social interventions like child and women welfare, education for scheduled tribe girls, consumer welfare, development of micro enterprises under Village Craft Scheme for the tribal artisans and watershed programmes. Its activities consist of production of khadi, promotion of bee-keeping, and marketing of agro-products like honey, turmeric powder, and arrowroot. The Samiti feels that promoting marketing of rural produce through a profitable enterprise can bring a change in the living standards of the poor.

Its registration under the Societies Act of 1860 precludes it from engaging in 'commercial' activities; however, its association and registration with the DIC has enabled it to engage in rural micro enterprise promotion through organization of non-farmer indigenous traditional artisans, assistance in value addition, and marketing. The Sarvoday Samiti has been implementing the craft village scheme with the help of DH&CI, UNIDO and DIC (Koraput) for the promotion of rural artisans in cluster basis. Two craft cluster are identified for the programme–terracotta craft is implemented in village Kusumi, Kuagaon of Kotpad block and Tala Limika, Kumbhar Limica, Mastiput, and Jhadiguda of Koraput block; and Iron craft in Girla and Kotpad in Kotpad block.

Sarvodaya Samiti had developed 18 numbers of SHGs with a membership of 270 artisans in the craft sectors of terracotta, bamboo and iron craft in the district of Koraput. The SHGs were formed at Kusumi, Girla, Bandhagaon, Goudaguda, Kasamguda, Mastiput, Jhadiguda. They had identified the socio-economically backward, SC and ST artisans to avail the developmental thrust of the Government of Orissa for eradication of poverty and sustainable livelihood. The Samiti had conducted 7 numbers of skill development training camps, 4 design and development training programs and 5 exposure visits for the artisans.

Kalaniketan: Kalaniketan, a leading voluntary organization established in the year 1986, and provides services towards development of various handicrafts and handlooms of Orissa and its practitioner. Its concentration is to meet the needs of the rural poor craft-persons and weavers those are downtrodden in the society and live until under a subsidence level. While formulating several programmes, it has first looks towards the protection of rights and cultural value from the base of the working procedure and initiatives are taken towards sublimate of skill development, design and technology development and marketing arrangements of various handicrafts with following by rehabilitation of rural artisans through various promotional programmes on various handicrafts at different places of Orissa. The districts covered under handicrafts development initiative are Ganjam, Khurda, Nabarangpur, Nayagarh and Cuttack.

Micro Enterprises: Their Forward and Backward Linkages

Introduction: KBK districts are characterized by its unparallel natural beauty–high mountains, deep valleys, perennial streams, dark forests, green fields and unadulterated tribal life and their culture. These districts are very rich in minerals and also have a lot of potential in agriculture particularly in plantation and horticulture, farm mechanization, fisheries, cattle rearing, agro and food processing and handicraft industries which need to be exploited to achieve the desired goal of poverty alleviation and self-employment. Crafts like stone carving, wood carving, tribal jewellery, terracotta, Dhokra casting, cane and bamboo works, brass and bell metal products, golden grass products have the potential to grow into serious commercial venture. These handicraft sectors in KBK districts operate with the following strengths, weaknesses, opportunities and threats.

Strengths:

1. Availability of a major cross-section of craftsmen with desired level of skill and competencies.
2. Low level of investment with little gestation period.
3. Generation of self-employment.

4. No/less power utilization in production process.
5. High level of value addition to investment.
6. Economic empowerment of women.
7. Utilization of local resources.
8. Easy adaptation of appropriate technology.
9. Eco-friendly.
10. Products having adequate demand in domestic and foreign market.

Weaknesses:

1. Highly unorganized and widely dispersed sector.
2. Lack of opportunity/willingness for adaptation to:
- Market oriented designs,
- Production diversification,
- Cross-culture innovation,
- Advanced technology.
3. Lack of exposure to different market segments.
4. Lack of enterprising and marketing skill.
5. In-adequate market intelligence.
6. Non-conducive policies on utilization of forest and mineral based raw materials.
7. Inadequate institutional credit flow leading to exploitative lending.
8. Inability of timely execution of large orders.
9. Lack of proper branding of products resulting in duplication.
10. Lack of awareness and measures for quality assurance.

Opportunities:

1. Availability of large manpower and labour force.
2. Ample scope of government schematic support for artisans under various schemes.
3. High export potential.
4. Least impact of WTO in this sector.
5. Availability of traditional skill.

Threats:

1. Imitation by other States due to lack of patenting.
2. Frequent occurrence of natural calamity.

3. Seasonal availability of raw materials needing huge fund for due time procurement.
4. Seasonal employment in crafts like terracotta.
5. High illiteracy rate to adjust with the changed scenario.

The handicraft sector in KBK districts is not that much grown up to be compared with that of state level in spite of enormous scope for the development. Though the craft is a traditional art-form mingled with traditional values and culture, due to lack of income generating abilities throughout the year, the crafts are going to be vanished from these areas. At present, these crafts are only seen in a very few places. Various developmental schemes and training programs were implemented earlier in these districts for the handicraft artisans.

However, the cluster development program for handicraft sector was initiated in KBK districts 2000-2001 by the Director of Handicraft and Cottage Industries (DH&CI). It is due to this intervention of DH&CI in these districts through identification of 21 different craft clusters and other intervening measures; an improvement has been experienced in the development of these crafts.

For the present study, three crafts viz., terracotta, dhokra casting and bamboo crafts have been identified among 21 crafts earmarked by the DH&CI for KBK districts. Data had been collected from various clusters situated in six different districts viz., Koraput, Sonepur, Malkangiri, Nabarangapur, Rayagada and Bolangir. Three different clusters with 75 artisan households in each craft (total 225 respondents) were selected to be studied. The details of the respondents are given in Table A2.

Analysis of Macro Environment of the Clusters

Features of the Crafts:

Dhokra Casting: Dhokra casting is one of the earliest known methods of non-ferrous metal casting known to human civilization. The oldest form of metal casting, 'Dhokra' is popular because of its primitive simplicity. This art style is the speciality of non-tribal and semi-tribal communities of central India located in Madhya Pradesh, West Bengal, Orissa and parts of Vindhya Range. It is a very important handicraft because of its more or less exclusive folk character. The Dhokra of Bihar, Orissa, and West Bengal are distant cousins of the Madhya Pradesh. They all perhaps belong to a tribal group of that area.

Table A2: Distribution of Households among the Crafts

S. No.	Crafts	Districts	Cluster	No. of HH
1.	Dhokra Casting	Nabarangapur	Dabugaon Cluster	75 HH
2.	Terracotta	Koraput	Kusumi Cluster	75 HH
3.	Bamboo Crafts	Malkangiri	Mathili Cluster	75 HH

Terracotta: Terracotta is an art form so universal in its scope, yet emblazoned with the distinct imprint of the native soil. The art of kiln burnt potteryware provides the perfect counterfoil to the amazing legacy of stone sculpture. Terracotta artifacts demand a very high degree of skill and motivation. Behind the polish on the final figure is concealed an enormous volume of tireless toil and watchful attention. These terracotta products have attracted admiration of art-lovers all over the country for their eternal beauty. The terracotta work is traditionally done by the non-tribals of Orissa. They use special type of clay and design to match their skills. Popular items are utensils like plates, khullars, or the earthen tea cups, jars and many other kitchen items. Artisans prepare many items, most of which are outlined and highlighted with colours. However, in many cases the finished product is left with natural terracotta colours. Animal figurines of bulls, elephants and horses are elegantly moulded in very natural strong forms.

Bamboo Craft: Bamboo craft, an age old traditional craft, is the mostly adopted by the artisans with varied designs and production process and with a distinct cultural reflection, as reflected in the produces. The artisans are traditionally associated with production of various traditional products like *dala*, *kula*, *tokei*, flower *changidi*, *maan* etc., for their livelihood. The long life of the bamboo made items, termite proof and flexible produces are the major causes for the wide acceptance and high demand of these products. After the design up-gradation, the demand of the bamboo products has gone manifold.

Procedure of Making Artifacts

Dhokra: The Dhokra castings of figurines and different animals with their antique look, fits in with interior décor. Dhokra is an alloy of brass, nickel and zinc that gives an antique effect to the castings. The hollow method (lost wax, cire-purdue) and the dense/solid method are the two processes of Dhokra casting. In the hollow method, a clay replica is prepared slightly smaller than the object to be cast. After this is bone dry, hand rolled wax are applied on the clay-core, till clay is covered by wax, and upper surface is smooth and uniform (usually up to 1.5 mm thick). Then another covering of clay paste made of cow dung, clay, paddy husk, jute pieces, and vegetable pieces is made. A pouring channel is made in this layer.

After that, melted metal alloy is poured into the passage. The wax melts out which is drained off from another channel leaving space behind which is filled by the metal. After cooling the outer clay layer is removed using a knife. The Solid form of casting is slightly different with the object to be made being of entirely wax. This results in better finesse of designs. After that, it is coated with a clay paste as in hollow casting. Then the wax is melted away by exposing it to fire and the molten metal is poured into the cast. After cooling the clay, cast is removed. The polishing was done traditionally using limejuice and vegetable alkalis, brushing with vegetable fibers. However, the artisans use very dilute sulphuric acid and sodium carbonate now-a-days.

Terracotta: The intermediary processes involved in pottery are many from identifying clay suited for earthenware, mixing it to get the right texture, using the wheel, making the kiln, arranging raw pottery in the kiln, etc. to ultimately firing the pieces. Votive figures of elephants, serpents, birds and horses are made.

Bamboo Craft: Bamboo has undergone a number of processing operations before they are converted into different products. The branches are removed and culms (joints) cut to required lengths. This is the primary preparation. If required, starch and gummy substances may be removed at the initial stage itself. Then depending on the end-product, a primary processing step such as splitting or bending, cross cutting, splitting knot removing is carried out. For certain products, the bamboo parts are subjected to a secondary processing like bleaching or dyeing. The products are finally finished using a series of other processing like finishing, painting and polishing etc. The products are thereafter ready for packaging and transportation.

Items of Production

Dhokra: Dhokra is notable for its strength and shapeliness of design. Its motifs are mostly drawn from folk culture. While among the animals, the elephant is most popular, other motifs include human heads, kings, manas or miniature replica of measures, containers with lids, with or without locking devices, images of deities like Ganesh and Durga, lamps and lamp stands (intricate designs in shape of trees and branches with as many as hundred lamps in one stand). Of late, some utilitarian articles like candle stands, ash trays, pencil box, bangle box, wall hangings, photo frame, glass cover, boxes and pen stands are also being made keeping the essential folk design intact. These artifacts are ritual and their themes are mostly animals, jewellery, and icon of gods and goddesses. The items like tribal elephant, horse, tortoise, deer, tiger, snake, camel, folk animals; human figures are produced by these artisans.

Terracotta: The diversity of traditional arts and crafts found in KBK districts is a colourful testimony to centuries of exquisite craftsmanship and creativity of the people. These arts and crafts have grown around the religious heritage of the state and strong tribal tradition. They are prepared by the *Kumbhara* (locally known as *medri*) community. Potters make earthen pots to be used in various religious and social functions. They are made in various shapes and sizes and are adorned with fish and flower motifs and geometrical designs. Horses and elephants in terracotta are made to meet local demands during religious occasions.

These are offered to the village-goddess (*grama-devi*) to ward off disease and danger. In size they range from six inches to five feet. The potter also makes clay toys and simple and appealing figures of human beings which capture and reflect the essential characteristics of real-life creatures. The toys are simple in design and bear a local touch and colour. Terracotta panels and storage jars painted white and decorated with tiny mirrors are common. This area has a charming tradition of decorative roof-top tiles, made partly by hand-moulding and partly on the wheel. These tiles, shaped like half tubes, have perched on top of them figures of elephants, monkeys, bears, reptiles, gods and goddesses and are considered a status symbol among the rural people. The potters mould distinctive clay horses, camels, elephants, tigers and bullocks that are then offered to the village deity or to a revered animal itself such as the tiger.

Bamboo Craft: The artisans of bamboo crafts possess adequate traditional skill to take up the craft as an entrepreneurial venture. For this purpose, they work in groups and create their own designs and production basis. They are making various bamboo products like flower stand, brush stand, boat, pen stand, pen, mobile stand, photo frame, wall hangings, etc. which are very attractive and artistic. The design development process has a greater impact on the production of various new and aesthetic items with high demands.

Raw Materials:

Dhokra: The basic raw materials used by the Dhokra artisans are brass, wax, pichu, jhuna, red clay, rice husks, wood, cow dung etc. The artisans generally procure the brass and wax from Jagdalpur (Chhatisgarh), and Nabarangapur, whereas other raw materials are available locally.

Terracotta: The basic raw materials used by the terracotta artisans are clay (soil—black and red), fire wood, straw (*pala*), fevicol and colours etc. The artisans generally procure all raw materials from local sources.

Bamboo Craft: Bamboo is the basic raw material for these craft but wood adhesives (fevicol), wooden polish (touch wood and spirit-lacquer polish), sand paper, plastic wire, nail, kerosene, plywood, paints etc. are also used.

It is found that no scheduled tribe is engaged in Terracotta craft. As the tribals worship earth as *Dharani Penu*, traditionally they are not engaged in any sort of activities which is derogative to the soil (like digging, burning etc.) Majority of the artisan households (HH) under study are coming under the Below Poverty Line (BPL) categories and also being identified by the block office that provided them with BPL cards. These artisans have been practicing this craft since their childhood as it is a part of their traditional occupation. The skill level varies according to ages and places.

It is also interesting to observe that the Dhokra craft involves very advanced process of production like moulding, and casting, which is generally not seen in any other forms of traditional crafts in these areas. The Kings, *Samants* and *Jamindaars* of these areas had patronized this craft and hired the artisans from the coastal areas like Ganjam, Paralakhemundi etc. who are known as '*odia*' by the locals (who in turn called as "*deshia*"). These locals (*deshia*) learned the crafts from these master craftsmen and by the effluent of time; the craft became the livelihood for these artisans. All the artisan households under study are coming under the Below

Poverty Line (BPL) categories and also being identified by the block office that provided them with BPL cards. These artisans have been practicing this craft since their childhood as it is a part of their traditional occupation. The skill level varies according to ages and places.

SHGs Formed by the Artisans: The individual entrepreneurship among the artisans are lacking and falling short of the expectation to solve the unemployment problems and to provide sustainable livelihood. Thus, the state Government and the Director of Handicraft and Cottage Industries formed the Village Craft Scheme which is based on the principle of joint responsibility and group entrepreneurship. Under the Village Craft Schemes, SHGs had formed to cater the sustainable developmental needs of the artisans. The MEP provides a pre-condition that a SHG has to be formed to avail the loan facilities from the banks and to avail the benefits provided by the government under the Craft Village Scheme.

Benefits Experienced: The SHGs formed by the artisans in the study areas have provided the following benefits apart from setting up micro enterprises, micro financing, credit linkage and marketing support.

One-on-One Group Training Sessions: When participants were asked which of the services received from NGOs and DICs were more valuable to them, the majority of the participants agreed that the one-one-one group sessions were highly useful, and it helped them in a variety of ways aside from getting their business started. During the one-on-one session, trainers provided valuable and personalized guidance, which helped individuals analyze their strengths and weaknesses and encouraged them to follow specific steps to achieve success. One entrepreneur mentioned "As entrepreneurs we have millions of ideas bumping around our heads. The program helps us narrow down our focus and assesses the situation to steer us away from failure, which I hear is very common when individuals try to start their own business". Thus, due to the time constraints (which all participants exhibited) and through substantive information and counselling received, the one-on-one sessions were the most valued service obtained from them.

Business Plan: Another service component that was unanimously agreed to be one of the most important attributes obtained from intervening authorities was the ability to create a business plan. Because loan providers, whether mainstream or catered to low-income individuals, require a business plan to ensure investment, the business plan becomes an important tool for the future success of their business. This is particularly important, as research has shown that completing a business plan does represent an important marker of an individual's likelihood to succeed as a business owner. This is confirmed by one of the interview participants—"The business plan was one of the most important things I got from the program. Having a business plan was the most valued thing for me. I could not have developed the plan without their help".

Individual Development Account (IDA) Enrolment: Saving money can be a challenging task. This can be even more demanding to those who don't have a steady and significant source of income. The difficulty of performing this endeavour can be reflected by the amount of individuals that were interviewed, as only 20 percent were involved in the IDA program. The benefits obtained through these services was echoed throughout this cohort and greatly emphasized. As a micro-entrepreneur narrated her experience and the benefits she received, in her opinion the advantage of having an IDA could not be understated – "It is a big deal when you match your funds with the help of the IDA and add the business plan component. I didn't know as much as I do now, it was all definitely worth it! All my funds from the IDA helped me buy goods for my business and household, which is part of my profit and income, and there is no way I could buy all I did without my matched savings". In addition, some individuals expressed that having the responsibility to save, once enrolled in the IDA, increases the person's awareness with regards to expenses and provides them with a sense of stability and pride:" What we really appreciated is that they helped us in being more realistic in the sense that it is not going to be easy to have income at the start of our business, but, having the savings account and knowing that we have to save every month has really helped us manage our family finances and provided us with leverage for the future".

Knowledge and Intangible Benefits: Due to the fact that many, if not all, of the clients that come to be a member of SHGs have no business background and just come with a traditional skill for their future business in mind, the changes in knowledge they experienced were highly valued. As a participant mentioned—"I really knew nothing about business; this was all very new to me and coming to MEPs definitely helped". In addition, another individual commented: "All the finer skills I've gotten from MEP have given me more money and financial stability". The knowledge gained was classified into many areas. For some, bookkeeping, market networking and management were keys to lessen their frustrations and increase their chances of success in business.

Aside from business specific knowledge, when participants were asked to describe any personal benefits they experienced, control and confidence were mentioned by a majority of the participants: "I definitely recommend MEPs all the time to all those with a traditional skill interested in starting their own business. The things that you get from here are priceless…I now feel I am in control of my future thanks to my business and all the help I got from them".

Another person's experience helps to confirm this benefit—"I feel I have more confidence because of the things I achieved thanks to the program such as my business plan. I felt the format met the criteria I would need for a future loan and I like knowing that I have that tool with me and I can use it whenever I am ready. So yes, I am more confident I can achieve my goals and my self-esteem has gone through the roof".

Overall, MEP clients expressed not only economic but intangible benefits as a result of the services obtained. From confidence to profits, stability, organization and funds, all were important components echoed by the micro entrepreneurs in this study.

Artisan Group Profile

The study covered 3 enlisted craft clusters, covering 3 districts out of 8 KBK districts. 15 artisan self-help groups were formed and got training on various cluster development programmes implemented in the districts. All these artisan groups cover 225 artisans, out of whom 144 (64 percent) are male artisans and 81 (36 percent) female artisans, almost a gender equalization situation where male and female artisans share an almost equal contribution towards the cluster development. In some groups it was found that there are both male and female members (3 SHGs). The reasons when explored about came out that male members were selected to help the group artisans in terms of marketing and purchasing raw materials.

Keeping in mind the socio-economic status of the districts there is a need for continuous support and follow up for all the activities undertaken by these artisan groups. The living standards of these artisans are not up to the level. The structure and conditions of the houses they live in are very poor. Access road to the craft village is also not suitable for all weather condition. There is an urgent need of improvement in all these basic livelihood parameters, which are directly linked with their profession they are engaged in at present. As we observed, they need a regular income source to support their families when they are engaged in craft activities. Other facilities like health services, education facility, childcare support, etc. also need to be provided to these artisans. During interaction with the group and group members, the following conclusions are drawn:

1. SHGs are formed for the sake of getting access to the bank for the credit linkage under the SHG schemes, and when benefit derived from the group activities, members are eager to form more SHGs for other diversified activities.
2. The groups were more eager to get the subsidy from the bank and were less fascinated in the utilization and repayment of the loan availed from bank.
3. Though there was monthly savings by every member, there was no regularity in it due to control over the income of the individual is having male dominance.
4. Need external support and guidance for book keeping and record updates. To improve the group function some training programme on record keeping, accounting and leadership management need to be designed for these groups.
5. Groups had hardly any experience even in internal lending. Thus groups have to start internal lending to have hands on experience on credit management.
6. Though they have entrepreneurial skill, they need a boost and motivation to turn it to a professional business activity.
7. Entrepreneurship development programme should be initiated for the artisan groups to promote private entrepreneurs who in turn will support the cluster artisans in several ways.
8. Need for capacity building training on converting SHGs into a marketing unit, rather than a producing units only. Training in storing, quality control, advertising and publicity, trading activities should be provided to the selected members of each group to make specialized functional sub-groups.
9. Artisans also need some exposures to a more developed place for the craft activity they are engaged in and in the fields where part time attention can be made for lateral diversification.

Production Cycle Analysis of Craft Clusters

From business point of view all the existing craft clusters are very new. Though a lot of funds have been invested in near past for the development of craft sectors, none of the craft has come up with a significant improvement ensuring its viability. Still the analysis of the production cycle and the overall business process of each craft will show a business pattern that has been adopted by these rural artisans.

Dhokra Casting Cluster: This cluster consists of two villages namely Jayanti Nagar and Jhaliaguda of Nabarangapur district covering 75 artisan households. All the artisans of these clusters are very new to this activity and have involved in it since last six years only in a scientifically way. They need a lot of inputs for the improvement in the quality of the products and for their skill upgradation. The present production cycle much depends on availability of brass. Normally, they procure ten kilos of brass from the market and go for the production. They consume the whole raw material in 20 days and produced items worth of ₹ 3,645. Though there is a. market for this precuts and raw materials are easily available in the local market, a lot of initiative is to be taken to improve the group cohesiveness among the cluster artisans to make its production viable.

Terracotta Cluster: This cluster consists of two villages namely Kusumi and Kuagaon of Koraput district covering 75 artisan households. The production cycle of this craft is normally one month. Artisans normally produce the Items every month. But, the availability of working capital and sometimes the raw materials increases their production cycle. Also this affects the rate of return period in the business, as they have to purchase and store the raw material for the whole year. Again, the pricing of the product depends on the variety of the product and finishing work done. It also varies to a great extent on the market location. Hence, artisans sell these items more in outside exhibitions and sales.

Rainy season is not at all suitable for these artisans to

make the products. Also a lot of care is to be taken to store the finished items in this period. As it is mostly affected by the environment condition, a proper place is highly necessary for storage of the items. No doubt about it, it is a very much profitable business, if done with proper planning and care. The value chain analysis of this craft provides that there will be on an average 30-45 percent profit margin for an artisan, who makes a good quality product. Hence, attempt should be made to focus on the quality and skill of these artisans in this cluster.

Bamboo Craft Cluster: This cluster consists of four villages namely Sardaput, Sankarpali, Nayakguda, and Sindhiguda of Malkangiri district covering 75 artisan households. The present production cycle for the bamboo craft is one week. In a week an artisan produces different artifacts of different sizes by using one full grown bamboo of 10-12 feet. The production cycle for these artisans is not at all fixed for any particular period. It depends on the variety of items they produce. The quality of the product depends on the quality of the raw materials and the price of the items depends on the decorative and artistic work done on it. The more the artistic works, the more value addition will give to the product. Normally, this craft gives a profit margin of around 20-30 percent. Hence, it will be a profitable business for the cluster artisans if they produce good quality items and sell it at a proper market place.

Value Chain Analysis

A value chain represents a series of activities of an enterprise that serve to deliver value in the form of goods and services to its final customers. The activities of the enterprise have a strong link and at each level there is a distinct values addition. The addition to the value is directly reflected in the customer's willingness to pay. The difference between total value (price of the product) and the total cost of performing (value creating) activities is the margin. Every enterprise is a collection of activities that are performed to design, product, market and service value to customers. A cluster where the entire value chain involving artistic work towards creating more customer value is one that is sustainable, dynamic and competitive. Greater consumer value is reflected in greater margins for it.

Analysis of a value chain also involves an analysis of the value chain of the suppliers to the enterprise and the value chain of its marketing channel. Value chain activities may be divided into two broad types, viz., primary activities and support activities. Primary activities are activities involved in the creation of products/ services and their sales and delivery to the customers as well as after-sales support and the support activities support the primary activities and include purchase of inputs, technology, human resources and other functions. The value chain has significance for issues like resource allocation, cost efficiency, control over resources and financial analysis of the firm. The value chain analysis in a cluster starts with an analysis on the marketing front backwards to the raw material purchase front.

Value Chain in Dhokra Casting Cluster: A diagrammatical explanation on each of the craft-clusters under study is given above with a craft specific analysis. The ultimate profit margin calculated herewith includes the labour cost. Hence, the net return to the artisans seems to be very less. But, when the artisan produces in a large volume, this profit margin scales up and makes the artisan sustainable. In addition to this, proper care has been taken to minimize the wastage of raw materials during production process. This will in turn minimize the production cost for the artisan and hence increasing the profit margin with a significant amount. Also, a techno specific intervention in value chain process will increase the price of the product in terms of quality and higher production.

Stake Holder Analysis and Their Role

Stakeholders can be identified with the following reasons:

1. Those whose interests are affected by the issue or those whose activities strongly affect the issue.
2. Those who possess information, resources and expertise needed for strategy formulation and implementation.
3. Those who control relevant implementation, instruments.

Stakeholder analysis is a vital tool for identifying those people, groups and organizations that have significant and legitimate interests in specific issues. The analysis ensures proper representation in relation to gender, ethnicity, poverty, or other locally relevant criterion. Cutting across these categories, the analysis can also look at stakeholders in terms of their information, expertise and resources applicable to the issue. The purpose of stakeholder analysis is as follows:

1. Ensure inclusion of all relevant stakeholders.
2. Maximize the role and contribution of each stakeholder.

Stakeholder analysis has been done in terms of three generally sequential stages of activity:

1. **Specifying Issue(s) to be Addressed**: Stakeholders were defined and identified in relation to a specific issue—people and groups only have a concrete "stake" in a specific issue or topic. Hence, the stakeholder identification process had operated in respect to a particular specified issue.
2. **Long Listing**: With respect to the specified issue, a "long list" of possible stakeholders, as comprehensive as feasible, were prepared with further sub-categories also identifying those which:
   - were affected by, or significantly affect, the issue;
   - had information, knowledge and expertise about the issue;
   - had control or influence implementation instruments relevant to it.
3. **Stakeholder Mapping**: The "long list" of stakeholders had analyzed by different criteria or attributes and determined clusters of stakeholders that exhibit different levels of interest, capacities, and relevance for the issue. Areas where capacity building is necessary were identified

for effective stakeholder participation, and highlighted possible "gaps" in the array of stakeholders.

All the stakeholders in the study areas are categorized in two levels, viz. district and state level and cluster level.

District and State Level Stakeholders:

1. **District Industrial Centre (DIC):** DIC is the primary agency at district level that is implementing the entire cluster development programme. At present, DIC of every district has appointed one cluster manager to look after all the cluster development work in the district with the support of its entire staff and trainers, and the NGOs. On the other hand, DIC engages all its IPOs in cluster development work as cluster supervisors, who will assist and monitor the work of the cluster manager work in their respective cluster area.
2. **District Rural Development Agency (DRDA):** District Rural Development Agency (DRDA) is a government undertaking, which is looking after all the developmental works undertaken in the district and monitors the programme implementations. It is the approving authority for all the financial expenses under various programmes. This, basically, works for infrastructure development and construction of roads and providing other basic amenities in rural areas.
3. **National Bank for Agriculture and Rural Development (NABARD):** National Bank for Agriculture and Rural Development is a nationalized bank, which has opened its branch office in each district. One AGM is appointed who becomes the official authority to deal with all the district level works and who basically coordinates and acts as a linkage between the district office and state office. The potential linked credit plan (Annual Credit Plan) prepared by NABARD not only helps banks but also all the agencies working for the development of the district including DIC for their individual planning in resource allocation and making an appropriate implementation

strategy.

4. **District Supply and Marketing Society (DSMS):** The District Supply and Marketing Society (DSMS) is the district level office of Orissa Rural Development and Marketing Association (ORMAS), which is a state government undertaking working for promotion of rural marketing. One Chief Executive Officer is appointed for this office. As far as the cluster development work is concerned, DSMS is confined only with the exhibitions. Besides this, it has opened a sales outlet called 'Pallavi' at district headquarters, where variety of handicraft items is kept for display and sales.
5. **Integrated Tribal Development Agency (ITDA):** Integrated Tribal Development Agency (ITDA) is working in the district for the development of Tribal. It provides financial support for establishment of various entrepreneurial units for Tribal groups for their income generation programme. It also provides infrastructure in terms of roads and bridges (missing link) for improving the connectivity in rural areas. Also it constructs market complex for the development of marketing of rural produces.
6. **Financial Institutions (Banks/MFIs):** Banks act as financial institutions that provide credit linkage to the artisans. All the banks including State Bank of India, UCO Bank and regional bank like Koraput Panchabati Gramya Bank (KPGB), Utkal Gramya Bank etc. are operating in these districts. Credit linkage is never felt as a problem from banker's side and what is more important is the dynamism of artisan groups which takes the loan from the bank and how productively they use it. Besides this, credit linkage activity, banks do have some social welfare schemes, under which they can do the capacity building of artisan groups and train them on credit need assessment, credit linkage and utilization, preparation of business plan of their individual units.

7. **Block:** What is DRDA to the district, the same is Block to the villages. All the developmental activities at village level is implemented and monitored by the Block Office and the Block Development Officer. Block helps the artisans in credit linkage, building of infrastructure like Common Facility Centres. It also implements some social welfare programme for the development of rural women under its Community Development Programme, where CDPO is in charge of it. Even at village level, the Anganwadi workers are engaged in strengthening the artisan groups.
8. **Non-Government Organizations:** Non-governmental organizations are happening to be more people friendly and the rural people trust them more in compare to any external agencies. Hence, these agencies can be used effectively in cluster development works in the KBK districts. In every district, NGOs are working as cluster manager, selected by DH&CI. They have opened their branch offices and appointed one District Coordinator who is looking after all the district level activities.

Cluster Level Stakeholders

1. **Artisans:** Artisans are key stakeholder in any of the cluster as they are directly involved in the cluster development process, starting from the raw material purchasing to the marketing of the final products. Unless and until they develop, cluster development cannot be possible. There are a number of clusters present in KBK districts with multiple crafts. Though in most of the clusters more number of new artisans are selected and trained for different crafts, if other basic facilities will be provided to them for building a regular source of income, then most of them will come up as skilled artisans in these sectors.
2. **Artisan Self-help Groups:** Artisans are formed into separate groups where 10-15 artisans come together and form the artisan self-help groups. All training programme

are implemented group wise in a cluster and all the groups come together to a common place for their work. It is a very good concept and if care is given towards the improvement of these artisan groups then the cluster development programme will be a successful one in the district.

3. **Master Craftsman/National Awardees/State Awardees:** Master craftsman and national awardees are the artisans who have gained special skills and expertise in a particular craft and who help a lot to other artisans in development of the skill and quality of the products by disseminating their own knowledge to others. Also due to their nationalized figure and expertise skill they are renowned throughout the state and hence they get a better access to national and international level markets in terms of receiving orders for supplying finished items. To capitalize their expertise and skill in cluster development of the district an appropriate platform needs to be built up which can support these resource persons and who in turn enhance the development of cluster artisans in a variety of ways.
4. **Artisan Societies/Federations**: This is a registered body formed by artisan groups. A number of artisan groups from different clusters come together and form this association, which is registered under Society Registration Act. The society basically takes care of marketing of individual artisan's products. As it is obvious, a single artisan cannot have access to bigger market or cannot get a big order in terms of quantity, the society in turn, can get the order, representing a group of artisans, where more than hundreds of artisans are the members of the society and work for the society. Hence, accumulating business of all the artisans becomes the business of the society, which can definitely attract big traders to do the business. Thus, society is a key point in providing regular market to the artisans.
5. **Service Providers:** This sector consists of various key

players who are actively involved in cluster development. The major players are raw material suppliers, design development support providers, insurance agencies, local traders, various marketing agencies at cluster level, state level and national level, transport agencies and outlet agencies. The existence of these is very much scattered.

6. **Local Money Lenders and Traditional Middlemen:** This group plays a very important role in the development of cluster in KBK districts. Generally, the artisans of these areas are illiterate and poor, the traditional money-lenders (generally the schedule caste like *Dombos* and Sundhis) are the sustainers of the traditional crafts. They, at the same time, are the traditional exploiters of the artisans. In the form of order givers, working capital providers and the sole purchaser of the finished products, they take the major share of the profit margin and very rarely they share them with the artisans. Material to material bargain (rice, annual crops of a mango tree etc. in lieu of finished products) is also practiced in these areas.

Marketing Network

Existing Marketing Status: The traditional, cottage industries and specially handicrafts enjoy a good national and international market but more needs to be done on upgrading quality and design, as well as production and also improvement in the marketing network. The current marketing scenario is not very encouraging. Marketing is considered to be the major thrust area as it reflects the successful implementation of all other activities. The artisans of KBK districts, used to sell their products in local market, door-to-door selling, local exhibitions. Sometimes the local businessmen directly contact these artisans and purchase their items at a low price. For handicraft products, the local market place does not fetch much money and it is only the NGOs and visitors from outside who purchase items at a fair price, which is not a very often process.

Few of the Artisans along with their products have also participated in the Ekamra Haat Exhibition, Adivasi Exhibition at Bhubaneswar, Khurda Mahotsav, District level Cultural *melas*, Handicraft Exhibition at Vishakhapatnam at Andhra Pradesh, exhibitions in Chhattisgarh and Delhi Haat etc. Exhibitions are a great way to promote the traditional industries of this area. Exhibitions are organized in different parts of the State including major cities and towns. Representatives of artisan members participate in such events and sell their products. The artisans also participate in a number of *melas* organized by other like-minded agencies. These *melas* stimulates the artisans to come out of their limited rural scenario and become market-savvy. They pick up new ideas from other more experienced exhibitors. Direct interaction with customers provides them with valuable feedback. A sense of interdependence among members is reinforced among the members as they help each other in selling their products.

Presently, the artisans are not selling their items to any individuals or groups directly, as the marketing of their products are taken care by the cluster managing NGOs. Their marketing activities aim at strengthening export potential by increasing contacts and thereby product sales. Intensive contact with trading houses within the state and out of the state also enhance orders; organizing exhibitions for handicraft marketing; local marketing through showroom outlets; productivity coverage of the product within and outside; market analysis, costing and pricing of the product, forward and backward linkage in production and marketing process, are all ways they assist in marketing.

Thus, the craft needs design and technical development, value addition along with product diversification. The earlier use of items of limited range could not provide adequate marketing support to the grass root artisans. The absence of profitable marketing network and the lack of appropriate processing facilities for manufacturing quality-finished products have resulted in most of the products being sold at uncompetitive prices.

Nature of Markets: Understanding the nature of markets in terms of their spatial dimension (neighbourhood, city, national, international) as well as market segmentation relating to current fashion trends, variant income levels of different client segments and class-cum-status distinctions is of vital significance for designing an integrated strategy aimed at promoting handicrafts. In the handicrafts sector, the main buyers can be classified as: local buyers; buyers in urban centres; private handicrafts shops; institutional buyers consisting of hotels, offices, clubs; temple authorities and cooperatives/handicrafts corporations; Indian and foreign tourists. In all the three crafts, the respondent enterprises were asked to indicate their "main buyers" out of the aforementioned typology of buyers.

In the terracotta crafts, the artisans pointed-out that local people were their "main buyers" (50.56 percent) followed by private handicrafts shops (16.22 percent) and the institutional buyers consisting of cooperatives/handicrafts corporations (14.29 percent) and temple authorities (4.29 percent). In the case of bamboo craft, artisans identified local people as their main buyers (57.14 percent) followed by private handicrafts shops (19.67 percent), persons in urban centres (11.20 percent) and institutional buyers (10.23 percent). In dhokra craft, artisans considered private handicrafts shops to be their main buyers (59.33 percent) and followed by local people (16.67 percent) and institutional buyers (18.50 percent).

In short, it is pointed-out that markets for handicraft goods are spatially organized and better profits can be reaped by trader entrepreneurs and merchant entrepreneurs who are capable of selling products in the distant parts of the country and abroad. Artisan products are the torchbearers of a community's identity in terms of its local culture, history and tradition. The artisans of these indigenous clusters have been marketing their products directly to the local buyers and through middlemen to export-markets throughout history. The very fact that the local artisans need to work with the middlemen for marketing their products to the upscale handicraft boutiques, art galleries and import stores, tells upon their financial output. Nevertheless, these establishments sell their pieces of arts and crafts at very high prices, at the end of it all the local artisans are left with just a fraction of the profit.

From the beginning, the primary mandate given by the artisans was to help them in developing the marketing network to gain a fair price for their products. This has not been without its challenges; design, quality, and packaging presented their own problems in the struggle to market handmade crafts. In this context that the NGOs took up two important tasks in the form of providing and strengthening the production base of the artisans, technically, and managerially. This encouraged the organizational aspect of the artisans; to operate collectively and act as a pressure group in terms of advocacy and lobbying to influence the macro level policy decisions. The marketing wing takes care of quality and timely production along with the marketing of the products in different market outlets. To its credit, it has occupied a position in local, regional and national sphere by way of showroom sale, order sale, exhibition sale. The following regular market channels are present for these artisans.

Problems Encountered in Marketing: A major shortcoming experienced by the artisans of the KBK districts is the marketing of their products. Lack of exposure to larger markets, absence of publicity and advertisement, non-existence of market research, etc. are the major causes for the dismal performance of the artisans in the marketing front. During the interaction with the artisans, peer-groups, NGO operatives and the district administration, the following major shortfalls experienced by them are derived:

1. To maximize the earning potential of the artisans and as a result this will put more money into the artisan's economy as well as local economies which resulted in higher

number of production without giving heed to quality aspect. To add as much value to handmade products, through quality in design and making for maximizing the earning potential of the artisans is the need of the hour.

2. Artisans are paid the price of the items unequally as based on gender, race and caste. Artisans are paid at the rate set by their groups or marketing association or a fair rate determined by the cost of materials and the time involved in the production of the goods. Thus, the artisans lose control over price of the items.
3. Necessary support in an integrated and comprehensive manner to upgrade skills and knowledge of artisans along with basic inputs for product development and its diversification are to be provided in order to have an easy access to both indigenous and foreign market. This aspect is completely absence in the handicraft cluster situated in the whole of KBK districts.
4. Absence of necessary support by various institutions to find suitable markets for the products, and the lack of research and developmental support
5. To support community initiatives through fair trade partnerships, which can involve paying a premium for a product, such as micro finance schemes (though this is dependent on what the market will bear).
6. To aware the artisans on market trends and provide sufficient support so that they can be self-dependent and confident in their own designs and marketing.
7. To ensure availability of infrastructure and common facilities which would enable development of better products and their diversification.
8. To make the artisans aware of the demands of the market and provide assistance for publicity for marketing of handicraft products.
9. To improve the mobility of the finished products from the cluster.
10. To make the artisans self-sufficient in marketing activities

as like in the production activities. The NGOs and the intervening agencies acts as a middleman for these artisans rather than working as a capacity builder in the marketing aspects in the real sense.

11. No specialized activities for the members of the group or SHGs. All the members are doing all type of activities like production, marketing, record keeping etc.

Technology Intervention

With the change in the global trade conditions and the shift in economic policy of Government of India there is a greater need for continuous design and technology up-gradation for sustainability in the highly competitive market and for higher value realization for targeting upper end of the market, for improved productivity and higher return. Technological intervention has the following sub-components:

1. Assistance for training the trainers (a type of certificate or diploma course for trainers/master craft persons who can work in close cooperation with clusters).
2. Financial assistance for development and supply of modern improved tools, equipment, products and process technologies.
3. Assistance for design and technological up-gradation

- Integrated design and technology development project.
- Design and technology workshop.

The present status of technology intervention in the existing craft clusters in the district is very poor. Hardly there is any intervention on technology front and it is not focused in near past. Almost all the craft clusters are doing the production process in their traditional way. They are using all the old tools and machineries. Even the non-availability of common facility centre and electrification in some cluster villages do not permit the installation of up graded machineries which of these were availed by artisans during their training programme. In the process of cluster development this intervention is highly necessary to go for production of market driven products with requisite qualities. By this, the production of each cluster will definitely improve a lot, giving an additional business to it, which in turn will make the cluster a viable unit. Both of the above interventions are equally important and necessary for the development of any craft. Both of these things combined will give quality and production of items as per the requirement of the market.

As it is rightly identified in the cluster profile, the requirement of technology up gradation is one of the upcoming needs of the cluster, which needs to be addressed immediately. There are various state and national level institutes who are supporting on this front. These institutions can be accessed and contacted for the said purpose, after going through a detailed study about their credibility and expertise on this field. Government support and in particular initiative form directorate of handicraft and cottage industries (DH&CI) is highly essential.

Design development and technical up-gradation in handicrafts sector is entirely different from that of small-scale industries. Each craft is highly complicated involving numerous processes and it is also very individualistic and local. Crafts differ from region to region. They have their traditional ways of production, their own designs, colour, shape and so on. Each craft, each centre needs careful study and understanding before new life can be injected into it. Therefore, in the very nature of the sector, there is need for great sensitivity and delicates handling and tireless service before any results can be achieved. The gradual alienation on handicrafts from their traditional use and their increasing commercialization has led to the development of new products. New designs and styles have been evolved to suit the tastes and preferences of the new generation.

State/Central Handicrafts Corporations, Craft Councils, Apex Societies, NGOs are eligible to avail assistance. In addition EPCH, CEPC, MD, NIFT and top designers are also eligible to avail assistance. Support from Development

Commissioner (Handicrafts), can be availed for this purpose as this institute is involved in technology development in the sectors of handicraft and small-scale industries. One of its units is established at Calcutta. It is known as regional technology development centre. This institute can be contacted for technology up gradation in these clusters.

Common Facility Centre (CFC)

Since handicrafts from a part of the informal and decentralized sector, it is not able to meet the challenges of free market economic forces and also not able to meet the standards required for international marketing. In order to address this problem, there is a need to put in place a centre/mechanism, which will ensure economy of scale, price competitiveness, quality control, application of design and technology. input on continuous basis, scope of product diversification and higher unit value realization and compliance with WTO compatible standards. Common Facility Centre (CFC) is therefore to be set up at cluster level to achieve these objectives.

The majority of the handicraft artisans of KBK Districts are facing the problems of good working conditions as their work place. All individuals and group artisans work around their houses or at a rented common place, which is almost impossible to accommodate the huge numbers of artisans to work in a common platform. Normally, the working space is insufficient and often it is not properly ventilated and lighted. Mostly these artisans work at their workhouses in a family environment, which may not always be conducive for production of quality handicraft appropriate to up market segment. This affects their productivity and income. For this, there is an immediate requirement of setting up an effective common facilities centre for the artisans of all existing clusters in KBK districts. The need of common Facilities Centre required with proper housing, basic necessities like provision of water, electricity, sanitation and up to date machineries and equipments etc. The CFC set up includes the following inputs:

1. Building (land to be provided wither by beneficiaries or by State government/panchayat etc.).
2. Hall type rooms with proper installation of tools and machinery and sitting arrangement of the artisans for production.
3. Rooms for storage of raw materials and finished products respectively.
4. Toilet and water tank facilities.
5. Crèches for children of the artisans.
6. Room for sale outlet.

Still there are CFCs constructed in some of the existing clusters. But these centres are tied with a number of problems. For example, in the bamboo cluster at Sandhiguda, Mathali, though there is the CFC, there is no electricity connection to this CFC. The same problem is experienced in dhokra cluster at Jhaliaguda, Malkangiri. Construction of CFC is not a problem, as quoted by the district collector. As he said, the major problem lies with availability of raw materials, which makes the craft viable. If this problem is solved, then there will not be any problem for any of the craft clusters to have their separate common facility centre.

Also focus is to be given towards using some of the common facility centres constructed by the government and which exist nearby to the clusters. These structures are unused now and are lying in defunct position or being used by the anti-social elements. In some cases there is government land available near the cluster for the Construction of the CFC. Where there is no government land available, some of the artisans are eager to donate their land for this purpose. Hence, negotiation should be done on this aspect, wherever possible to construct a common facility centre, keeping in mind the business growth of the cluster and the viability of the product.

Function of the Production Sub-System

The function of the production sub-system within the

composite social system can be examined with reference to:

1. Terms of services.
2. Technological process of production.
3. Terms of trade.
4. Nature of markets.
5. Working and living conditions.
6. Access to social security.

Terms of Service: The terms of service relates to wages/income levels as well as the working and living conditions. This analysis shows that there is considerable variation in the monthly income of artisan households even within each craft. Further, the analysis shows that workers in the dhokra craft are least remunerated amongst the three crafts. The study also shows that the modal income of both terracotta and bamboo craft households are between ₹ 7000 to ₹ 8000 per month whereas for dhokra craft, the modal income is only between ₹ 6000 and ₹ 7500 per month and the modal income is between ₹ 7300 to ₹ 8000 for terracotta artisans.

This is despite the fact that more than 80 percent of the respondents in these crafts belong to the highly skilled/skilled categories.

The Economic Survey of Orissa (2007-2008) states that the per capita income was ₹ 9119 at current prices. In comparison, the per capita income of artisan households in the selected three crafts comes to ₹ 8341.00 for terracotta craft, ₹ 8769 for bamboo craft and ₹ 6345 for the dhokra craft. In short, the per capita income of artisan households in the three selected crafts is significantly lower than the per capita income at the all-Orissa level.

Further, the per capita income of Orissa is significantly lower than the national level which was computed at ₹ 18682 at current prices in 2007-2008. In this manner, it emerges that the Orissa State is at the lower end of the national economic spectrum and within Orissa, artisan households reflects a very poor state of affair which needs to be specially arrested.

At this stage, it would be appropriate to examine the

income of artisan households with the below poverty line (BPL) income in Orissa. The Tenth Five Year Plan pegged the Orissa BPL at ₹ 16000 per annum for rural households and ₹ 18000 for urban households. The study shows that 8.93 percent of the terracotta households and 38.33 percent dhokra households fall below the poverty line. The sectoral study, therefore, shows that despite the aesthetic excellence of the artisans of KBK districts, they earn very modest incomes. It is pertinent to note here that craft-based income is a major source of income of artisan households: 46.67 percent worker households of terracotta, 71.42 percent households of bamboo and 66.66 percent households of dhokra craft generate more than 60 percent of their total household income from craft-based employment.

In terms of working and living conditions of the artisans concerned, the worst scenario is that of bamboo craft where 75 percent of the artisans work for 9-12 hours. In the terracotta craft, a little over one out of every four worker (28.6 percent) work for 9-12 hours. The study also examines the artisans who work for the whole week without availing a rest day; two-third of the workers in the terracotta craft, 46.7 percent workers in the bamboo and 16.10 percent workers in the dhokra craft work for the entire week.

Examining the entitlements in relation to paid leave, medical allowances and monetary help in the event of casualty it shows that the availability of these benefits ranges from 2 percent to 13 percent. Focus group interviews have revealed that these benefits are not built-into the terms of service of the members. Instead, the foregoing benefits are provided once in a while on a paternalistic basis. In short, these benefits are not available to artisans as a matter of right.

Technological Leverage: Introduction of intermediate technology which reduces drudgery without displacing a sizeable proportion of labour force is a significant means of improving workers' productivity. 'Enhancement of workers' productivity increases the surplus value available to micro entrepreneurs and therefore, can render valuable impetus to provision of terms incorporating decent work. While examining the possibility of using technological leverage in promoting decent work in terracotta, bamboo and dhokra crafts we may come across; power driven potter wheels, electric clines, bamboo cutting and wood cutting machines, sizing machines and shaping/dressing machines can be installed with a view to reducing the drudgery of handicrafts' workers as well as enhancing their productivity.

Further, in the case of bamboo craft, the introduction of diamond chisel available in Rajasthan can enable a carver to do crude carving at a much faster pace. Again, the use of electric-fret saws and shaping machines for making ornamental pillars and canopies can embellish the presentation of finely carved bamboo statues. These ornamental pedestal-cum canopies can also be used for the effective lighting of the artifacts placed below them. In the case of dhokra work, computerized designing can lead to the introduction of more versatile designs as well as adoption of modern motifs. Moreover, superior furnaces can be used for removing impurities from brass leading to financial saving, higher productivity as well as greater safety of operations. Again, time spent on drawing of fine wires and their plaiting can be reduced by introduction of appropriate technology.

Terms of Trade: The terms of trade refer to the nature of relationships between different role players in the processes of production and marketing. The key role players in the production and marketing of handicraft items in these clusters are: the handicraft workers or artisans; the artisan entrepreneurs; the trader entrepreneurs; cluster managing agents (the NGOs), suppliers of raw materials; commission agents or intermediaries procuring orders for either the trader entrepreneurs or artisan entrepreneurs; Handicrafts Corporation of Orissa; private show-room owners in the major cities of Orissa; and agents of exporters in Orissa as well as metropolitan cities like Delhi, Mumbai, Kolkata, and Chennai.

In the terracotta craft, wages of ₹ 100 to ₹ 150 per day is usually paid to a skilled artisan depending upon his skill and experience. A semi-skilled worker is paid between ₹ 80 to ₹ 100 per day and an unskilled worker is paid between ₹ 40 to ₹ 80 per day. Sometimes skilled artisans are given work by entrepreneurs on a piece rate basis. Generally, a skilled artisan working on piece rate basis never succeeds in earning more than ₹ 7000 per month despite strenuous efforts. It is only when a skilled artisan procures direct orders from consumers that he manages to earn more than ₹ 7000 per month. In case a skilled artisan supplies items on piece rate to a cooperative/SHG, even then he is unable to earn more than ₹ 7000 per month. The artisan entrepreneurs who generally work at home or in a small workshop using their family labour and/or a few hired hands tend to earn between ₹ 7000 to ₹ 10000 per month depending on the marketing season.

It is the bamboo craft artisans who have the best terms of trade at the local level. For a standard batch size production of a particular item, the cost component of raw material is estimated to be 20 to 30 percent of the wholesale selling price depending on the quality of bamboos used.

The wage component of the wholesale selling price varies between 50 to 60 percent. In this manner, an average entrepreneur keeps a profit margin of 25 to 30 percent. The profit margin of them is higher than this average when he produces goods on his own as well as selling the items through his own means.

The terms of trade in dhokra craft are similar to those of terracotta craft. An artisan is the key role player who procures latest designs from designers manufactures a significant proportion of the artifacts which he sells through his own workshop, as well as sub-contracts work to artisan entrepreneurs by supplying raw materials or by providing cash advances on securing large orders. Under the sub-contracting system, the entrepreneur collects the finished products from artisans at pre-fixed prices which are generally lower than the wholesale market prices. In the case of items manufactured at his own workshop, he invariably ends-up with a net profit margin of 5 to 10 percent of the net selling price and in case he procures items from artisan entrepreneurs, his margin comes down to 2.5 to 3.0 percent depending on whether it is a standard batch production, small sized items batch or production of intricate and larger items.

The artisan is invariably a master craftsman and tends to earn, on an average, ₹ 7000 to ₹ 8000 per month. His profit margin goes-up when he is able to procure direct orders from customers. In this manner, on a direct order, he can earn 50 percent or more of the purchase price depending on the aesthetic excellence of the item. At the top of the ladder in terms of profit margins are a few merchants who control the trade along with the middlemen. On account of the exploitative nature of the relationship between the artisans and middlemen, the total quantity of artifacts being produced is declining. It is, thus, apparent that craft work is in a state of decline and requires immediate redressal measures for saving the employment of artisans engaged in such work. Given the considerable export potential of craftwork, there is considerable potential for generating even additional employment provided superior intermediate technology is used and the terms of trade are organized in a more equitable and symbiotic manner.

Working and Living Conditions of Artisans: With respect to the availability of social amenities at the CFC; workers are not provided with the basic facilities—residential accommodation at the work site. As regards to provision of food at the CFC, no worker is provided with. However, in relation to provision of electricity, the situation is less favourable with 30 percent of terracotta, 29.69 percent of dhokra and 33.3 percent of bamboo workers availing this facility. The simple provision of toilet at the CFC is extremely poor and no workers being provided with this facility. When enquired about drinking water, almost nine out of 10 workers in all the three crafts enjoy the benefit of this facility. Finally, in relation to proper ventilation at the work site, only about half the workers in the three crafts are well endowed in this respect.

In relation to living conditions of the three craft artisans, one finds that one out of every five terracotta artisans (21.7 percent), about half bamboo artisans (46.4 percent) and two-thirds of dhokra craft artisans (65 percent) live under a thatched roof. It is further noticed that because of paucity of funds majority of handicrafts' workers in KBK districts live under a `kuchha thatched roof or in a semi-concrete dwelling unit. This is indicative of their modest standard of living.

Social Security: Social security is another basic criterion that every worker/artisan must enjoy. As found, in case of the terracotta, bamboo and dhokra crafts, benefits such as provident fund, gratuity, medical allowance or group insurance are not available to any category of artisan workers. A simple and limited form of Paternalistic social security cover is available to workers in the form of some assistance/advances during serious illness and marriage or death rituals. In addition, festival advance is given to members during Dussehera/Pooja holidays in the form of one or two day's wages accompanied by new clothes. Single migrant workers are sometimes provided free accommodation. In a nutshell, social security cover available to handicrafts' workers is limited and generally restricted to some assistance during emergencies and nominal benefits during a specific festival season.

Ideational Framework

The ideational framework relates to labour laws, traditional norms and work-place conventions that constitute the `super-structure' of the social system. It is this super-structure which determines the content of the role-expectations associated with different role-players in the production sub-system. The fulfilment of their role-expectations by different role-players can be viewed as one useful barometer of the quality of relationships between employers and workers. Further, the progressive adoption of international labour standards and their effective implementation on the ground is indicative of a qualitative improvement in the ideational framework.

Organization: The right of association and collective bargaining has been embodied in the Indian law relating to formation of unions. Unionism or protection of artisans' rights through the formation of associations is not a regular and well developed feature of the informal sector. In the case of terracotta, dhokra and bamboo crafts, the scenario in the KBK Region of Orissa is characterized by lack of unions/associations of artisans. Given the substantial supply of artisans who are ready to work without laying claims to social protection, it is felt that artisans are concerned about losing their benefits in the event of their forming unions. In a nutshell, it is amply clear that the handicrafts sector in Orissa is largely un-unionized.

Law and Administration: The cardinal component of the ideational framework is the set of laws applicable to a given micro industry, service or business. The main labour laws which constitute the ideational framework for the handicrafts sector are given below:

1. **Minimum Wages Act, 1948:** which authorizes the State Government to fix and revise a minimum rate of wages for time work (minimum time rate, the minimum rate of wages of piece rate (minimum piece rate), a minimum rate of remuneration to employees employed on piece work for the purpose of securing to such employees a minimum rate of wages on a time work basis (a guarantee time rate).
2. **Payment of Wages Act, 1936:** This Act regulates the payment of wages to stipulated establishments and seeks to ensure disbursal of such wages to employees within a prescribed time limit and without retention of any part thereof to be paid in future.

3. **Equal Remuneration Act, 1976:** The Act provides for payment of equal remuneration to men and women workers for the same work or work of similar nature and for the prevention of discrimination on grounds of sex.
4. **Trade Union Act, 1926:** This Act seeks to protect the right of workers by enabling them to form a Trade Union and collectively bargain with their employers with regard to their wages; conditions of work at the work site and provision of various types of welfare benefits.
5. **Maternity Benefit Act, 1961:** This Act seeks to regulate employment of women in certain units for specific purposes before and after child birth and to provide maternity and allied benefits.
6. **Employees' Provident Fund (Miscellaneous Provisions) Act, 1952:** This Act enables workers working in factories and other establishments to avail of benefits accruing from Provident Fund, Pension and Deposit-linked Insurance Fund.
7. **Employees' State Insurance Act, 1948:** This Act seeks to provide certain benefits to employees in case of sickness, maternity and employment injury. It is applicable to factories where 10 or more persons are employed or were employed for wages and the manufacturing process is carried on with the aid of power or where 20 or more persons are/were employed for wages in a day of the preceding 12 months where the manufacturing process is carried on without the aid of power.
8. **Factories Act, 1948:** This Act provides for the health, safety and welfare of workers in factories where 10 or more persons are employed. Provisions relating to health cover issues like cleanliness, ventilation/temperature/ dust/fumes, artificial humidification, overcrowding, lighting, drinking water, toilets etc. The provisions relating to safety cover issues like fencing of machinery, rules concerning work on or near machinery in motion, prevention of employment or young persons in dangerous

machines unless fully trained. Provisions relating to welfare cover issues such as proper washing facilities, facilities for sitting, first aid, shelter, rest room, lunch room, canteens, crèches etc.

9. **Orissa Shops and Commercial Establishments Act, 1956:** This Act applies to Shops and Commercial Establishments in the urban areas of Orissa and has provisions relating to working hours, half an hour daily rest, overtime, weekly paid holiday, sick leave, gratuity and leave entitlement for those who have completed 240 days of work.

The general perception amongst the Labour Inspectorate staff in Orissa is that the production of handicrafts falls in the cottage industry sector and, therefore, Acts such as Factories Act and Shops and Commercial Establishments Act are not enforceable but the factual position is that in case piece rated workers and home based workers are taken into account, many of the workshops where handicrafts are manufactured would have workers exceeding 20 without power and exceeding 10 with power. It would be pertinent to point-out that in many of the handicraft workshops, the manufacturing and selling process operate side-by-side within the same premises. Some of the comparatively larger units also have their own small show rooms.

Spatial Intervention in Clusters

Another way of supporting a large number of livelihoods is supporting activities in a cluster. Usually a cluster arises around a particular activity, and eventually a number of related and supporting activities emerge leading to all round livelihood promotion. These enterprises closely depend on each other for sustenance. On the one hand, the stone polishing units in the area support these enterprises, at the same time; these supporting enterprises have helped the informal units to grow. The advantage of growth of such a cluster is that, related and supporting services become available to all participants, reducing the transaction costs for all. The cluster attracts various suppliers to the area, as it provides economies of scale.

The strong competition attracts consumers, who are assured of choice, competitive quality and price. Growth of clusters attracts policy attention increasing the availability of skilled workers. Clusters also enhance ability to cope with changes in the environment as information flow becomes faster. Usually a cluster starts growing with one pioneering unit, which very often sets up an enterprise serendipitously. If this unit fails, the cluster never grows; but if it succeeds, many others follow; providers of support services get attracted. This in turn makes setting up similar new units more economical. At this stage, the policymakers get involved; infrastructure in the cluster gets developed; associations get established. These associations play a role in policy lobbying, start sharing market information, training and production facilities, etc.; cluster gains market share. However, this process can be further accelerated with dissemination of information to different key players. There are many agencies such as United Nations Industrial Development Organization (UNIDO), which have adopted development of a cluster as their strategy for livelihood intervention.

When the participants were asked what types of services they received from NGOs, an overwhelming majority (80 percent) received some sort of training or technical assistance either through classes, workshops or one-on-one counselling and received a small business group loan. Although some individuals expressed the need to apply for a loan, some hesitated to go through the application process as they thought they would not qualify or were afraid of being rejected. Regardless of their hesitation to apply for a loan, most participants did show interest in obtaining one and knew that through the work they did with SHGs their chances of becoming more "bankable" were greater than if they went on to apply for a loan without the services and help from NGOs. Meanwhile, the majority preferred individualized group sessions when obtaining guidance and or getting their questions answered.

Attitudinal Orientation

There are many factors that both "push" and "pull" individuals into becoming a micro entrepreneur and self-employed. "Pull factors" are those that attract an individual to start a business. These include distinct market opportunities, the desire to be "one's own boss" and the potential to make more money than in a wage or salary job. On the other hand, the factors that "push" individuals into micro-entrepreneurship are for the most part negative factors such as unemployment, discrimination, being disabled and low wage levels among others.

Out of the 225 individuals that participated in this study, 17 fall into the "push factors" category as many of them were people who were in need of an extra source of income for their families to make ends meet. The remaining eight individuals can be categorized into the "pull factors" of micro enterprise development. These individuals emphasized their need to be self-employed and fulfil their dream of having their own business as the income opportunities in other sectors are curtailed and they can use their traditional skill to earn the livelihood. Some of these individuals were artists who wanted to profit from their skills, while others simply had the desire to become their "own boss".

When interview participants were asked why they chose to become a micro-entrepreneur and the reason they chose to be a member of SHGs, the number one answer was to obtain a livelihood. This is evident due to the nature and mission of MEPs, where individuals seek the opportunity to make more money in order to change their economic status through group activities. However, shortly after stating their financial needs, several respondents reflected upon other reasons behind their choice to become self-employed. In addition, some participants mentioned the need to learn modern skills that would allow them to enhance their business, as well as achieving a sense of pride and success as a result of owning a business. With regards to skill acquisition, one participant mentioned, "The further you get into the program the more you realize all the skills you need". Another participant joined the ME program simply for the cash benefit, but later came to realize that he knew nothing about cash flow statements, supply and demand, product analysis and product design. After enrolling with SHGs and receiving training, a participant pointed out—"Money was not as important, because without the business skills to put into practice, the money was relatively useless, so it was crucial for me to obtain those skills".

On a different note, a women artisan responded the following when asked their reason behind their enrolment with SHGs—"Being a destitute and single mother is hard...I was at a time where I needed a lot of help and emotional support; a friend told me about the program and told me they could help me start a small business. It was comforting to know that I could use my artistic knowledge and skills...having the help from SHG definitely helped me lift up my spirits and gave me hope and a sense that I could gain some sort of income without leaving what I love doing".

As noted, even though for many individuals money was their main driver to be a member of SHG, there are also many other aspects that play an important role when deciding to become self-employed and enrol with SHG, be it skills, training or simply personal encouragement.

A worker's attitude with respect to the young members of his family adopting the same vocation is considered as a useful indicator of his views about his profession. In the case of terracotta, bamboo, about one out of every four workers (26.7 percent terracotta and 23.2 percent bamboo) expressed a positive view suggesting that they would like their children to follow their vocation. In contrast, only 5 percent of the dhokra artisans expressed similar views. This is understandable on account of the current decline in this craft in Orissa. It is also worth noting that one out of every three terracotta artisans (33.33 percent) and a little over one out of four bamboo artisans (26.50 percent) wanted to set-up their own unit on a self-proprietary basis whereas only one out of five dhokra artisans (19.95 percent) supports that view.

Viability of the Craft Cluster

To study the viability of the cluster, triangulation methodology had been adopted. Scores have been given for respective crafts based on the five major parameters taken for the triangulation. Then the total point for each craft is calculated summing of all scores it received across all the parameters taken. The five parameters taken for the study of viability of the crafts taken into account are as follows:

1. Availability of critical mass which includes all factors of production.
2. Potential of the artisan growth with respect to the skill and technology.
3. Livelihood dependency of artisans on the craft.
4. Market potential of the craft.
5. Status of basic infrastructure, which includes roads, road connectivity, CFCs, electricity connection and other basic facilities like medical, education etc.

The status of the basic infrastructure like road connectivity, power, water facilities etc. is an area of concern for the development and growth of the artisans. Though the availability of the critical raw materials and the market demand shows a higher figures (more than 7 points) as well the dependency of the artisans for livelihood shows a 6.33 points in average, the hindrance for the development and growth is the basic infrastructural facilities.

Suggestion for Improvement in Marketing Network

The twin constraints for the growth and development of the indigenous artisans of the study area are the provision of infrastructural facilities present in the areas and the restricting marketing performance of the artisans. The skilled artisans faced the problems to sale their elite products to the target markets. The hands that create these exclusives fail to give a two full day meals to their family members. To enhance the sale and to create an avenue for development and growth, the following measures are suggested:

1. Creation of an atmosphere conducive to handicraft growth, taking into consideration the available natural resources and the local socio-economic environment.
2. Promotion of the traditional handicrafts and artisan sector, by providing adequate support in the form of common facilities like service centres cheap raw material, technical inputs, marketing network skill development, etc.
3. Proactive participation of all concerned Government agencies and non-government agencies for the development of handicraft sector.
4. Rapid development of basic infrastructure so that handicraft growth is facilitated.
5. Encouraging self-employment and identification of avenues for the same.
6. Human resource development through appropriate skill and entrepreneurship development programs behavioural training, etc., at district, sub division, block and village level, to meet the emergent skill requirements of the district within a stipulated time frame.
7. Specialized training should be given to the members by forming sub-groups within the group apart from their artistic skills. Capacity building measures should be taken to make the artisans be self-reliant in activities like marketing, publicity, record keeping, quality control etc.
8. Encouraging joint ventures between local entrepreneurs and industrialists from outside the state.
9. Simplification of procedures and opening up of Orissa with a view to attract both internal and outside investors and buyers, with respect to prospects whose long term

viability is carefully evaluate.

10. Strengthening physical and social infrastructure like power generation, railway and road network.
11. Simplification of rules and procedures of bank for credit linkage.

Establishing Alternate Marketing Channel: To create a regular market base at district level, various alternate market channels should be explored. These local NGOs working for the craft sectors and individual skilled artisans can be promoted as marketing agents for the craft products produced in a cluster. Otherwise, a formal agreement should be done with the cluster development agent who will also provide the market linkage to cluster artisans.

Establishment of District Handicraft Museum: To make the publicity and enhancing the present marketing situation of the craft products, there should be a district level handicraft museum. This museum will display about all the art and crafts available in the district. This will attract all the outside visitors and delegates from foreign countries who will in turn publicize about this at their respective countries. This will open a new market channel for the products and will definitely help a lot in ensuring a regular market channel for the district artisans.

Findings and Suggestions

Micro enterprise development is not a panacea for the working poor and low-income individuals. It does not replace the need for different governments to develop coherent and effective macroeconomic policies. Rather, this approach to socio-economic development embodies the recognition that macro level policies alone have not significantly reduced poverty nor materially improved the living standards of the poor in both the developing and developed world. As a result, microfinance services and micro enterprise development cannot be considered as the panacea to help low-income individuals gain access to financial services or to achieve their micro enterprise goals.

However, it does provide an important tool for reaching to underserved populations and, coupled with sound development policies, it has the capacity to reach and change the lives of many. With a rich potential traditional background and traditional knowledge, business viability, and presence of skilled manpower, KBK districts are the place for the most poorest and underdeveloped manpower. The sustainable livelihood is a distant dream for them. The MEP and MFP are the programs what can bring them the sigh of relief from the clutches of acute poverty and underdevelopment. The use of their traditional knowledge, not making the indigenous artisans alien to their culture and tradition, the MEs can make them socio-economic independent and sustainable.

Major Findings:

The specific findings of the present study are as follows:

1. In general, there is a positive impact of the MEPs on the livelihood of the indigenous artisans of the KBK districts. The analysis of the household income had shown a quantum jump as so the asset acquisition by the artisans, in both aggregate and in per capita income. The MEP intervention has increased the security in the income generation by increasing the employment work days for the households, not only for the artisans but for also his family members. Thus, the income of the household had shown a remarkable increase. The rise of the household income gives rise to change in the expenditure pattern and thus, more expenses is made in the form of medical, child care, fooding etc. which ultimately lead to quality life style for the artisans.
2. The significant change, as depicted through the analysis of the sample households, in housing sector, asset building and land acquisition is a symbol of life style change. The MEPs not only make the indigenous artisans to develop assets but also it is observed that they are diversifying their activities to increase their income laterally. The secondary

occupations like cow and goat rearing, poultry, small shops, agricultural etc. were taken up in a substantial scale to increase the household income.

3. Education and health are the two most important indicators for the stationing of quality life. In the education front, the present analysis ended with a mixed bag of conclusions. In one hand, where the enrolment of boys has improved over time, the artisans have a little interest for the girl education. The drop-out rate in the secondary level for the girl is the major concern for the policy makers.
4. A marked growth has been experienced in the revenue generating capacity of the MEs due to timely intervention of various governmental and non-governmental organizations in the fields of finance. The net worth of the MEs has shown a quantum jump as also the profitability. The artifacts produced by the artisans have a good demand in the national and international market but due to poor marketing activities and strategies the financial result of the MEs were dismal, but the MEPs holds that limitation at bay and the result is significant and positive.
5. MEPs had a significant effect on income diversification. All of the moderating variables like diversify through horizontal growth, diversify in lateral ways, through own effort, through the help of family members, as a member of a group and with the help of others, seemed to make much difference over time and due to the interventions. Many households have multiple sources of income because the income from any one source would not be enough to sustain the household; many households shift or diversify income sources across the year to take advantage of seasonal peaks and to compensate for seasonal troughs.
6. MEPs leads to superior transactional relationships with suppliers, intervening agencies, govt. departments etc. but they were unable to show any impact on transactional relationships with customers as the major marketing activities has done by the intermediaries, NGOs and the

marketing agencies set up by the government.

7. Current participation in MEPs through borrowing and/or saving did have a clear impact, however, on the informal sector earnings of respondents (including income from other informal sources as well as micro enterprise revenue). It also raised the total micro enterprise revenues and informal sector earnings of the household as a whole. There is also some indication of a significant impact on employment, but average employment in these micro enterprises is very small. Although the income level of the society, and even of the sample households, is rising, there is little scope for an individual micro entrepreneur to expand his or her enterprise because others are likely to compete away any gains. In addition to this general constraint, specific constraints apply to the entire trades in which the artisans in the sample engage. They face constant conflict with the moneylenders and the middlemen. They have been locked in a long-running struggle with the employer/traders and may also be facing a decline in the demand for their product. The NGOs engage in struggle (lobbying activities) on behalf of all tribal artisans engaged in some of the major trades in which the respondents in our sample participate. They have, for example, fought for higher piece rates, sub-contracting, and incense making. Similarly, they have pushed for improved government services and benefits—such as those provided for under the informal workers welfare activities. They have worked to reduce police and moneylenders' harassment of artisans and obtain better space in the income generating zone.
8. Most of the laws under which the microfinance institutions are operating seem to have fallen short in dealing with their institutional and operational aspects. Micro finance institutions, which are basically NGOs providing financial services, do not fall under the government regulations that are applied to banks and other non-bank financial

intermediaries. Actually, they are in need of appropriate regulatory frameworks. The absence of a single registering, monitoring and supervising organization appropriate for the microfinance institutions in Orissa/ India has made it difficult to decide if they have been targeting the right people and for the right purpose.

9. The intervention of the NGOs are only limited to two or three years for cluster development which is not sufficient to make the artisans self-sufficient and self-reliant. Sometimes, it is found that the positions of the artisans are back to square one again. The MEs become sick and the SHGs become non-operating.
10. The tribal artisans are generally very apprehensive and suspicious in nature when approached to form the groups or for opening of bank accounts. It is due to the lack of education and exposure for them, and due to the previous bad experiences.
11. MEs can become a mechanism for promoting the inclusion of women into broader social processes. In the front of women empowerment, the following findings are experienced:

- A marked difference in the earnings of the women entrepreneurs is seen due to the micro enterprises and timely intervention of NGOs and GOs in developing their skill level and proper marketing of the products.
- The awareness level of the women artisans had shown a tremendous change and the damsels of the conservative tribal and underdeveloped male-protagonist society are more aware about their rights with respect to property, equal wage, equal food as husband, access to government schemes, to give votes and to medical care etc.
- It has been noted that when women members play leadership roles, as group leaders and/or centre leaders, they experience an increased sense of self-confidence and self-worth.
- Exposure visits, training programmes, and participation

exhibitions provide women with opportunities to travel outside the village and expand their knowledge of the world outside the household and immediate community. The increased mobility leads to a greater sense of self-confidence, and is empowering in its own right.

- The position of women artisans in the male-dominated tribal society has changed in a positive direction such as reduction of wife beating, family violence, and positive change in respectability towards women, their significant role in the decision-making in the family etc.
- Lack of attitude towards diversification of trade is observed among the conservative tribal women artisan population in KBK districts which is due to lack of change agents, and the alienation to their culture.

Suggestions: Despite many shortcomings about the function, impact and sustainability of the micro enterprise programmes in KBK districts, microfinance institutions, have made a successful breakthrough in reaching the target group mainly because of the easy availability of funds and close supervision. It is pertinent to further gear up the activities of the intervening institutions for the sake of poverty alleviation and also to deal with socio-economic-financial issues of the rural areas. Although micro credit is not the panacea for poverty alleviation and rural upliftment, the supportive services of microfinance institutions for primary requisites (such as health, education, and infrastructure) and financial services (such as savings schemes, consumption, investment and insurance services) are essential for the smooth operation of micro credit. In order to improve the performance of the microfinance institutions and micro credit for targeting the poor, the following measures have been suggested:

1. **Coherence with Macro Policy Agenda:** MEPs as local socio-economic systems are essentially a part of the global and national socio-economic system. They not only draw from the wider context but also contribute towards it. Within the national socio-economic policy arena, there are

specific sectoral policies that have a direct bearing on the MEs. Industrial developments being a 'state subject', MEs also fall under the state policy domain. These are highly employment intensive and are an important source of non-farm income in a multi-livelihood space. Thus, they deserve special attention and inclusion of social and environmental aspects in ME initiatives need to become integral with the economic agenda.

2. **Compatibility with Current National Policy:** The micro enterprise clusters are culturally and socially important from the view point of employment generation and poverty alleviation. The cluster policy therefore has seemingly contrasting tasks to balance the need for flexibility to meet diverse requirements and yet coordinate among those diverse efforts for ensuring synergy. Thus, a coherent policy has to be provided which has a compatibility with current national, state and localized policies to gain the biggest output.

3. **Role of Public, Private and Knowledge-based Institutions:**

A. National Government: It is proposed that a National policy be framed to integrate with the macroeconomic policies and social development objectives. In specific, the national government should undertake the following:

- Build up new database on ME clusters particularly in terms of social and environmental parameters and classify the existing database of clusters to identify common areas of assistance.
- Make available adequate funds to the implementing agencies (public or private institutions) through various schemes of assistance administered through different ministries and help up-grade their capacities to manage the initiatives.
- Enable knowledge sharing across states and institutions.
- Coordinate common programmes of technical assistance to ME clusters that cut across different states and draw upon

common sources of knowledge, institutional framework and best practices.

- Initiate common programmes for thematic inter-linkages around common needs of clusters to build an interface between specific union ministries and state departments.
- Undertake capacity building initiatives for local development institutions, industry/micro enterprise based associations and regional resource institutions through largely public funding.
- Ensure that public development schemes focus on inclusivity of growth and accordingly relevant monitoring and evaluation frameworks to ensure greater effectiveness of expected outputs.

B. State Government: The state level governments should essentially be responsible for coordinating implementation of ME initiatives in their respective states through national and state level funding, leveraged by private sector pooling of fund. The state governments should be expected to draw state policy framework on MEs that in specific should ensure:

- Draw state level policy framework on clusters that integrates with the overall macro economic and social development policy and objectives at the national level.
- Provide funding and policy support for capacity building to the nationally funded and coordinated initiatives for local development institutions and industry/micro enterprise based associations.
- Set up a separate cluster cell in the department and designate a nodal resource organization to coordinate, support and monitor cluster initiatives in the state.
- Undertake initial cluster analysis of the chosen clusters for intervention in the pilot phase and developing vision for them.
- Draw up specific activity framework in the short, medium and long term with stakeholders.
- Coordinate the execution of collaborative action plan in

the clusters.

- Undertake a process review of initiatives and assessing the gaps therein.
- Based on the learnings drawn from the pilot initiatives, expand the scale and scope of interventions.

C. Private Sector: ME development cannot be expected to succeed without an active participation and sharing of responsibility by the private sector in terms of conceptualization on development initiatives, partial funding and significant role in implementation.

- They have to play an active role to increasingly undertake development initiatives in partnership with public institutions, knowledge partners, R&D institutions and value chain partners. Smaller groups of enterprises need to join hands as networks and consortia to undertake initiatives for their limited private interests.

D. Knowledge Institutions: Technical institutions, research organization, vocational training centres have an important role to play:

- Joint research with cluster stakeholders including machinery suppliers, speciality input suppliers and major customers.
- To assess emerging skill requirements, develop suitable joint (along with industry) training curricula along with local industry and run training programmes jointly funded with the government and the industry.

4. **Policy Agenda for Action:** A detailed list of specific policy measures expected to lead to effectiveness of the ME based development approach by ensuring an enabling environment, to be put in place.

- To establish an inter-ministerial coordination focal point: To target the review of all ongoing development initiatives, identify areas of synergy, suggest necessary institutional arrangements for implementation, get studies organized, draw upon international best practices and finally evolve a communication strategy to disseminate them.

- To prefer cluster activation to new cluster creation: Activation of existing cluster will be preferred over cluster creation, unless the conditions warrant otherwise.
- To undertake a national initiative on export promotion across specific clusters that has a high potential to grow.
- To undertake a national initiative to achieve environmental compliance across specific clusters to ensure environmental compliances. This initiative should also be nationally coordinated through Ministry of Environment with support drawn from specialized agencies and implemented by a range of public and private institutions.
- To undertake a nationally coordinated initiative on select social issues such as working conditions, provision of micro-credit needs of workers community, living conditions and safety aspects around specific clusters with scope for significant improvement.
- To establish cluster-oriented free trade zones, industrial parks and other common facilities that can help ME clusters realize their growth potential and upgrade facilities that individual enterprises may find difficult to achieve.
- To undertake national and regional initiatives to augment the supply of key business development services (BDS) like international marketing, technology, financial services, designing and management inputs.
- To follow an appropriate framework for monitoring and evaluation (M&E) to enable corrective action during the ongoing process and provide policy lessons to re-work strategies at the cluster level and across the clusters for policy makers.

5. **Promotion of Formalization of the Informal Economy:** The major setback the rural and traditional entrepreneurs faced is the lack of formalization of their micro-organizations. High business costs and the informal sector are mainly caused by ill-designed and unstable rules and

regulations (particularly in relation to taxation, labour policy and business registration); the lack of well-defined and secure property rights; poor quality or non-existent public services; deficient capacities and resources of government agencies to administer and enforce laws and regulations; a lack of transparency, accountability and political autonomy of governmental institutions (particularly the judiciary); as well as high degrees of macroeconomic instability, unemployment and corruption. The following measures can be taken at macro level to eradicate the hindrances for the informal sectors to be formalized:

- Fostering macroeconomic stability as a precondition for economic reform, growth and informal sector formalization.
- Increasing public participation and transparency in the policy making and legislative process by instituting transparent, inclusive decision-making procedures and providing regular opportunities for the public to comment on existing and proposed laws and regulations.
- Clarifying and streamlining legal and regulatory codes by eliminating duplicative, superfluous laws that increase the costs of doing business and invite for corruption.
- Making private property rights accessible to all, clearly defined and strongly enforced.
- Simplifying business permits and licenses and making them affordable so that becoming part of the formal economy is within reach for entrepreneurs of modest means.
- Reforming tax systems in order to encourage profitable economic activity and promote widespread compliance.
- Overhauling labour laws to allow for more flexibility.
- Reforming excessively bureaucratic government agencies and strengthening their administrative and enforcement capacities.
- Making essential business-related information available to

all.

- Providing high quality, efficient, and cost-effective infrastructure essential for a democratic, market-based system so that entrepreneurs benefit from joining the formal sector.

KBK Specific Suggestions: Establishment of common facilities centres for imparting training, marketing, providing market intelligence, establishing linkages with financial institutions, providing raw materials, providing managerial inputs is the need of the hour. Following recommendations are suggested for development of promotion of tribal handicraft in KBK districts along with a provision for sustainable socio-economic development of indigenous artisans.

- Use of indigenous knowledge and practices: Whenever any policy decisions will be taken for the development of the indigenous artisans, the cultural aspects have to be taken into consideration and should be based on the knowledge system that prevailed in those areas.
- Availability of raw material at reasonable rates: It is suggested that raw material depots may be set up in craft concentration tribal pockets to facilitate uninterrupted supply of standard raw material to craftspersons in appropriate quantity and quality at reasonable rates. In such circumstance the state governments may supply raw material like seasoned wood or wool at cheaper rates become incentive for the tribals to continue producing crafts.
- Provision for infrastructural facilities: It is suggested to develop and provide the worst hit infrastructural facilities and connectivity to the place of production to place of consumption or market.
- Provision for Special Fund for establishing training and design centres at block level in those districts where tribal population is more than 50 percent.
- Credit Facilities/Financial Support: Instead of craftspersons approaching to bank individually, the bank

should camp at specified place to get completed the documents and distribute the loan to the tribal artisans. Further, it has been suggested that finance should also be made available through post office.

- Upgradation of technology and production techniques: Design development, production of new items and improvements traditional tools and age old techniques need to be attempted in such items where the originality of the tribal designs is retained. Introduction of new items with improved models may be designed continuously to attract new customers and explore new markets by the present design and training institutes Therefore it has been recommended that central and state government should organize regular seminars to upgrade the technology and production of techniques. There is need for upgrading their skills, product diversifications, product designing, market oriented products, participation in exhibitions in India and abroad.
- Setting up of Institute of Design and IITs in tribal concentrated areas: It has been suggested that the various State Government might consider setting up an Institute of Designs under the aegis of Directorate of Small Scale Industries at some suitable place which will work with the mission to become professional centre of design excellence and innovation, disseminate technical knowledge and develop skill based upon the topographical requirement of rich human resource base of artisans. The design centre shall also work for value addition of products of art-wares leading to higher demand of the products while preserving the traditional skill and excellence and blending with contemporary marketing content and taste for handicrafts. The central or state government should also explore the possibility of involving ITI for skill development and training in handicraft sector especially in tribal districts
- Parity between handloom and handicrafts sector.

- TA/DA to artisans for marketing programmes: It has been recommended that like J&K, North Eastern States and some districts of Orissa, TA/DA/transportation charges should be provided to artisans in the old pattern.
- Consultancy for handicrafts sector: It has been suggested that consultancy/seminar should be organized from time to time in different crafts for the benefit of artisans/exporters and dissemination of market intelligence, up-gradation of technology, standardization of quality and packaging for higher value addition of products.
- Publicity of tribal handicrafts: Since not much documentary literature is available, it has been suggested that facilities for putting handicrafts profile of tribal state on website and publication of brochures etc. should be provided to promote the state handicrafts.
- Exemption of sales tax/trade tax on tribal handicrafts products like many other states.
- Implementation of welfare schemes for artisans: It has been reported that welfare schemes like insurance, pension, workshed, workshed-cum-housing etc. should be monitored and implemented with faster pace.
- Creation of handicrafts cell in Directorate of Industries: To give the priority to solve problems of crafts and craftspersons of the state, an exclusive handicrafts cell should be created in the Directorate of Industries.
- Setting up of urban haats/sale-cum-demonstration centres: In order to promote handicrafts at the places of tourist spots and urban centres to provide regular marketing channel to artisans. Sale cum demonstration centres may be established at important cities with more than fifty lakh population by involving TRIFED.
- Skill dissemination by master artisans in each district: It has been suggested that state government should take initiative by identifying master artisans at state level to identify district level artisans and impart training for trainers to them.

- Human resource development can be a tool to escape poverty: Education is an important tool to escape poverty, but only if the education system reaches the right people with the right contents. But education alone will also not bring automatically progress, if it is not supported by economic opportunities. Thus, training efforts should be modularized into flexible, cost-effective and puzzle-like units. This also facilitates the access to continuous education systems and trainings which are tailor-made to the needs.
- Streamlining bank activities: Regional rural banks and the commercial banks should establish separate functional relations with the micro finance institutions to provide the required guidelines, supervision and financial assistance. Close cooperation among the microfinance institutions, banks and organs of the government for social welfare activities is essential for the effective coordination of their activities. Accounting systems, management information systems services, the calculation method of the recovery rate of the micro finance institutions should be streamlined and transparent.
- Facilitate group interaction: Although the content of the classes and the knowledge obtained from them was not deemed as valuable as other services provided by MEP, participants did appreciate the opportunity to interact with their peers and the ability to share ideas, provide support or simply be able to relate to others going trough the same process. In doing so, social capital–defined as shared norms, personal trust and reciprocity, highly valued for community development and relationship building—would increase along with a sense of belonging for many of MEP clients.
- Work towards establishing a permanent service catered to rural residents: In rural KBK communities, one in five jobs are attributed to micro enterprises. The difficulties of these individuals to constantly travel to urban areas and

towns, in addition to the lack of access to financial services catered to low-income individuals, makes a valid ground to asses the potential to establish a permanent resource similar to that located in urban areas and towns.

- Create a network of experts from different fields, including successful MEP clients.
- To undertake survey to assess skill level and needs of future clients.

Bibliography

Bibliography

Ackerly B.A. (1995), Testing the Tools of Development: Credit Programmes, Loan Involvement and Women's Empowerment. IDS Bulletin, Vol. 26 No 3, pp. 56-68.

Ahluwalia, M.S., 'Planning' in Kaushik Basu (ed.), Oxford Companion to Economics in India, 2007, New Delhi, Oxford University Press.

AIAMED (2000), Good Practices of NGOs in Setting Up Alternative Development Financial Institutions, AIAMED, New Delhi.

AIMS (2000), Learning from Clients: Assessment Tools for Microfinance Practitioners, The Small Enterprise Education and Promotion (SEEP) Network, Washington, DC.

Allerdice, A. and Rogers, J.H. (2000), Renewable Energy for Micro enterprise, National Renewable Energy Laboratory (NREL), Colorado, USA.

Amin R., S. Becker and A. Bayes (1998), NGO-promoted Micro credit Programmes and Women's Empowerment in Rural Bangladesh: Quantitative and Qualitative Evidence, The Journal of Developing Areas, Vol. 32, No. 2, Winter 1998, pp. 221-236.

Ankuram-Sangamam-Poram (2000), Making a Difference-Where It Matters Most, Approach Paper, Hyderabad.

Antia, N.H. and G.K Kadekodi (2002), Dynamics of Rural Development: Lessons from Ralegaon Siddhi, A Joint Study by the Foundation for Research in Community Health, Pune and Centre for Multi-disciplinary Development Research, Dharwad, pp. 53-56.

Arunachalam, Ramesh (1999), Alternative Technologies in the Indian Micro-Finance Industry-A Study for Action Aid, Bangalore.

Ashe, J., Christopher, E., Cosslett, R. (1993), Credit for the Poor-Past activities and Future Directions for the United

Nations Development Program (UNDP), UNDP Policy Discussion Paper. New York: UNDP.

Atteh, O.D. (1991), Indigenous Local Knowledge as key to Local-level Development: Possibilities, Constrains and Planning Issues in the Context of Africa, Seminar on Reviving Local Self-reliance: Challenges for Rural/Regional Development in Eastern and Southern Africa, Arusha, Tanzania, 21-24 February.

Audit Report on Implementation of RLTAP in KBK Districts- for the period from April 2002 to March 2006.

Bandyopadhyay, Kaushik Ranjan, Poverty Alleviation and Pro-Poor Growth in India, Asian Institute of Transport Development, New Delhi, 2007.

Barton, C. (1998), Micro enterprise Business Development Services: Defining Institutional Options and Indicators of Performance, Micro enterprise Best Practice Project, USAID, Washington DC.

Basu, Kishanjit and Krishan Jindal (eds.), (2000), Microfinance: Emerging Challenges, Tata McGraw-Hill, New Delhi.

Baumgartner, R. and Högger, R. (eds.) (2004), In Search of Sustainable Livelihood Systems-Managing Resources and Change, New Delhi, Sage Publications.

Beijing Platform for Action, Fourth United Nations World Conference on Women (Beijing, 1995), paragraph 41.

Bell, M. (1979), The Exploitation of Indigenous Knowledge or the Indigenous Exploitation of Knowledge: Whose Use of What for What?, IDS Bulletin, 10: 44-50.

Benería, Lourdes (2003), Gender, Development and Globalization: Economics as if People Mattered, New York: Routledge.

Bhat, M.K. (2000), SHGs: Delivery Mechanism or Empowerment Tool?, Paper presented at the Workshop on Best Practices in Group Dynamics and Micro Credit, 15-17 February, Manesar, Gurgaon.

Bhatt, Nitin and Tang, Shui-Yan (2001), Designing Group-based Microfinance Programs: Some Theoretical and Policy Considerations, International Journal of Public Administration. 24, 1103-1125.

Bhattacharya, R.N. and Z. Hussain (2004), Attitudes and Institutions: Contrasting Experiences of Joint Forest Management in India. Environment and Development Economics, 9 (4): 40-50.

BIRD, (2001), Sustainable Microfinance Challenges Facing MFIs, Report of a workshop organised by SIDBI and BIRD, Lucknow, 15-17 January.

Biswas, Soumen, Expanding NGO-SHG-Bank Linkage Across the Country-Some Issues and Recommendations (mimeo), PRADAN.

Bosch, Ellie (2001), SHG Development in India: Some Issues Relating to Quality and Sustainability, I/C Consult, The Hague, The Netherlands.

Bosch, Ellie and Pieter Damen (2000), Self-help Groups Landscape (Draft), I/C Consult, The Hague, The Netherlands.

Bose, S., Lal, P., Pareek, P.S., Verma, M. and Saigal S. (2006), Forest-based associations in India-An Overview, Winrock International India and the International Institute for Environment and Development (IIED), London, UK.

Bouman, F. (1995), Rotating and Accumulating Savings and Credit Associations: A Development Perspective, World Development, 23: 30, pp. 371-384.

Bruntrup, M., Alauddin, S. M., Huda, A. and Rahman, M., (1997), Impact assessment of the Association of Social Advancement (ASA).

Cameron, Sara (n.d.), India: Convergent Community Action (CCA) in Bihar and Jharkhand (Draft), Reaching the Unreached Case Studies, UNICEF.

Canadian International Development Agency (CIDA), "CIDA's Policy on Gender Equality" (Hull, Canada: CIDA, 1999), 5.

Carney, D., Drinkwater, M., Rusinow, T., Neejes, K.,Wanmali,

S. and Singh, N. (1999) 'Livelihoods Approaches Compared;. London: Department for International Development (DFID).

Carr, James H. and Tong, Zhong Y. (2002), Replicating Microfinance in the United States. Washington, D.C.: Woodrow Wilson Centre Press.

Charmes J. (1998:12), A Critical Review of Concepts, Definitions and Studies in the Informal Sector, in Employment and Development: A New Review of Evident, edited by D. Turnham et al., Paris, OECD.

Chattopadhyay, Suhrid Sankar, Anguish in Bolangir, Frontline, Volume 21, Issue 5, February 28-March 12, 2004.

Chen M. (1984), Developing Non-craft Employment for Women in Bangladesh, New York, Seeds.

Choudhury, S. (1995), Awareness of Rural Women and their Development: A Study, Kurukshetra, September: 44-48.

Christodoulou, N.T., Kirsten, M.A. and Badenhorst, J. (1993), Financing South African Micro-entrepreneurs, Development Bank of South Africa: Midrand.

Cleaver, F. (2005), The Inequality of Social Capital and the Reproduction of Chronic Poverty, World Development, 33(6): 893-906.

Cobo, Jose Martinez., Study of the Problem of Discrimination against Indigenous Population, 1986.

Colchester, M. (2006), Forest Peoples, Customary Use and State Forests: The Case for Reform, paper presented at the 11th Biennial Congress of the International Association for the Study of Common Property, 19-23 June, Bali.

Coleman, B. (1999), The Impact of Group Lending in Northeast Thailand, Journal of Development Economics, 60, pp. 105-141.

Collier, M and Batty. P., Micro enterprises and Third world Countries, World Bank Research Paper, Washington, pp. 491-492, 2003.

Craig G. and M. Mayo (1995), Community Empowerment: A Reader in Participation and Development, Zed Books,

London.

Cronwell, D.W. (2003), The SEWA Movement and Rural Development: the Banaskantha and Kutch Experience, Sage Publishers, New Delhi, pp. 5-30.

D'Silva, E. and S. Pai (2003), Social Capital and Collective Action: Development Outcomes in Forest Protection and Watershed Development, Economic and Political Weekly, 38(14): 1401-1415.

Das S. (2005), People's Banking is Here to Stay, Economic Times, February 5, 2005.

Das, Biswaroop (2001), Role and Impact of Microfinance on Poor, Friends of Women's World Banking, India, Ahmedabad.

Dasgupta, S., C. M. Deichmann, and D. Wheeler (2005), Where is the Poverty-Environment Nexus?-Evidence from Cambodia, Lao PDR and Vietnam, World Development, 33 (4): 617-638.

Dash, Anup (2003), Strategies for Poverty Alleviation in India: CYSD's Holistic Approach to Empowerment through the Self-help Group Model, IDS Bulletin 34(4), 133-142.

Datar, C. and A. Prakash (2004), Engendering Community Rights: Women's Access to Water and Wasteland in Gujarat, Maharashtra, Andhra Pradesh and Karnataka. Livelihood and Gender-Equity in Community Resource Management, Sage Publishers, New Delhi, First Edition, pp. 137-170.

Datta, K.L. and Savita Sharma, Facets of Indian Poverty, 2002, New Delhi, Concept Publishing.

Datta, Sankar and Vijay Mahajan (n.d.), Savings and Credit Movement of Andhra Pradesh-Lessons for the Rest of India (mimeo), BASIX.

De Soto H., The Other Path: The Invisible Revolution in the Third World, Harper & Row, New York, 1988.

Department of Women and Child Development and Gender Equality Fund, CIDA (2000), Best Practices in Group Dynamics and Micro-Credit, Report of a Workshop, 15-17

February, Manesar, Gurgaon.

Devi, M. (1994), Rural Poverty Alleviation Programme, New Delhi, Anmol Publications Pvt. Ltd.

Devi, U. (1982), Status and Employment of Women in India, New Delhi, B.R. Publishing Corporation.

Dewes W. (1993), Traditional Knowledge and Sustainable Development in Southern Africa, Proceedings of a Conference held at the World Bank, Washington DC, September 27-28, Environmentally Sustainable Proceedings, Series No. 4.

Directorate of Handicraft and Cottage Industries, Government of Orissa, Annual Report, 1999-2007

Dreze, J. and Sen, A., (1989), Public Action for Social Security: Foundation and Strategy, DEP No. 20, The Development Economics Research Programme, London School of Economics, London, August.

Eade D. and S. Williams (1995), The Oxfam Handbook of Development and Relief, Vol. I, Oxfam, Oxford.

Economic Review of India, 2006-2007, Government of India, New Delhi.

Economic Review of India, 2007-2008, Government of India, New Delhi.

Edgcomb, Elaine L., and Klein, Joyce A. (2005), Opening Opportunities, Building Ownership: Fulfilling the Promise of Micro enterprise in the United States, Fund for Innovation, Effectiveness, Learning and Dissemination, 1-140.

Elkan, W. (1988), Entrepreneurs and Entrepreneurship in Africa, World Bank Research Observer, 3(2): 171-187.

ETFRN (2005), Forests and Conflicts. European Tropical Forest Research Network News No. 43-44, ETFRN, Wageningen, Netherlands.

Fernandez, A.P. (1998), Self-help Groups in Watershed Management, ILEIA Newsletter, July 1998: 12-13.

Fernandez, Aloysius Prakash (1994), The MYRADA Experience-Alternate Management Systems for Savings and Credit of the Rural Poor, MYRADA, Bangalore.

Fernandez, Aloysius Prakash (1999), Is Micro Credit heading toward a Macro Mess?, Search Bulletin, January-March.

Fernandez, Aloysius Prakash (2000), Putting Institutions First Even in Micro credit, Paper presented at the Workshop on Best Practices in Group Dynamics and Micro Credit, 15-17 February, Manesar, Gurgaon.

Friedmann J. (1992), Empowerment: The Politics of Alternative Development, Blackwell Publishers, UK.

Gain, Raji T.S. and P. Satish (1995), A Micro Study on Group Dynamics and Group Functioning, Working Paper No. 6, Banker's Institute of Rural Development, December.

Galab, S. and N.C. Rao (2003), Women's Self-help Groups, Poverty Alleviation and Empowerment. Economic and Political Weekly, 38(12 and13): 1274-1282.

Ghate, R. (2003), Ensuring Collective Action in Participatory Forest Management, Working Paper No. 303, SANDEE, Nepal, Pp. 1-20.

Gittinger, J. Price, (1984) (Indian reprint), Economic Analysis of Agricultural Projects, The Johns Hopkins University Press, Baltimore.

Goetz A. M. and R. Sengupta (1996), Who Takes the Credit? Gender, Power, and Control Over Loan Use in Rural Credit Programs in Bangladesh, World Development, Vol. 24, No. 1, pp. 45-63.

Gorjestani, Nicolas (Chief Knowledge Officer, Africa Region, The World Bank), Indigenous Knowledge for Development: Opportunities and Challenges, This paper is based on a presentation made by the author at the UNCTAD Conference on Traditional Knowledge in Geneva, November 1, 2000.

Government of Orissa (2002), Health Statistics 2000-01, State Bureau of Health Intelligence, Directorate of Health Services, Bhubaneswar.

Government of India (1993), Employment Assurance Scheme, Guidelines, Ministry of Rural Development (Primary

Source), New Delhi.

Hailey, J. and Harper, M., Management Development for Enterprise Promotion, Paper to IHRD Conference, Manchester, 1989.

Harper, Malcolm (1998), Profit for the Poor-Cases in Micro-Finance, Oxford and IBH Publishing Co. Ltd., New Delhi.

Harper, Malcolm (2002), Indian Self-help Groups and Bangladesh Grameen Bank Groups: A Comparative Analysis, Discussion Paper, Friends of Women's World Banking India, Ahmedabad.

Harper, Malcolm, Ezekiel, Esipisu, A.K. Mohanty and D.S.K. Rao (1998), The New Middle Women-Profitable Banking Through On-Lending Groups, Oxford and IBH Publishing Co. Pvt. Ltd., New Delhi.

Harper, M., Small Business in the Third World, Wiley, Chichester, 1984.

Hindess, B. (1996), Discourses of Power: From Hobbes to Foucault, Blackwell Publishers, Oxford.

Hoff, K. and J. E. Stiglitz (1993), Imperfect Information and Rural Credit Markets: Puzzles and Policy Perspectives, in K. Hoff et al. (eds.), The Economics of Rural Organisation, World Bank/Oxford University Press, Oxford, Chs. 1 and 2.

Holcombe, S. (1995), Managing to Empower: The Grameen Bank's Experience of Poverty Alleviation, London: University Press Ltd.

Hulme, D. and P. Mosley (1996), Finance against Poverty. Volume I & II, Routledge, London.

Hulme, D. (1991). The Malawi Mundi Fund: Daughter of Grameen, Journal of International Development, 3(4), pp. 427-431.

Hulme, D. and Mosley, P. (1996), Finance Against Poverty, Vol. 1, London: Routledge.

Hulme, David (2000), Impact Assessment Methodologies for Microfinance: Theory, Experience and Better Practice, World Development, Vol. 28, No. 1, pp. 79-98.

Hulme, David and Paul Moseley (1996), Finance Against Poverty, Vols. 1 and 2, Routledge, London and New York.

Hussain M. (1984), The Impact of Grameen Bank on Women's Involvement in Productive Activities, Dhaka, Grameen Bank.

ILO (2001), Social and Labour Dimensions of the Forest and Wood Industries on the Move, International Labour Organization, Geneva, Switzerland.

Jahan, R., G. Kelkar, and D. Nathan (2004), Redefining Women's Samman: Micro credit and Gender Relations in Rural Bangladesh. Economic and Political Weekly, 39(32): 3627-3640.

Jaquette, Jane S. and Summerfield, Gale (2006), Women and Gender Equity in Development Theory and Practice, Durham and London: Duke University Press.

Jayaraman, B. (2001), Micro-Finance-Retrospect and Prospects, Occasional Paper No. 20, NABARD, Mumbai.

Jodha, N.S., (1988), Poverty in India: A Minority View, Economic and Political Weekly, Special Number, November, pp. 2412-2418.

Johnson S. and B. Roglay (1997), Microfinance and Poverty Reduction, Oxfam, UK.

Johnson, Susan and Ben Rogaly (1997), Microfinance and Poverty Reduction, Oxfam and Action Aid, UK.

Jose, A.M. (1989), Role of Women in Rural Development, Trichur, Kurukshetra, July: 13-18.

Joseph, M. (1982), Women Participation and Development Strategy, pp. 120-25, New Delhi: Kanishka Publishers.

Kabeer N. (1994), Reversed Realities: Gender Hierarchies in Development Thought, Kali for Women, New Delhi.

Kabeer N. (1999), Resources, Agency, Achievements: Reflections on the Measurement of Women's Empowerment. Development and Change, Vol. 30, No. 3, pp. 435-464.

Kabeer N., (1999), The Conditions and Consequences of Choice: Reflections on the Measurement of Women's

Empowerment, UNRISD Discussion Paper No. 108 (1999), 49; www.unrisd.org.

Kabeer, N. (2003), Assessing the Wider Social Impacts of Microfinance Services: Concepts, Methods and Findings, IDS Bulletin 34(4), 106-114.

Kakwani, N. Khamdker S. and H. Son, Pro-poor Growth: Concepts and Measurements with Country Case Studies, Working Paper, Number I, International Poverty Centre (IPC), August 2004, available at: http://www.undp-povertycentre.org.

Kantor Paula (2003), Women's Empowerment through Home-based Work: Evidence from India, Development and Change 34 (3):425-445.

Kar, G. C. and R. K. Meher (2001), An Evaluation of Anti-poverty Programmes in Koraput District of Orissa (Mimeo), Nabakrushna Choudhury Centre for Development Studies, Bhubaneswar.

Kar, G. C. and R. K. Meher (2001), An Evaluation of Anti-poverty Programmes in Nawarangpur District of Orissa (Mimeo), Nabakrushna Choudhury Centre for Development Studies, Bhubaneswar.

Kar, G. C., Poverty and Human Development: An Enquiry into the Causes of Rural Poverty in Orissa, Department of A & A Economics, Utkal University, Bhubaneswar (Mimeo).

Karekezi, S. and Majoro, L. (2002a), Improving Modern Energy Services for Africa's Urban Poor, Energy Policy, Vol. 30, pp. 1015-1028.

Karmakar, K.G. (1999), Rural Credit and Self-help Groups-Micro-finance Needs and Concepts in India, Sage Publications, New Delhi.

Kaur, S. (1992), Women in Rural Development, New Delhi: Mittal Publications.

Khandker, S. (2005), Microfinance and Poverty: Evidence Using Panel Data from Bangladesh, The World Bank Economic Review, 19(2), pp. 263-286.

Kilby P., T. Kidder N. Nayar, M. Leach and N. Mule (2000),

Report of Phase 1 of the Oxfam Development Finance Institution Feasibility Study and Review of Oxfam Interventions in Micro-Finance, Oxfam, January.

Kirsten, J. van Zyl, J. and Vink, N. (1998), The Agricultural Democratization of South Africa, Cape Town: AIPA/Francolin Publishers.

Kishanjit Bash and Krishon Jindal, Bankers Institute of Rural Development, Lucknow, 2000, Micro Finance: Emerging Challenges.

Kumar, V. (1994), Women's Employment in Himachal Pradesh-Some Reflections, Extension Education Programme, Yojana, September: 26-28.

Lal, D. (1999), Unfinished Business: India in the World Economy, Oxford University Press, Oxford.

Lal, D. and H. Myint (1996), The Political Economy of Poverty, Equity and Growth-A Comparative Study, Clarendon Press, Oxford.

Lepenies, P. H. (2004), Exit, Voice and Vouchers: Using Vouchers to Train Micro-entrepreneurs-Observations from the Paraguyan Voucher Scheme, World Development 32 (4), pp. 713-724.

Lewis, H.T. (1989), A Parable of Five Hunter-gatherers in Canada and Australia, in Johannes, R.E (eds.), Traditional Ecological Knowledge: A Collection of Essays, IUCN, Gland, Switzerland, pp. 11-19.

Lindholm. C. and Mead, D., Small Scale Industries in Developing Countries: Empirical Evidence and Policy Implications, MSU International Development Paper No. 9, East Lansing, 1987.

Littlefield, E., Murduch J. and Hashemi S., (2003), Is Microfinance and Effective Strategy to Reach the Millennium Development Goals?', Focus Note 24, CGAP, Washington, DC.

Macqueen, D.J., Dufey, A. and Patel, B. (2006), Fair Trade Timber, Background paper presented at an international meeting on "Enhancing local returns from trade in forest products, 27 September 2006 at Royal Botanic Gardens, Kew. IIED, London, UK.

Mahajan, V. (2004), De-regulating Rural Credit, Paper presented in New Priorities: Symposium on a Social Agenda for India, www.India.seminar.com.

Mahajan, Vijay (2002), Microfinance Policy: Review and Prospective Suggestions, Presentation to the Sa-Dhan Subgroup on Policy, January.

Mahajan, Vijay and G. Nagasri (1999), Building Sustainable Microfinance Institutions in India, Paper presented at Seminar on New Development Finance, Frankfurt, September.

Mahajan, Vijay, Bharati Gupta Ramola and Mathew Titus (2000), Dhakka-Starting Microfinance in India in K. Basu and K. Jindal (eds.), Microfinance: Emerging Challenges, Tata McGraw-Hill, New Delhi.

Majumdar, Vina (1978), Role of Women in Rural Development: Report of an International Seminar, UK, Delhi: Allied Publishers.

Mangetane GK, Asibey EAO (2001), An Overview of African Indigenous Knowledge for Sustainable Development, Scandinavian Seminar College: African Perspectives of Policies Supporting Sustainable Development.

Mathew. P.M. and Nair. M.S. (1986): Women's Organization and Women's Interest, p. 123.

May, P.H., Da Vinha, V.G. and Macqueen, D.J. (2003), Small and Medium Forest Enterprise in Brazil, Grupo Economia do Meio Ambientee Desenvolvimento Sustentável (GEMA) and International Institute for Environment and Development (IIED), London, UK.

Mayoux, Linda (1998), Women's Empowerment and Micro-Finance Programmes: Approaches, Evidence and Ways Forward, DPP Working Paper No. 41.

McGuire P. B. and Conroy, J. D. (2000), The Micro-finance Phenomenon, Asia Pacific Review, Vol. 7, No. 1, pp. 90-108.

McNamara, Nora and Stephen Morse (1998), Developing Financial Services-A Case Against Sustainability, On Stream, Cork, Ireland.

Meher, R.K. (1999), Development Disparities in a Backward Region-A District Level Analysis, APH Publishing Corporation, New Delhi.

Meyer, Richard L. (2001), Microfinance, Poverty Alleviation and Improving Food Security: Implications for India (Draft), IDS Bulletin, Volume 29, Number 4, October.

Micro-Credit Summit 1997, Declaration and Plan of Action, Available from:
http//www.microcreditsummit.org /declaration.htm.

Misra, S. N. and M. Behera (2000), An Evaluation of Anti-poverty Programmes in Mayurbhanj District of Orissa (Mimeo), Nabakrushna Choudhury Centre for Development Studies, Bhubaneswar.

Mitlin, D. and Satterthwaite, D. (2004), Empowering Squatter Citizen-Local Government, Civil Society and Urban Poverty Reduction, Earthscan, London, UK.

Mohanty, M. (1995), Studies of Farm Women in Rural Orissa, Kurukshetra, August: 91-93.

Montgomery R., D. Bhattacharya and D. Hulme (1996), Credit for the Poor in Bangladesh: The BRAC Rural Development Programme and the Government Thana Resource Development and Employment Programme, In Hulme D. and P. Mosley 1996, Finance against Poverty. Volume II, Routledge, London.

Morduch, Jonathan (1999), The Microfinance Promise, Journal of Economic Literature, 37, 1569-1614.

Moser C.O.N. (1989), Gender Planning in the Third World: Meeting Practical and Strategic Gender Needs. World Development, Vol. 17, No. 11, pp. 1799-1825.

Moser C.O.N. (1993), Gender Planning and Development: Theory, Practice and Training. Routledge, London.

Mukesh Gulati, UNIDO Cluster Development Program for Micro and Small and Medium Enterprises.

MYRADA (1998), Guidelines for Working with Self-help Groups, Rural Management Systems Series Paper 30, (30A, 30B, 30C).

MYRADA, (1999), A Concept Paper on Federations of Self-help Groups, Rural Management Systems Series, Paper 32, Bangalore.

NABARD, (1999), Task Force on Supportive Policy and Regulatory Framework for Microfinance-A Report, NABARD, Mumbai.

NABARD, (1995), Report of the Reserve Bank of India's Working Group on Non-Governmental Organizations and Self-help Groups, NABARD, Mumbai.

Nanda, Y.C. (2000), Marketing Microfinance in India-The NABARD Way, Paper presented at the Workshop on Best Practices in Group Dynamics and Micro Credit, 15-17 February, Manesar, Gurgaon.

Narayan, D., Patel, R., Schafft, K., Rademacher, A. and Koch-schulte, S. (2000), Voices of the Poor-Can Anyone Hear Us? World Bank, Washington, USA.

Narendranath, D. (2000), Experiences in Promoting Savings and Credit Self-help Groups-Best Practices in Group Dynamics and Credit Plus Interventions, Paper presented at the Workshop on Best Practices in Group Dynamics and Micro Credit, 15-17 February, Manesar, Gurgaon.

Neck, P. and Nelson R., Small Enterprise Development: Policies and Programmes, ILO, Geneva, 1987.

Nelson, N. and S. Wright (1995), Power and Participatory Development: Theory and Practice, Intermediate Technology, London.

NSSO (55th Round), Report on Unorganized Manufacturing Sector in India, 1999-2000, September, 2001, New Delhi.

NSSO (56th Round), Report on Unorganized Manufacturing Sector in India, 2000-2001 (Report No. 477(56/2.2/1), September 2002, New Delhi.

Nunes, S. (1998), Women and Small Business Development, Pretoria: Ntsika Enterprise Promotion Agency.

Oakley P., B. Pratt and A. Clayton (1997), Outcomes and Impact: Evaluating Change in Social Development, INTRAC, Oxford.

Orissa Agricultural Statistics 2000-01, Directorate of Agriculture and Food Production.

Osmani, S., Defining Pro-poor Growth, One Pager, No. 9, January, 2005, available at: http://www.undp-povertycentre.org.

Ousmani, S., Macqueen, D.J. and Robert, G. (2006), Development from Diversity: Guyana's Forest-based Associations, Guyana National Initiative for Forest Certification (GNIFC) and the International Institute for Environment and Development(IIED), London, UK.

Panda, S.K. (2003), Micro-finance in Economic Empowerment of Weaker Sections, Yojana, 47 (3): 21-25.

Parveen, S., Aktar S., De Costa, N. and Kamal M.M. (1996), Dropout in Micro-credit Operation, Dhaka, Association for Social Advancement.

Pattnaik, B. (1994), Women Work Participation and Family Welfare, Yojana, May: 28-30.

Pearce, D., Markendya, A. and Barbier, E.B., (1989), Blueprint for a Green Economy, Earthscan, London.

Planning and Evaluation Organization, Various Evaluation Reports, Planning Commission, Plan Documents of Five Year and Annual Plans.

Poverty Estimates for 1999-2000, Dr. N. C. Saxena, Planning Commission, Government of India.

Prahlad, C.K. and A. Hammond (2002), Serving the World's Poor Profitably, The Harvard Business Review, 2002.

Prahlad, C.K. (2005), The Fortune at the Bottom of the Pyramid, Wharton School Publishing.

Price J. (1992), Women's Development: Welfare Projects or Political Empowerment?, Amesterdam Conference, Mimeo.

Puhazhendi, V. (2000), Evaluation Study of Self-help Groups in Tamil Nadu, NABARD, Mumbai.

Puhazhendi, V. and K. J. S. Satyasai (2000), Microfinance for Rural People-An Impact Evaluation, NABARD, Mumbai.

Puhazhendi, V. and K.J.S. Satyasai (2001), Economic and Social Empowerment of Rural Poor through Self-help Groups, Indian Journal of Agricultural Economics, 56(3): 459.

Putney, A. (2000), An Approach to the Identification and Assessment of Non-material Values, Parks Magazine, 10 (2).

Radhakrishna, R. and Shovan Ray (eds.), Handbook of Poverty in India: Perspectives, Policies and Programme, 2005a, New Delhi, Oxford University Press.

Rajasekhar, D. (2004), Micro finance and Poverty Alleviation Issues Relating to NGO Programmes in South India, ISEC Working Paper No.146, pp. 1-25.

Rajashekhar, D. and S. Madheswaran (2005), Economic and Social Benefits of Micro-Finance Programmes: An Economic Analysis, Studies in Microeconomics and Welfare, Academic Foundation, pp. 383-404.

Rao, D. S. K., P. Satish, Girija Srinivasan and D.S. Chauhan (1999), Study of SHGs as Financial Intermediaries, Working Paper No. 15, BIRD, February.

Rath, N. (1996), Women in Rural Society: A Quest for Development. pp. 14-29, New Delhi, MD Publication.

Ravallion, Martin (2000), Should Poverty Measures be Anchored to the National Accounts?, mimeo, ARQADE, University of Toulouse.

Ravallion, Martin, Pro-Poor Growth: A Primer, Policy Research Working Paper, Number 3242, World Bank, March 17, 2004.

Report of Tour of the KBK Districts, July 2005, Planning Commission.

Robinson, M. (2001), The Microfinance Revolution, The World Bank, Washington, DC.

Roche, Chris (1999), Impact Assessment for Development Agencies-Learning to Value Change, Oxfam/Novib, UK.

Rogerson, C.M. (1997), Rural Electrification and the SMME Economy in South Africa, EDRC, University of Cape Town.

Rowcroft, P., Studley, J. and Ward, K. (2006), Eliciting Forest Values for Community Plantations and Nature Conservation, Submitted to Forests Trees and Livelihoods.

Rowlands J. (1997), Questioning Empowerment: Working with Women in Honduras, Oxfam. UK.

Rural Development Statistics 2002-03, National Institute of Rural Development.

Russell, H. (1995), Poverty Close Home: A Christian Understanding. New York: Mowbury.

Rutherford, S. (2000), Raising the Curtain on the Micro financial Services Era, Focus Notes, No. 15, Consultative Group to Assist the Poorest, World Bank, Washington.

Rutherford, Stuart (2000a), Self-help Groups as Microfinance Providers: How Good Can They Get?, Paper presented at the Workshop on Best Practices in Group Dynamics and Micro Credit, 15-17 February, Manesar, Gurgaon.

Rutherford, Stuart (2000b), The Poor and their Money, Oxford University Press, New Delhi.

Sa-Dhan (2001), Microfinance Regulation in India, Sa-Dhan, New Delhi.

Sahoo, B. (1990), Women Employment in India. Bhubaneswar: Satanetra Publication.

Satish, P. (2000), Self-help Group Promotion-The Institutional Framework, Working Paper No. 17, Banker's Institute of Rural Development, March.

Schreiner, Mark (2004), Evaluation and Micro enterprise Programs in the United States, Journal of Microfinance, 4, 67-91.

Schubert, Michael (2004), Replicating Microfinance in the United States, Journal of the American Planning Association, 70, 230-231.

Schurman, F.J. (2003), The Politico Emancipatory Potential of a Disputed Concept, Third World Quarterly, 34(6):991-

1010.

Scoones, I. (1998), Sustainable Rural Livelihoods: A Framework for Analysis, IDS Working Paper 72.

SEARCH (1999), Microfinance sans Empowerment: Quickfix Approaches to Poverty Alleviation, SEARCH Bulletin (January-March), Bangalore.

Sebstad, Jennefer and Gregory Chen (1996), Overview of Studies on the Impact of Micro enterprise Credit, AIMS Project Report, USAID/G/EG/MD, Washington, DC.: Management Systems International.

Sebstad, Jennefer, and Monique Cohen (2000), Microfinance, Risk Management, and Poverty, AIMS Project Report, USAID/G/EG/MD, Washington, DC.: Management Systems International.

Sebstad, Jennefer, Catherine Neill, Carolyn Barnes, and Gregory Chen (1995), Assessing the Impact of Micro enterprise Interventions: A Framework for Analysis, USAID Managing for Results, Working Paper No. 7, Washington, D.C.: USAID.

Seibel, Hans Dieter (2001), SHG Banking: A Financial Technology for Reaching Marginal Areas and the Very Poor, Rural Finance Working Paper No. A 9, IFAD.

Sen, A. (1981), Poverty and Femines: Resources, Values and Development, Basil Blackwell, Oxford.

Sen, A. (1987), The Standard of Living, The Tanner Lectures, Clare Hall, Cambridge, 1985, Cambridge University Press, Cambridge.

Sen, A. (1990), Development as Freedom, Oxford University Press, Oxford.

Senapati, N. and D.C. Kuanr (1980), Orissa District Gazetteers-Kalahandi, Government Press, Cuttack.

Senapati, N. and N.K. Sahu (1968), Orissa District Gazetteers-Bolangir, Government Press, Cuttack.

Senapati, N. and N.K. Sahu (1968), Orissa District Gazetteers-Bolangir, Government Press, Cuttack.

Sengupta, Rajdeep and Aubuchon, Craig P. (2008), The

Microfinance Revolution: An Overview, Federal Reserve Bank of St. Louis Review, 90, 9-30.

Servon, Lisa J. (2002), Fulfilling the Potential of the U.S. Micro enterprise Strategy, In Jim Carr and Zhong Yi Tong (ed.), Replicating Microfinance in the United States, (pp. 169-190), Washington, DC: Woodrow Wilson Centre Press.

Servon, Lisa J. (2006), Micro enterprise Development in the United States: Current Challenges and New Directions, Economic Development Quarterly, 20, 351-367.

Seth, M. (1995), Women's Development: Indian Initiatives, Kurukshetra, August: 33-55.

Shiva, V. (2002), Saving Lives or Destroying Lives? World Bank Sells Synthetic Soap and Cleanliness to Kerala: The Land of health and Hygiene, AgBioIndia.

Shiva, Vandana et al. (1991), Ecology and the Politics of Survival: Conflicts over Natural Resources in India, UN University Press, Japan, and Sage Publications, New Delhi.

Shylendra, H. S. (1999), Micro-Finance and Self-help Groups (SHGs): A Study of the Experience of Two Leading NGOs, SEWA and AKRSP in Gujarat (India), IRMA Research Paper No. 16.

Simeen, M. (2003), Actually How empowering is Micro credit? Mahmud, Development and Change 34(4):577-605.

Simon, H. A. (1984), Models of Bounded Rationality, Volume 1, Cambridge, MA: MIT Press.

Singh, S.K. and R. I. Singh (1987), Impact of Rural Development on Economic Status of Women in U.P. Kanpur, Kurukshetra, May: 13-18.

Sinha, F. and S. Sinha (2002), Sustainability and Development: Evaluating the Performance of Indian Micro-finance. Beyond Micro credit: Putting Development Back into Microfinance, Vistar Publishers, New Delhi, First Edition, Pp. 264-298.

Sjöstrand, S. (1992), On the Rationale Behind "Irrational" Institutions, Journal of Economic Issues, 26(4), pp. 1007-1040.

Smith, Stephen C., Ending Global Poverty: A Guide to What Works
www.palgrave-usa.com/ Catalog/product. aspx?isbn=140 965 4X.

Srinivasan, Girija (ed.), (n.d.), Building a Future Group by Group-Case Studies on Self-help Groups in India, BIRD, Lucknow.

Srinivasan, Girija (n.d.), Group Approach to Empowerment of Rural Women-IFAD Experience in Tamil Nadu State, Working Paper 5, BIRD, Lucknow.

Srinivasan, Girija and P. Satish (2000), Transaction Costs of SHG Lending-Impact on Branch Viability, Research Paper No. 5, BIRD, March.

Strong, Maurice (1992), Required Global Changes: Close Linkages between Environment and Development in Change: Threat or Opportunity?, United Nations.

Swift, J. (1989), Why are Rural People Vulnerable to Famine?, IDS Bulletin, Vol. 20, No. 1.

Swift, J. (1989), Why are Rural People Vulnerable to Famine?' IDS Bulletin, Vol. 20, No. 2.

Tankha, A. (2002), Self-help Groups as Financial Intermediaries in India: Cost of Promotion, Sustainability and Impact, Report for ICCO and Cord Aid, Netherlands, pp. 1-89.

Tankha, Ajay (1998), The Problem of Forced Savings in Some NGO-run Savings and Credit Programmes, Exchanges, No. 21, June, Action Aid India, Bangalore.

Tankha, Ajay (1999), Some NGO Dilemmas in Reaching the Poorest with Microfinance, Search Bulletin, Bangalore, January-March.

Tendler J., Whatever Happened to Poverty Alleviation, in J. Levitsky, (ed.), Micro enterprises in Developing Countries, IT Publications, London, 1989.

Tendulkar, S. D. and L. R. Jain (1995), Economic Growth and Equity: India 1970-71 to 1988-89, Indian Economic Review, Vol XXX, No. 1.

Tenth Five Year Plan (2002-07), Volume III, Planning Commission, Government of India.

Thakur S.G. and Tiwari A.M. (2005), Whether SHG-based Micro credit Programs Can Remove Poverty?-A case study of SHG-based programmes in Patan district of Gujarat. Women in Informal Employment: Globalizing and Organizing, Conference Paper, pp. 1-21.

Thomas, J. (2002), An Evaluatory Study of the Activities of Peermade Development Society and its Research Institute in the Environmental Perspective, M.Sc. thesis, Mahatma Gandhi University, pp. 46-74.

Thorp, R., F. Stewart and A. Heyer (2005), When and How Far is group Formation a Route out of Chronic Poverty? World Development, 33(6): 907-920.

Tiwari, K. (1995), Women and Development in Bilaspur, Madhya Pradesh, Kurukshetra, August: 53-55.

UNDP, 1995 Human Development Report, New York, UNDP, 1996, 4.

UNESCO, (2002), Universal Declaration on Cultural Diversity. United Nations Educational, Scientific and Cultural Organization.

UNESCO, (2005), Convention on the Protection and Promotion of the Diversity of Cultural Expressions, United Nations Educational, Scientific and Cultural Organisation.

UNIFEM, Progress of the World's Women, New York: UNIFEM, 2000.

United Nations Economic and Social Council, Working Group on Indigenous Populations, 1996, Report of the Working Group on Indigenous Populations, 14th Session at para.35,U.N.Doc.E/CN.4/Sub.2/AC4/1996/2.

United Nations, Agenda 21: Programme of Action for Sustainable Development, United Nations Conference on Environment and Development, Rio de Janeiro, Brazil, 3-

14 June 1992.

USAID, Micro enterprise Development in a Changing World: U.S. Agency for International Development Micro enterprise Results Reporting for 2000, Arlington, Va.: Weidemann Associates, 2001, 31.

USAID, Reaching Down and Scaling Up: Focus on USAID's Development Partners: USAID Micro enterprise Results Reporting for 1999, Arlington, Va.: Weidemann Associates, 2000, 22.

Vaidyanathan, A. (2001), Poverty and Development Policy, Economic and Political Weekly, Vol XXXVI, No. 21, May 26-June 1.

Vasimalai, M.P. (2000), "Kalanjiam Federations" in Kishanjit Basu and Krishan Jindal (eds.), Microfinance: Emerging Challenges, Tata McGraw-Hill Publishing Company Limited, New Delhi.

Vatta, K. (2003), Micro finance and Poverty Alleviation, Economic and Political Weekly, 38(5): 432-433.

Vatta, K. and P. Singh (2001) The Performance of Self-help Groups in Punjab: A Study of Hoshiarpur District, Indian Journal of Agricultural Economics, 56(3): 452.

Vijay Mahajan and Tom Dichter, A Contingency Approach to Small Business and Micro-enterprise Development, Small Enterprise Development, 1.1 (March 1990), BASIX, Hyderabad.

Vinding, Diana (2003), Indigenous Poverty: An Issue of Rights and Needs, Indigenous Affairs, 1/03, Copenhagen, IWGIA, p. 5.

Vishwanathan, M. (1994), Social Framework and Strategies in Womens' Development, Jaipur: Rupa Books Pvt. Ltd. Jaipur, 1994.

Von Pischke, J.D. (1999), Microfinance in Developing Countries, Office of Development Studies, United Nations Development Program, Washington DC.: Fannie Mae Foundation.

Vyas, Jayshree, Dinesh Harode and Hetal A. Patel (1998),

SEWA Bank at the Doorsteps, SEWA.

WCED (1987), Our Common Future: The Brundtland Report, World Commission on Environment and Development, Oxford: Oxford University Press, UK.

WCED, (1987), Our Common Future, The Report of the World Commission on Environment and Development, Oxford University Press, Oxford, New York.

Woller, Gary M. and Woodworth, Warner (2001), Micro credit as a Grass-Roots Policy for International Development, Policy Studies Journal, 29, 267-282.

World Bank, Engendering Development: Through Gender Equality in Rights, Resources, and Voice Summary, Washington, D.C.: World Bank, 2001; World Bank, 2000. World Development Report 2000/1, New York, Oxford University Press.

World Development Report, 1996, World Bank, Washington DC.

World Survey on the Role of Women in Development, (1999), New York, United Nations.

Xavier Institute of Management (1997), Self-help Groups in Orissa and their Linkages with Formal Financial Institutions, Centre for Development Research and Training, Bhubaneswar.

Young, K. (1993), Planning Development with Women: Making a World of Difference. Macmillan, London.

Zaman, H. (1999), Assessing the Impact of Micro-credit on Poverty and Vulnerability in Bangladesh, Washington, The World Bank Policy Research Working Paper No. 2145.

Index

Index